Life Is Not a Stage

Life Is Not a Stage

From Broadway Baby to a Lovely Lady and
Beyond

✌

Florence Henderson

with Joel Brokaw

**CENTER
STREET**®

New York   Boston   Nashville

Center Street
Hachette Book Group
237 Park Avenue
New York, NY 10017
www.centerstreet.com

Printed in the United States of America

RRD-C

Originally published in hardcover by Hachette Book Group.

First Trade Edition: September 2012

10 9 8 7 6 5 4 3 2 1

Center Street is a division of Hachette Book Group, Inc.
The Center Street name and logo are trademarks of Hachette Book Group, Inc.

The Hachette Speakers Bureau provides a wide range of authors for speaking events. To find out more, go to www.hachettespeakersbureau.com or call (866) 376-6591.

The publisher is not responsible for websites (or their content) that are not owned by the publisher.

The Library of Congress has cataloged the hardcover edition as follows:

Henderson, Florence.
   Life is not a stage : from Broadway baby to a lovely lady and beyond / Florence Henderson ; with Joel Brokaw. – 1st ed.
      p. cm.
   ISBN 978-1-59995-388-5
   1. Henderson, Florence. 2. Television actors and actresses–United States–Biography. 3. Singers–United States–Biography. I. Brokaw, Joel. II. Title.
   PN2287.H4265A3 2011
   792.02'8092–dc22
   [B]
                                                          2011007490

ISBN 978-1-59995-387-8 (pbk.)

To my children, who inspire me and teach me about love every day
To my grandchildren, who fill my life with light and joy
And to my sister Emily, who has walked every step of the way with me

Acknowledgments

As I will mention in the introduction to this book, there were many reasons why the idea of writing a memoir was a daunting task that I had avoided for years. But just as it has often happened throughout the course of my life, the support and help I needed to move forward seemed to manifest once I truly committed. Here are some of those special people to whom I am so grateful:

Joel Brokaw put a lot of miles on his tires over many months to work with me to put my thoughts and words on the page. His sensitivity, dedication, and patience made the process far easier and more enjoyable than I could have envisioned.

David Brokaw and Rick Hersh came forward to suggest the idea that the time was right and found a publishing home for it.

My friend Ruth Helen truly understands and taught me the meaning of the word "friend."

Kayla Pressman was there as always with her steadfast hand

and keen oversight. She has been a cornerstone of friendship and professionalism in my life for almost forty years.

My brothers and sisters have loved me and supported me unconditionally.

Christina Boys brought her loving red pen to the process. Every author should have such an enthusiastic, supportive, and adroit editor. Rolf Zettersten, the publisher of Center Street, believed in the potential for the book and made it all happen.

The Orland family—Paul and Malcolm—manage my business affairs as they have for over half a century.

Cheryl O'Neil, my hypnotherapist and friend who was trained by my husband John, has helped me over many a rough spot.

Araceli (Shelley) Loza and Angela Burton are my indispensable and loving in-house support team. They run a tight ship. I would also like to thank Dr. David Kipper, who took over my healthcare after Dr. Giorgi passed away.

It would take many pages to express my gratitude and appreciation for all the friends who have blessed my life. Many of these relationships have lasted almost my entire lifetime while some are more recent. Their loyalty, acceptance, love, and kindness have been a constant in both good and more challenging times.

Teachers continue to inspire and excite me about how much more there is to learn and discover. Whether it was during my school years, professional training, or in unexpected forms in my everyday encounters today, I have been so thankful for the many ways teachers have turned up in my life and continue to share important lessons.

Lastly, special thanks go to the fans, some of whom have been part of my life since the beginning of my career. To the newer and younger ones who have recently discovered me on the tube and think I'm still thirty-five years old, you don't know how good you make me feel.

Contents

Introduction   xi

CHAPTER 1—The Faith of a Child   1

CHAPTER 2—Singing for My Supper   12

CHAPTER 3—Growing Up Fast   27

CHAPTER 4—Wide-Eyed and Confident   36

CHAPTER 5—Wish You Were Here   53

CHAPTER 6—Hitting the Road   60

CHAPTER 7—The Big Break   73

CHAPTER 8—Yes, I Was a Virgin!   88

CHAPTER 9—The *Today Show* Girl   98

CHAPTER 10—Do Re Mi   108

CHAPTER 11—The Girl Who Came to
Supper Loses Her Appetite   116

CHAPTER 12—The Pill   125

CHAPTER 13—The "No Door Act"   136

Chapter 14—Detours and Other
             Digressions   152

Chapter 15—Hollywood...Finally   160

Chapter 16—Brady-monium   170

Chapter 17—Good Help Is Hard to Find...   192

Chapter 18—Days of Wine and Roses...
             and Clam Chowder and Chicken   206

Chapter 19—Cutting Through the Layers
             to the Truth   220

Chapter 20—D-Day   231

Chapter 21—The Dragonflies   242

Chapter 22—The Horse Stays in the Game   253

It Will Never Be Noticed on a Galloping Horse

∽

Meet me at Route 2 and Darby Lane by the blue mailbox. I can't be with my family anymore. I'll be there waiting for you. Please take me away with you."

So reads a recent letter from a young girl that is not unlike hundreds of others I've received over the last four decades. Between 1969 and 1974, I played the role of Carol Brady on a television show called *The Brady Bunch* that hit a deep chord with millions of people around the world across all cultures. Astoundingly, it has never been off the airwaves over the past forty years. That is why the letters and e-mails such as this one keep coming.

I have taken each and every one of these letters to heart, deep in my soul. You see, what I have kept private for all these years is that I too was one of those children waiting at the crossroads. My real family, although similarly large in size, was the polar opposite of the Bradys. Truth be told, Carol Brady came alive in my portrayal because she too was the mother that both I and the young girl who wrote me the letter so desperately wished we had.

Throughout the years I resisted offers and simply sidestepped the whole topic of writing an autobiography. Most accepted my excuse that I was too busy to sit down and write a book, since my hectic schedule spoke for itself. I had followed my mother's advice all too well, words I first remember hearing when I was a little girl no more than six years old.

"I can't wear this to school, Mother," I cried, referring to a dress that was made out of feed sacks. In the 1930s, bags of flour, seeds, and oatmeal came in colorful muslin patterns as a sales incentive because many Depression-era families could not afford to buy new cloth or ready-made dresses. The fabric was bright although mismatched, but worst was how the bottom ruffle was partially missing. It left a gaping hole in the front and made the dress stick out like a sore thumb. "Please don't make me wear it! Everybody at school will make fun of me."

"Of course you're going to wear it. That's all you have. Think nothing of it. *It will never be noticed on a galloping horse.*"

Those words grew to have enormous meaning in my life. In fact, they were so pervasive, I almost used them as the title of this book. They were a way to deal with adversity and a standard operating procedure for a good part of my life. When terrible things happened, they dictated that no matter what, you picked yourself up and put yourself back in the saddle. You got busy and you stayed busy. But as the stories in this book will testify, that is only a temporary solution.

Not writing this book was also symbolic of an avoidance of a larger issue that I hadn't been prepared to deal with nor had summoned sufficient courage to heal. It is what kept me in constant motion on that galloping horse, relentlessly kicking up dust so I couldn't easily see the truth.

Why dredge up the past? Am I prepared to discuss difficult and uncomfortable things about parents, family members, friends, colleagues, and of course, about myself? Wouldn't it be better for those memories just to rest in peace? What's the point? I had plenty of good excuses not to write a book. But one thought countered them. Perhaps the connection that Carol Brady opened up in the hearts and minds of millions was just preparation, a gateway for me to do more. Perhaps my story could inspire and help others who continue to face similar challenges in their lives.

I realized that all my doubts about doing a book were completely normal for someone who as a young child had endured abuse and abandonment because of alcoholism. We suffer a guilt syndrome in one form or another because we were so powerless to help at the time. If we're not paralyzed by fear, anger, and hatred, or numbed by our own addictions, we have to overcome deep-seated reactive patterns. In addition to being workaholics who are stuck on the galloping horse, some of us also grow up to become control freaks to keep real and imagined chaos away. Others become gregarious caregivers trying to please everybody, except ourselves. And many, including yours truly, end up doing most of the above!

This book is written as a natural consequence of forgiveness and compassion, not only for those whose actions may have caused harm, but most important, for myself. I say this because victims have to forgive themselves for what they did or didn't do in response or for holding on to negative emotions like sadness, anger, and hatred. I too have made my fair share of mistakes and gone through periods of personal turmoil that certainly created upheaval around me. Without that sense of honesty and forgiveness, it is nearly impossible to clean the slate and move forward to a happier and healthier life.

I've chosen not to go into any great detail about my childhood up to this point for a very simple reason. I wasn't comfortable talking about it. I have come to realize that my decades-long silence was a classic pattern of normal response to an abnormal circumstance of deprivation and neglect. It is a syndrome that millions of others, both children and grown-ups, may be dealing with at this very moment, regardless of whether it is happening right now, stuck in constant flashback, or, worse yet, recycled in continuing and escalating drama in our lives.

At the heart of my silence is the sense of guilt that I surely felt as a little girl living under such conditions. Realistically, a small child living in an abusive environment has few choices and little power to change things. That guilt keeps the victim not just quiet but makes them seek out the approval and affection of the abuser. "Perhaps it was all my fault." "If only I could have done more." So thinks the child so often in that situation. It is no wonder why I so gladly took on the role of a relentless caregiver in relationships later on.

Regarding my parents, I came to accept that they were coping the best they could with the hand they were dealt. If Joseph and Elizabeth Henderson could read the pages that speak of their lives, I hope they would view the content as healing for themselves as well. Who knows how far back the cycle of dysfunction had gone unchecked through generations of their ancestors. There were many things that remained largely unspoken during their lifetimes that I hope these pages might serve to bring forward and clarify.

Obviously, this is not a book about only the good times and success I've had. Yes, I have had a lot of laughs along the way, and I trust you will see in these pages how my sense of humor has been a steadfast companion throughout it all. What's more important is what happened when things were not good and how adversity was handled. Our choices in those moments have important and often dramatic consequences. Any success I've had has drawn upon the lessons learned and strength tempered through difficult times. Out of that mix of drama and pathos, comedy and farce, and laughter and tears that make up our daily lives, I hope my story will remind us that no matter how serious or dire our situations may be, each of us has unbounded potential to transcend the most formidable of obstacles.

The book will also deal with some of the more significant health challenges I've faced and conquered. I'll speak specifically about bouts of postpartum depression, hearing loss, and heart problems. You don't have to scratch the surface so deeply to see how the mind, body, and spirit are so indelibly linked. I share these too with the spirit that they will awaken a greater awareness of how imbalances in our lives find expression in our weakest links.

It took a long time, but I was ultimately able to create a life of more profound joy and purpose. The process has not been easy, you'll understand in frank detail as you read on. Although my life has been a dream come true in so many ways, success didn't make all my problems go away. Reliving things in the writing of this book that happened many decades ago has brought back a mix of fond memories and others that I'd have rather chosen to forget. The lumps in my throat and tears in my eyes remind me that much sadness still remains.

I know that for the rest of my life I will remain a work in progress, with wounds still to heal and lingering pain in old scars. But thankfully, I did something about it. Piercing through the many protective layers of illusion does require painful self-examination and a fair measure of courage. I have learned it takes courage to be happy. But as we begin to make progress, we see how much easier it is to begin to connect the dots and make better sense of our chaotic journeys. Surprisingly, I realized how much energy it took to hold back all the things in my mind that I thought were terrible and wanted to hide. Looking back, I sometimes want to cringe at all the mistakes I readily made in the pathology of those circumstances. But hang in there. There is a reward, because the end product is unmistakable—an ever-expanding state of joy and fulfillment bound up in the daily adventure of our lives.

When I was seventeen years old, I stood at the crossroads. All I had was a suitcase, a talent for singing, naïve ambition, a scholarship, and a one-way ticket on a small DC-6 plane bound for New York City. As you will learn in the next few pages, I was very fortunate to be there, to have survived given everything that had happened to me in my young life. Unbelievably, doors would open quickly. My talent would soon be discovered and I would be taken under the wing of Rodgers and Hammerstein and the other giants of Broadway. Television also beckoned, and good fortune followed me there too. But through it all, I feel in some ways that I still remain that hopeful, wide-eyed, and excited teenager on that first trip to New York City, eager to explore the farthest boundaries of where our talents and our determination can take us.

What I hope will come through to you on these pages is how I cherish my past, both the good and the bad. It has made me who I am. It has given me the gift of knowing how every day there is something joyful to discover. I love living in the present. I am fascinated by the people I meet every day. I love studying how they behave and how they think.

A short time ago, I was in St. Louis visiting my son and his family. I was staying at the Ritz-Carlton Hotel. The doorman, a tall man, came over to me when I was standing outside in front of the hotel.

"Are you being picked up?" he asked me.

"Yes." I told him that I was waiting for my son.

"Would you like to sit over there?" He pointed at a comfortable chair just inside the lobby.

"No, I'm loving looking at the trees. The air is so refreshing."

"I could tell," he replied. "You're very serene and peaceful." As I took my sunglasses off to look at him, he looked at me and said very calmly and assuredly, "I see heaven in those eyes." His words hit me deeply because I knew what he meant. When we take the moment to look into the eyes of another person, even a stranger we may never see again, we understand how it is a golden opportunity to learn.

He had no idea who I was. Being Florence Henderson or Carol Brady didn't matter to him. I learned his name was Dewitt, and he turned out to be a very wise man. Each morning I came down early just to have a few extra minutes to speak with him. We talked a lot about spirituality and many other things. I wish I could remember all the pearls that came out of his mouth. One in particular I cannot forget: "Attitude determines altitude." It is something that I certainly believe and have put into practice.

Like my time with Dewitt, I hope that our time together on these pages will be a similar "moment of grace." In that spirit, I dedicate this book to that child who wrote the letter and to millions like her, young and old, who are looking for hope and promise but feel trapped in their sadness and pain. Come along with me.

Life Is Not a Stage

CHAPTER I

The Faith of a Child

cᴏ

Please, can I go home?"

When I got the news of my father's death, I asked for a leave to travel back to Indiana. His funeral was to take place in two days. I had just been cast in the lead in the last national touring company of *Oklahoma!* We were set to open the next night in New Haven. It was the big break, a dream come true for an eighteen-year-old girl. It had come only months after I had moved to New York City to study theater and hopefully to find work.

At the first opportunity during the rehearsal, I had gone over to Jerry White and Richard Rodgers. The director and the composer were seated in the audience of the empty theater in New York. "We don't have an understudy for you yet, and the place is sold out," Mr. Rodgers told me in sympathetic but no uncertain terms. He was *the* Rodgers of Rodgers and Hammerstein, the legendary duo behind such other Broadway classics as *The Sound of Mu-*

sic, *The King and I, South Pacific,* and *Carousel.* Jerry White told me about all the publicity they had done. There was a lot riding on this first performance. They went out of their way to tell me how bad they felt about the situation. It made me feel even worse, which almost immediately manifested in a painful medical problem that made me wonder if there was some divine payback as a consequence for my actions. Strange how the mind works, but I'll get to more on that later.

Ironically, I knew that this dilemma, as gut-wrenching as it was at that moment, was within the natural flow of an improbable, sometimes horrific, and often miraculous young life. Despite the abandonment, neglect, and poverty I experienced as a child, I had an abiding faith I would do better than just survive. I knew with absolute certainty that everything was going to be okay in the end. I felt the undeniable presence of a guiding and protective hand from a higher power above. This gave me a sense of optimism, as if my spirit were still free in spite of my circumstances.

As I look back on that time, I wish I could recapture the unswerving faith of that child. Unfortunately, my doubts grew with time as life circumstances and relationships became more complicated and challenging. Thankfully, my spirituality remained intact and prevented me from the kind of nihilism people often develop in that situation.

That I was standing on the rehearsal stage with this legendary composer was, in my mind, a miracle of sorts. Only a few years earlier, when the conditions around me were at their worst, I would escape from my house to go to the local movie theater. Musicals like *Easter Parade* were my favorite. I would sing and dance on the street all the way home, mimicking the tunes I had just heard.

I decided at a very young age that performing was what I

wanted to do. To make it happen, more was required than just natural talent. To go beyond singing in church or in the shower, a performer needs an endless supply of grit, determination, and a passion for performing. If I was having a bad day or things were just not going my way, these qualities helped keep my priorities in focus and made me more tenacious in my commitment.

For many reasons, it would have been impossible to tell Mr. Rodgers that my family came first and they would have to get along without me. Mr. Rodgers's "the show must go on" mentality was not to be violated.

Naturally, I felt tremendous guilt about the situation. But secretly, deep down inside, there was a sad truth. I was relieved that I didn't have to go to the funeral. True to character both in life and now in death, the situation with my father, Joseph Henderson, was both complicated and problematic.

"Gal, rub my back," my father had said to me one of the last times I saw him alive. Since I was the last of his ten children, he called me "Gal" rather than rattling off the long list of names of all of his girls to remember it.

A dirt-poor tobacco tenant farmer, my father was nearly fifty years old and my mother twenty-five years younger when they married. Both of my parents were from Kentucky and each came from very large Catholic families. One plausible explanation why my father married so late was that he had spent years taking care of his immediate family. That responsibility also turned him into quite an accomplished cook, something I'm sure would have given him a more successful and fulfilling career than growing tobacco and tomatoes for the canning factory. We maybe never had all the delicacies, but he sure knew how to whip up a great vegetable soup from whatever was handy or plentiful.

By the time my next oldest sister, Babby, and I were born, my father was getting close to seventy. The family had moved across the Ohio River to a small farm in Dale, Indiana. One of my earliest memories from that time was going out to the fields to "worm the tobacco." And if you ever had to worm tobacco, you wouldn't forget it either! First of all, working with tobacco is very gummy. The resin sticks to the little hairs on your arms and it felt highly unpleasant when anything would brush against us— our skin became like Velcro. My brothers and sisters and I would have to inspect every leaf. When we found the green, two-inch creatures holding on to the back sides of the leaves with their many legs, we'd pick them off, pull them apart, and throw them on the ground.

One day, my brothers said that they'd give me a dime if I bit the head off of one of the worms. I did it. I got the dime. It tasted as you might expect, but it was worth it. I went out and bought some candy with it. They also challenged me to do things like carry a big canister of coal oil from the little store. We used it to fuel the lamps that lit our house at night. I was competitive in nature even back then. The canister must have weighed more than I did at the time, but I dragged it for the required distance. The end of the dares officially came another day when they asked me to swing from one rafter to the next in the barn. I fell and almost killed myself, and that sure scared the heck out of them.

During my early childhood, we moved from that farm to another farm, and to a successive number of homes (possibly to evade the landlords due to unpaid rents?). Finally, we ended up in a small house in Rockport, population 2,400. By then, most of the other eight children had grown up and moved out of the house, my older sisters having married and my brothers gone off to the war. In the end it was just Babby and me. She was three years older and sported a short dark Buster Brown hairstyle of the time. Babby's real name is Emily, which was what I called her then. The nickname Babby came much later. In our early twenties, we were goofing off role-playing from a wonderful film we had just seen called *The Little Kidnappers*. The young actors had Scottish accents, and we loved the sound of their voices. So I played the "Grandmommy" with my faux Scottish brogue, and Emily was the baby, pronounced "Babby." Babby has stuck to this day, but mercifully not Grandmommy!

My father was a big and powerful man in the eyes of a little girl, but by the time I reached high school age I had surpassed him in height. He had dark eyes and a nice smile, and he was considered to be a handsome man of strong Irish stock. Both of his parents and their families happened to travel together on the same boat from Ireland to America, but met only after they were settled in their new country. He had been bald since his late twenties, with only fringes of hair on the sides, so he was never without his favorite hat. The worn-out fedora had a ring of dried sweat from his being in the hot sun while he tended the fields. He smoked a pipe, and his clothes, which were never so clean to begin with, were pockmarked with burn holes from embers that would fall from his pipe when he fell asleep in his chair. As he dozed off, his suspenders would sag and his dime-store eyeglasses would go down the bridge of his nose.

I could see the good in my father, but his alcoholism had a devastating impact on himself and his family. When he wasn't drunk, he could be the sweetest, kindest man. He could stay sober for weeks and months, and remarkably, sometimes for a whole year. During those tranquil periods, he would get us up to go to mass every Sunday morning. He loved to read, especially books about Wyatt Earp and the Wild West and Abraham Lincoln.

He was also a man full of considerable wisdom and advice, which he'd share with Babby and me in a repetitious manner that made it stick. When we heard that familiar tone in his voice, we would roll our eyes and say under our breaths, "Here it comes again."

"Gal, now, you know, you have to be careful," he would tell us. "You've got to watch your reputation and your character. We don't have much money and we don't have many material things, but you've got a great reputation and a great character. People can take your money and your possessions, but they can't take your good reputation and your character. *You give that away*."

Perhaps, in the final analysis, his words to us had more impact on us than we could have imagined at the time. It is one possible reason among others why, despite the harsh poverty and other difficult circumstances, all ten of his surviving children (one of my siblings died before I was born) went on to lead very productive lives. I've used what I have learned in my life and as a parent of four children myself to look back and understand both my father and my mother with a clearer perspective. The sadness and disappointment I had in my early years diminished gradually with time. It has made it easier to regard them not just with forgiveness and compassion, but also with a degree of awe and admiration.

My father was dealing with a terrible disease, although it was hardly recognized as such back in the 1930s and 1940s. I know his condition really bothered him. But what could he have done short of abstaining? There were no twelve-step programs or other social services in our community that addressed this problem. Alcoholics Anonymous was only just getting started at the time.

When he was drunk, all hell would break loose. I couldn't have been more than five or six years old when I first noticed that there was something terribly wrong. At that time, we were still living on the farm. One night, I heard my mother yelling at my dad. I snuck close by the door and looked in through the crack. My mother was standing by an ironing board, shaking her finger at him. My father was sitting in a chair in his long underwear. He looked so sick and so sad. Then he started to cry. Seeing my father in that condition was devastating. It just about killed me.

My mother, too, would drink with my father from time to time. On Saturday nights, they'd go uptown to a saloon. Babby and I would be outside waiting on a bench for them to come out. Invariably, once home, they'd get into a fight. I worried about my older sister Ilean, who was out on a date with a new boyfriend. "Ilean's going to be home soon," I'd say, going into the kitchen where they were yelling at each other. "He [the boyfriend] is going to hear you. He won't like us. He won't like Ilean. Please don't fight."

"Think nothing of it," my mother snapped back in her customary rhetoric. "We're fine. Just say your prayers and go to bed."

My mother was not an alcoholic. She had more self-control. I think she went along with it just to try to cope with him. As crazy as it appeared to me, maybe it was their form of relaxation, a form of self-medication against the pressures and strains of their life together. They didn't have the skills to channel it in a healthier way. Nevertheless, when my mother was drunk, usually on beer, I learned to stay out of her radar range. Years later, when we'd go out to a fancy restaurant, I'd cringe every time the waiter would ask her what she wanted to drink. "Bring me a beer. In a can."

If things were not interesting enough, my father was also a moonshiner. He made a corn whiskey that was popularly known back then as white mule. During the years of Prohibition, my father told my older sister, "Pauline, gal, if anybody comes asking if we've got any white mule, tell 'em, 'Yeah, it's standing there way out in the pasture.'" He also brewed his own beer.

When my father would go on a binge, Babby and I would find empty bottles everywhere, in the house and piled in the garage.

He could have a beer or two without a problem, but once he got a whiff of hard liquor it was all over. It was hard to say what would set him off. I once asked the great comedian Jackie Gleason about this issue when we were having lunch one day, and he brought up the subject of his problems with alcohol. "Yeah, I drink a lot," he admitted. I asked him if there was any pattern to when he got drunk. He laughed. "No, any excuse will do. A leaf has fallen from the tree. There's a cloud in the sky. Better have a drink."

When my father would go on a toot, Babby and I would take turns taking care of him. In this state, he would beg us to go uptown and get him a beer. We would walk into a bar, I'd ask the bartender, and most of the time they obliged. But we found that the best way to slowly get him off the stuff was to give him a protein cocktail of whiskey with milk and a raw egg.

"Come on, Daddy, you can't keep doing this," I'd tell him, imploring him to straighten up. Lying down on the sofa as he did for days on end, he looked sick and melancholic. In response, he sounded almost sweet and apologetic. He would tell me what most drunks say. "Oh, Gal, it will be okay. Now don't worry. I'll be fine."

"Would you just rub my back?" he'd often ask me. Within a few moments, he'd try to take advantage of the situation. I'd find his hand touching one of my calves. Looking back on these incidents, I know they could have been so much worse than they were. No matter how young or innocent I was at the time, I always had an inbuilt sense of my surroundings and knew when something might be dangerous or harmful. While things never degenerated to a more severe degree of sexual assault, the sacred bond of comfort, protection, and safety that a child wants to have with her father was damaged forever.

If there are any explanations for what triggered his binges, I think it was a combination of factors. As I described before, grow-ing tobacco and farming the land were hard work, and the years had taken a toll on him. He also had the daunting responsibility and pressures of raising ten children.

It might sound Pollyannaish, but my faith made it possible for me to always be optimistic and feel that there was help available to me to face any situation. It also made me feel a sense of love for everyone. I recently read a passage by the great spiritual teacher Paramahansa Yogananda. He wrote that when you really expe-rience being in union with a spiritual force, you begin to more easily see the good in everybody. This was a bit confusing for a small child confronted by the unpleasant sides of humanity—that I could still love that person despite their hurtful actions. It had made me feel guilty at times.

It is true that my upbringing stressed loyalty and God forbid you should say anything negative about anybody, especially your family. But that will only take you so far. I did not want to go the other way where anger and bitterness take the place of love. I found a piece of writing I did in a notebook when I was six or seven years old. It read, "Dear God, give me the gift of under-standing." That's the way my little mind worked. I think I realized that I was in a situation for which I needed to have more com-passion and understanding. Maybe I understood my situation far better at that early age than I thought.

In the months before my father's death, I returned home from my studies at the American Academy of Dramatic Arts in New York to see him. That particular visit haunted me the most. No different than I had seen him hundreds of times before, he was on a big toot. But on this occasion he also had a large swelling on his face that was hard not to notice. As I rubbed his back, I told him, "Daddy, I hate it when I see you like this."

Without pausing, I said, "I'd rather see you dead."

"Don't say that, Gal."

Not long after, I came back from New York and saw him for what proved to be the last time. I shaved him. I had no idea that he was so sick. Despite the abuse I had suffered, my prophetic words to him about wanting to see him dead and the fact that I did not attend his funeral disturbed me greatly.

I was so troubled that I went to confession and told the priest about the situation. His advice was to try to go easy on myself. "Don't feel bad about it. As young people, we all feel these things about our parents. We all go through rough times. But as we get older, we learn that we didn't know everything." He went on to speak to me about forgiveness. Easier said than done. The incident continued to bother me for years and marked the first onset of my insomnia.

There was a strange irony as I accepted my fate that I would not be attending my father's funeral. There was a sense of gratitude that, for once, finally, I got a free pass from the trauma. Instead, with *Oklahoma!* and the whirlwind of work that would follow with my success, I was in full stride on my mother's notorious galloping horse. The ensuing adventures in my life are proof positive that it would be many years before I would feel safe enough to slow down and relax.

My father used to say his prayers every night before bed when he was sober. I once asked him what he prayed for. He replied, "I pray for everybody but I also pray for a happy death."

Because of my studies in New York, I wasn't there when he took ill. My sisters Pauline and Babby took care of him. He had a terrible form of cancer that started in the sinuses and spread from there. It was the root of that swelling I had noticed during my visit. Pauline told me that he repeatedly apologized for taking so long to die. When the time was nearing, they called for the priest to give him the last rites and to hear his last confession.

Pauline said that she could overhear laughing and carrying on from his room. From those sounds, I think my father's prayer was answered, but he was also given an extra bonus. From my sister's account, I have some peace and gratitude knowing that he also had a courageous death.

CHAPTER 2

Singing for My Supper

ᶜᵛᵒ

My mother, Elizabeth, left when I was about twelve or thirteen years old. For Babby and me, it was par for the course. Like the other traumas we had experienced, we had learned that there was little other option than to accept it and try to cope the best we could. We knew that sitting by the door hoping that she would return was a waste of energy and would set us up for more disappointment. It was a nebulous time, of which the memories are a little bit foggy around the edges.

There was also a part of me that understood that the situation was perhaps not as harsh as it could have been, and for one good reason: From as far back as I can remember I had experienced so little maternal love in the first place. Kind words or any gestures of affection from her were virtually nonexistent. I was, after all, the last of her ten children, and she had no doubt already reached the end of her rope. It was the way things were. I didn't give my mother's absence that much more thought, I blocked it out. Things would be okay. I put my energy instead toward staying optimistic.

Years later, when I faced a crisis in my own marriage, I had a different perception of what my mother did. I pondered the courage that it took for her to leave. It gave me the courage to change my life. Curiously, both my sister Pauline and I left our marriages at the same age my mother did.

Along with my father's alcoholism and all the children to care for, my mother had little material comfort or support. There was no running water or electricity at home for much of the time. And medical care for childbirth and everyday problems was basically unaffordable. When Babby and I got a bit older, my mother brought in a little extra money working at a nearby café, but that didn't improve matters greatly. She also cleaned houses. One day when I went along with her to one of the homes, I could not resist the temptation of a real luxury item within my grasp. It was a stick of gum. My mother read me the riot act that theft was still theft no matter how small the item was, and gave me a whipping to make sure I didn't forget it.

My sister Ilean, who is ten years older than I, thinks that our parents went "a bit crazy" soon after she left home. She could recall that Daddy went for a decade at one time without drinking. She wrote to me in a recent letter that she was certain he was hurt badly when Mother didn't come back. She said that life was hard before I was born, but admitted that she had grown up under more tranquil conditions than what Babby and I had to endure. Like me, she also has an appreciation for the fact that our parents instilled in all their children the values we needed to get through life. Despite the hardship and all the traumas, they left us with the skills to take care of ourselves, do the right thing, and have integrity.

Ilean also remembers our mother from her childhood as being

strict but fair, with a bark that was far worse than her bite. She thought that behind her toughness was a more loving manner toward all of her children, but that the hard life forced her to be on the defensive. "She didn't want to leave herself open to get hurt," Ilean surmised. Our mother didn't really think she was abandoning Babby and me, according to Ilean's recollection, perhaps part and parcel of that defensive shield.

Babby and I were only told that she was going to Cleveland to work. Although she left, I still longed for my mother's affection and never gave up hope for the rest of her life that things would improve in that regard. We spent more time together periodically as I got older and became successful in show business. But she remained a tough nut to crack.

She was a beautiful woman with black hair and bluish-green eyes. Her colorful and larger-than-life character was the kind an actress might dream of playing. She also had a large physical presence, accentuated as she went up and down in weight as she got older. She was tough-talking and strong-willed. No doubt if she were alive today and read this book, she'd probably be angry and try to "beat the gizzard out of me," even though I write of my father and her after the passage of time with love and forgiveness (along with candor). My father, on the other hand, would have cried melancholic tears of remorse.

Regretfully, I know so little about her life before she met my father, especially about her childhood, because she hardly ever wanted to talk about it. Her maiden name was Elder and her family was primarily from England, with ancestry linked to Sir Isaac Newton. There was also Irish mixed in, and some of her features also looked distinctly Native American. The irreverent joke in the family was that an Indian in the woodshed might have had something to do with her conception.

Questions like how she met my father and why she chose

to marry such an older man are mysteries that no one remains around to answer. When I spent more time with her as an adult, some details leaked out from time to time. I asked her once, given all the ten children, whether she and my father had a good love life. "Yes," she answered, "when he was sober." She also told me about what happened when she got her first period, a story that shines some light on why her personality was the way it was. She said she was swimming in a pond when she noticed the blood. She immediately ran home and told her mother the news. What did her mother do? She promptly gave her a whacking. Such was parenting in those days.

When my siblings and I get together, we can tell stories about our mother and laugh in retrospect, although things weren't always so funny at the time. One such episode that best epitomizes the kind of love/hate relationship I had with my mother was about my high school prom. Although I had a job after school working at a soda fountain and lived with the Chinn family taking care of their kids, I didn't have very much money and not nearly enough to buy a dress. So I wrote to her in Cleveland to ask if she could help me out with this all-important milestone in my life. I would have been overjoyed if she had sent me a couple of dollars, but instead a box arrived. I opened it up, and my heart sank. Inside was a white frilly dress, the kind that a young girl might wear to first communion or confirmation in the church. God knows why she sent it to me. Was it because she had no money? Stinginess? Or was it simply that she was ignorant of what was appropriate for a teenage girl? Or all of the above?

I told my brother Joe about it. I guess I had loaded my entire inventory of disappointment onto this single event. It was impossible to hold back how deeply upset I was about the situation. Like he did in many situations, he came to my rescue. He sent me ten dollars, and I got a dress.

One other memorable example of when Joe stuck up for me happened a few years earlier. It was during World War II, and he had come home on leave dressed in his sailor uniform with the white hat. Mother was fed up, exasperated by how I was asking too many questions all the time. But he had a question of his own. "Why do you think she's so smart?" he asked her. "It's because she's asking questions. Don't ever stop her from doing that."

My memories of my mother's departure from the family seem shrouded in fog. I was resigned to it, but I also didn't want to think about it because it would remind me that my situation was not okay. It was the child's mechanism for coping. That was the way it was. I put it off to the side. "If she comes back, she comes back," I thought. You just go about your business. I was the optimist, convinced that everything was going to be all right. At the same time, my father was beginning to get terrible headaches, probably the precursor of his cancer, so I was frankly more focused on his well-being than my mother's.

I would see my mother from time to time after she moved away, and I grew much closer to her late in her life. But she never came back to Rockport, not for my hospitalization for appendicitis nor for my high school graduation. In fact, she never set foot in our family home again.

No one outside the immediate family except my best friend Oscar came over regularly to visit. There wasn't much to see. It was exactly how you would imagine Depression-era poverty to be. From the outside, it didn't look that bad—a small, well-built wood-frame house. In fact, it still stands there today, albeit in much better shape than when we lived there. Downstairs, there was a small kitchen and a living room with a stove for warmth and a radio that my father often tuned in to listen to the boxing matches.

One bright spot in the sitting room was a sofa covered in a yellow plastic-like fabric. To the best of our abilities, Babby and I tried to fix the place up. We painted and put up curtains. Where there were holes in the walls, we stuffed old clothes and rags into them to protect against the cold. We then put paper over the hole and painted it. It didn't look too bad.

Another downstairs room just by the staircase was full of some old storage trunks, mostly things that my mother had left behind and other assorted junk. Since we didn't have a car, the adjacent garage was also used for storage, including the stockpile of emptied liquor bottles.

Upstairs, there were two small rooms, one more filled with junk, and the other a bedroom where my sister and I slept in one bed and my father in the other. The bedroom closet was also short on amenities. The few clothes we had hung from hooks on the wall instead of the customary bar with hangers. In the winter, the bedroom's broken windows gave no protection against the cold air, overwhelming any warmth that might rise from the woodstove in the living room below.

To deal with the cold, my sister and I often slept like spoons, turning over systematically in intervals, switching when one side was warm to heat up the other side. On really cold nights, my father put a big old overcoat on top of our blanket.

Inside our Rockport house, Babby and I had more serious things to deal with than the cold. We always had to be on guard, hypervigilant around our father because we never knew what to expect around him when he was drinking. Since there was no one else there to protect us, we saw up close and took the full brunt of the daily reality of the destructive nature of alcoholism. We learned quickly how all semblances of human dignity, morality, and judgment of what's simply right and wrong can evaporate into thin air.

"Pauline, I know he thinks that I'm Mother," I told my oldest sister one day when she was visiting.

"You made that up," she snapped back. "Dad wouldn't do that." But she saw that I wasn't joking.

"I'm going to wait outside the door, and we'll see," she said.

I went back in the room. My father grabbed me, trying to hold me too close. Pauline came in yelling and broke it up. Had she not come in, who knows what would have happened. I probably would have spoken up and told him to stop. I was about fifteen and as tall as he was, so if that didn't work I could have probably overpowered him. He felt terrible because he was caught in the act.

Another time, Pauline and her husband and children were staying with us. Again, my father was not behaving, and my brother-in-law Charlie, who was a terrible drunk himself, took great offense at what he was witnessing.

"Pauline, we're going," Charlie announced and abruptly signaled for my sister and their children to pack up their things and get to the car. Babby and I begged them, "Please don't leave us." Pauline was painfully torn as she did what her husband asked. "I have to go with Charlie," she called out to us as she was hurrying to leave. She said that she regretted her action that night for the rest of her life.

The trauma of alcoholism was not limited to within the four walls of our home. One hot summer night, Babby and I were staying across the river in Owensboro with my cousin, who had a house across the cornfield from her parents, my uncle Jim and aunt Loretta. They were closer family than most: Loretta was my mother's sister, and Jim was my father's brother. My aunt and uncle's daughter was married to another raging alcoholic. He came home that night horribly drunk. Anticipating this, my cousin had locked all the screen doors and the windows that were left open because of the heat. Once he discovered he was locked out, he went on a rampage.

We heard him rip the screen door off its hinges as we were huddled together on the kitchen floor waiting for the hurricane to pass. Then he turned over a table covered with glass jars filled with food my cousin had canned that afternoon. With the sound of the smashing glass, I crawled over and opened the lock on the bottom of the kitchen door. We bolted out of there running for our lives, tearing across the cornfield petrified that he would catch us. Once at the farmhouse, we woke up Uncle Jim. He got his shotgun and went back after him. I don't know what else happened that night, but this was hardly the last of these incidents my sister and I had to endure.

Even though I was just a young girl, I had developed a fairly thick skin. I had no other choice. Maybe it helped that I had nothing else to compare it to, so I accepted it in that spirit.

When I look back at pictures of myself from those early years, I see a lot of sadness in the eyes of that little girl. But there was also a lot of pride. I want to go back and hug that child. Remarkably, portraits of me taken in recent years seem to look more youthful than those from my childhood. I think it was because my spirit got lighter as I got older. I came more to terms with what happened. That was the way it was. This is the way it is now. Now, get on with it. I never wanted anybody to feel sorry for me. No different than children caught in the middle of a war zone who find a way to play even in the smoldering rubble, I found a source of inner joy. It came from the simple act of singing.

To her credit, my mother recognized from early on that I came into this world with a gift—a musical voice. In fact, I cannot remember a time in my life when I wasn't singing. My mother loved music and played the guitar. She taught me lots of songs from age two, fifty songs, in fact, that I knew note perfect. It was mostly what they called hillbilly music back then, like "Down on the Levee" and spirituals such as "The Old Rugged Cross." Years later, I found out in a rather unusual way that music was in the ancestry of my mother's family. An aunt was touring the Mammoth Caves National Park in Kentucky when she saw etched on the wall of one of the caverns some graffiti from two Civil War soldiers who were hiding down there. They wrote, "Isaac and Henry Newton, musicians and composers." They were on the family tree on my maternal grandmother's side.

As a young child, singing was also an antidote for my shyness. I had the belief that if I closed my eyes the people around me would also not be able to see me. My mother made me get up and sing in public wherever there was a gathering of people (sometimes in the local grocery store). I was more afraid of her than of being shy. Quite often I'd pass the hat. So I guess it can be said that I've always been singing for my supper. Sometimes Babby would join in, and we'd fall easily into harmony. We even won a contest. Our prize was hot fudge sundaes at Wyndall's Market.

I never had any musical instruction until the nuns put me in the church choir when I was eight. They taught me how to sight-read Gregorian chants. They had me sing two Latin masses on Sundays. If the tenor or bass didn't show up that particular day, I'd sing their parts too. People started to recognize that I had talent. Had my mother stuck around, I'm sure she might have become a great stage mother.

Often when I sang, some people in the gathering would cry. It is unlikely at the time that I fully comprehended on a conscious level the reason why they did this. But Rockport was not a large town. The conditions Babby and I lived under were no secret. And we convincingly looked the part of two little ragamuffins fending for ourselves, living precariously close to the edge.

Babby was three years older, and that age difference gave her a certain authority in watching out for me. She had brown hair and eyes and was very pretty. Being older, she was a big step ahead of me in knowing the ways of the world and especially about boys. When puberty erupted and the hormones kicked in, she stepped in as a form of guardian angel because there was no mother or grandmother figure around to rein me in.

"When he comes into your mind, just think about things you hate about him," she told me. That was her form of psychology to help rid me of puppy love. She thought my feelings had become a little too hot and heavy (nothing beyond kissing!) for Gene Springer, the boy who worked at the taffy counter at the carnival. She was also concerned about another boy named Doc Bush, and for good reason. He was five years older than I was! And I was crazy about him.

Temptation was all around, and had I been a little freer in spirit and not so Catholic, I might have gotten in some serious trouble. Case in point: Babby, Oscar, and I often went dancing at the Rendezvous Dance Hall in nearby Tell City. When I was out on the dance floor, I really felt the music and wasn't shy about expressing it—which would later prove to be a good thing when I became a Broadway performer. "Don't shake your behind like that," Babby warned me. Guys were always asking me to dance, and I was only thirteen.

Along with Babby's loving influence, religion also served to hold me in check. When I was a child, I had to go to mass nearly every day. And once a week, we all lined up to go into the little box for confession. "Bless me, Father, for I have sinned," was how I would begin. Our parish priest was on the other side of the perforated slot. When I was little, my sins were fairly predictable: "I disobeyed my parents"; "I fought with my brothers and sisters." As I got older and when it was something I thought was really a bad sin, I tried to disguise my voice, because the priest knew us all. My voice would go into a higher register: "I lied"; "I had impure thoughts"; "I touched myself impurely."

Confession is a fairly serious sacrament in the Catholic Church. It's all tied to owning up to our shortcomings, expressing genuine sorrow, receiving penance of some sort, and finally, absolution. Also, one of the other big rules is that what is said in the box stays in the box. One day, this rule provoked a particularly severe case of soul-searching for the simple reason that our priest absentmindedly forgot to close the slot on my side before he had finished with the person in front of me. As I entered, he had already begun to hear the confession of an older girl named Maria—better known as "Maria with the big boobs" among us other less endowed girls. Maria launched into her confession, and it was much better than listening to the radio. "Oh my God," I said to myself, realizing that I would probably be compelled to add this inadvertent eavesdropping to my already prepared list of sins. But this was juicy stuff. Maria said she was truly sorry how she let her boyfriend Simon have his way with her ample breasts. I decided to leave well enough alone.

A short time later, our priest revealed that he too fudged on the rules. At the end of one of my confessions, he asked, "By the way, *Florence*, how's *Carl*?" He was referring to my brother, who was gravely ill at the time. So much for the pretense of anonymity!

Our priest had no doubt a fair good bit of material for his own confession. It was clear that he thought that all of us blossoming young girls were pretty cute. As a group of us were graduating from the eighth grade, he called us to his rectory upstairs. He had us all line up. He was seated in a chair with his legs spread wide. When it was each girl's turn, he would rub us against his crotch. At least he kept his clothes on. I remember thinking, "That's Father So-and-So. Oh my God! What about confession? Is this his sin or ours?"

One of the girls must have told her parents about the incident. My mother got wind of it and asked me about it. "Yes," I admitted to her, "but I don't think he meant anything bad with it." I was always trying to make everything right, which was not always a good thing. The priest had been at the parish for many years, but was transferred somewhere else soon thereafter. Many years later, he came to see me performing on Broadway in *Fanny*.

In general, when those kinds of things happened, whether it was going on in the home, at church, or anywhere, kids didn't speak up as promptly as they should have. In high school, I was living with another family, and their friend came to visit one afternoon in quite a drunken state. "Now, you'll be very sorry," I said to him, trying to talk him down while circling the table in order to get close enough to escape through the door. Even though that self-preservation instinct luckily worked in our favor, we always had a blurry line of what was appropriate and what was not. Someone touching your private parts or hitting you was not called sexual abuse or domestic violence back then. You didn't tattle on anybody. Even though Babby certainly went through the same things with our father, our attitude was to try to work things out internally, silently. Be forgiving. See the good in everyone. That's life on the farm.

That farm life in a large family with older brothers did not give you a free pass from their sexual curiosity. My mother had one solution for it all. "If your brother tries to touch you, you tell him the devil will take him straight to hell." That devil must have worked overtime in our house, ready to spring into action whenever anybody did anything wrong. If I didn't get to sleep right away, my mother had that same devil standing by. Maybe that's why I still don't sleep so well. I'm not joking—it took me years before I had the courage to watch *Rosemary's Baby*.

"Come on, Florency, run faster, run faster." I can still remember how Babby cried out. We were walking home one night, and a stranger was following us all too close. Terrified, I cried back,

"I can't run any faster." Thankfully nothing happened. It is scary how much free rein we had to come and go as we pleased. On another night out past dark, when we were too tired to make it home, we crawled into the outhouse of a family we knew in town, the Berrys. We got up early the next morning and went home. Nowadays, a child protective agency would have probably intervened.

To my knowledge, no such entity of that kind existed in Rockport in the 1940s, with one notable exception, the truant officer. Babby and I would skip school sometimes, usually because we had no proper clothes to wear. So we'd take the day off and stay in bed. We'd hear the truant officers coming to the porch of our house on Eureka Road where we lived prior to moving to the two-story home. We'd hear them talking outside, followed seconds later by a knock on the door. With no answer, they'd walk around the house and look in the windows. We pulled the blankets over us and stayed very quiet until they left.

One silver lining of that house on Eureka was that it was located next door to an African American church. Their services were quite different from what I was used to in the Catholic Church. Instead of long liturgies, a young woman would sit down and play the organ, and the music seemed to take over from there. It was contagious. From the moment I would go into that church, I could not stop dancing. I learned there at a young age a valuable lesson on how to "get down" musically and otherwise.

Behind the church was a house where a black family lived, the Rowans. Mr. Rowan and Daddy would sometimes get drunk together. It was quite a sight to see them walking on the street, stumbling home together. His daughter would sometimes sit and kiss her boyfriend on the front steps of the church. I remember thinking, "Hmm, that doesn't look like such a bad thing." And the memory of Mrs. Rowan is still quite vivid. One night,

I was supposed to take the garbage out. For whatever reason, I was afraid to go back where the garbage cans were, so I came up with the excellent idea of dumping it conveniently over behind the Rowans' house. Well, Mrs. Rowan came over the next day. My mother didn't bother to count to ten after the screen door closed behind Mrs. Rowan. With no hesitation, she beat the tar out of me.

Whether I was singing and dancing at the African American church or performing in the grocery store, people must have sensed a positive life force in me in spite of my circumstances. I was, as far back as I can remember, a "glass-half-full" personality type. I was optimistic even in the worst of times when nothing around gave cause to be so. Any kind of inner strength and confidence that were communicated through my singing voice perhaps stemmed from that optimism and the protective faith I felt. Despite my listeners' tears, they were hopeful, as I was, that somehow I would persevere.

To my great delight, some of the people from that period of my childhood have turned up sporadically. A short time ago, a letter arrived from Missy Mason, the town doctor's granddaughter. Back in the old days, I held her in high regard, "the cat's meow," and the real height of sophistication in my mind. "It was just so semi!" was her favorite expression, and whatever that meant, it had to be good. She wrote in this letter some six decades later, "I've seen you so many times on TV and always feel so proud of all you've accomplished. Who would have thought it way back when we were so young. Maybe you did." Another unforgettable encounter was with Bananas, or 'Nanas for short, a tough African American kid whom I would say hi to on the street when he wasn't being a terrifying bully (or so he seemed to me). Sometime in the 1960s, I was performing a concert for Oldsmobile in Flint, Michigan, with a wonderful choir made up of their workers. At that event, a very handsome black man came up to me. "Florence, I'm 'Nanas from Rockport." We hugged each other with such joy. He took a step back with one of those "just look at us" looks. He laughed. "Yeah, we both got out."

No doubt I rode out of Rockport on my mother's galloping horse. As I mentioned before, Elizabeth Henderson was a survivor and a fighter, and give her credit, it was advice that worked for her for her whole lifetime. I didn't recognize until much later on just how courageous she was. She dealt with her difficulties with a lot of grit and sheer determination. I followed her example without totally being cognizant of it, and it's been one hell of a ride! For the greater portion of my life, I barreled through problems and obstacles as if my very existence depended on it. And certainly, in the difficult years of my youth, it did. But logic dictates that there comes a time when all of that is no longer necessary, when you can relax and loosen your grip on the reins, slow the horse down, and enjoy the ride. Nice thought. Why not? But that's easier said than done. Such behavior becomes an ingrained and stubborn pattern. It had a powerful presence lurking in all of my thoughts, actions, and choices. At the same time, it was seamless and nearly invisible, unnoticed like a painting hanging on a living room wall that fades into the background with time.

Heavy lifting would be required to deal with the emotions I held inside from early childhood, and, in my case, more than a few Kleenex boxes processing it all in therapy. As I've gotten older and somewhat wiser, I've come to better understand and deal with the past. But the scars are always there. We just deal with it the best we can. Even the very act of recounting these old stories has had a definite healing effect.

CHAPTER 3

Growing Up Fast

ᴖ

One of the brighter spots of my early life came in the form of Oscar. She was my saving grace and my best friend from the time we were five years old until she died all too early from asthma at age fifty-three. I'm not sure exactly how my lucky break happened, but Oscar was going to attend St. Francis Academy, the Catholic high school on the other side of the Ohio River in Kentucky. She came from a well-to-do family, and I think her grandparents didn't want her taking the Greyhound bus alone every day back and forth to school. I never found out how it was paid for, but regardless, it was all arranged. I got to go with her on the bus.

On those bus rides, we'd laugh and talk about girly things: school, making fun of teachers, boys, and movies—usually in that order. But beyond that, we usually didn't dwell on our problems. Oscar had her share of misfortune with her home situation too, albeit markedly more benign than mine. Her mother gave birth to her at seventeen. Due to alcohol problems, her father was not in the picture, but she was raised by his parents.

Oscar would visit her mother, who rented a room in the home of a wealthy Rockport family. Sometimes I'd come too, and we'd spend the night together in that room, all three of us packed in the same bed. Often I would stay at Oscar's house as well. During one sleepover, Oscar had an asthma attack. She couldn't breathe and got very frightened. We were alone, and I didn't know what to do and felt powerless to help. I tried to comfort her. It was terrifying, but it shocked me into a real state of compassion and gratitude when the calm was restored. It reduced things to basics. We supported each other the best we could. We were both trying to fit in and live as normal a life as we could imagine.

In that regard, going to St. Francis with Oscar was made to order, even down to the fact that we wore uniforms, since I didn't have any decent clothes. Still, often I'd get off the bus in the morning with a soiled uniform or wearing something other than the clean white blouse required as part of it.

"Why aren't you in your uniform?" Sister Mary Auxilium, the wonderful mother superior wearing the full nun's habit, asked me when I was sent to her office.

"I spilled hot chocolate on it," I replied, trying to mask the truth. Hot chocolate? I hadn't even had breakfast.

"Oh, I see," she said in a neutral tone. She offered me something to drink. Sitting there with the cup in my hand, I was completely clueless that she or any of the other teachers knew of my circumstances. How could I have been so naïve?

Thinking it might help, Sister Mary would send me to the school's spiritual director, Father Saffer, for counseling. I don't remember any particularly profound insights from our conversations, but there was something more powerful in the unspoken, in his gesture of caring kindness. As I sat in his presence, there was another thing about him that I couldn't resist. Even back then, I guess I was preparing to be an actress and conducting my own character study. He had a nervous manner about him that I found fascinating. And I had the audacity to imitate him, to everyone's delight, including his (I think!), when we had school assemblies.

"How's everything?" was how he'd usually start the conversation.

"Great," I'd say, but he knew I really meant, "Not so great."

"Would you like a candy bar?"

"Oh, thanks." So we would just sit and talk, and I'd eat the candy bar. That treat seemed extra sweet with his nurturing energy.

On a few occasions, my geometry teacher, Father O'Bryan, would make me leave the classroom because I was talkative and laughed a lot in class. He had been a Navy chaplain during the war, and he ran a tight ship in class. If you misbehaved or weren't listening, he was prone to throw erasers at you. Chalk does not taste good even when you're hungry—take my word for it.

I was staying temporarily with my older sister Marty during this time. She was not a happy person, and for good reason. She was married to a man who had a short fuse, to put it mildly. Being fifteen years old and his wife's youngest sister gave me no immunity from his treatment. I once tried to pull him off my sister when he was hitting her. He was a big man. He picked me up and threw me against the wall. Then he picked me up again and literally threw me out the door. I ran over to the neighbors and told them, "He's going to kill my sister." Mr. Wilkie calmed me down. But I don't remember them going over there or intervening in any way. Another time during this stay, I was babysitting for them. They came back late one night, and my brother-in-law discovered that I hadn't done the dishes as he had asked.

"I've got a good mind to shoot her right now," he told my sister. He owned a nightclub in Owensboro and always carried a gun on him.

"Stop talking like that," I could hear Marty pleading. Although Marty's husband didn't drink, his anger was terrifying, and I couldn't wait to get out of there. My grades, which were usually good, understandably went downhill. My conduct at school wasn't the best either.

When my behavior was not to his liking, Father O'Bryan would say, "Henderson, take a walk!" The classroom had a large glass window. From the outside, I could peer in and watch what was going on during my detention. One of the students would be sent to get me after a while. Father O'Bryan loved my singing, so his message to me would always be the same. "You can come back in if you sing an Irish song."

Many years later, I received an honorary doctorate at nearby Brescia University in Owensboro. All my old teachers from St. Francis came and some as well from my elementary school in Rockport. During the ceremony, I talked about my time at the high school, especially of the extraordinary kindness of the teachers and the enormous impact it had on me. They remembered what I had been through during that time of my life. They all were crying, but Father O'Bryan cried the most. When I left for New York, he gave me a beautiful crucifix he had made. It still hangs in my house.

One of the other duties I had as a child was to sing at funerals. If there was anything that wounded my childhood faith, it was the death experience. The poorer Catholic families usually had the viewing of their deceased family member in their living room. The rosary would be said, and I would sing the funeral mass. As part of it, they always wanted me to touch the dead body, which scared me half to death.

I'll never forget the time when two men and a woman were killed in a gangster war in Chicago and dumped in a field near our town. Everybody lined up outside the mortuary, adults and children alike (including Oscar and me), waiting to view the bodies and see the bullet holes up close. Their deaths were turned into a festive carnival in Rockport. It gave me nightmares.

No matter how much I believed in prayer and saw its power in action, it could not defeat death. My beloved brother Carl had survived World War II only to come home and die of peritonitis from a ruptured appendix a short time thereafter. He left behind a wife who was eight months pregnant. How shocking it was to see his once handsome, curly dark hair turned suddenly straight as I viewed his corpse laid out in his home. I didn't know him as well as some of my other siblings, given our age difference and the fact that he had been gone for a greater part of my childhood. But that didn't diminish my grief, just as the standard line that he was going on to heaven only comforted me so far. That body didn't look anything like him in real life. But the child finds a way to shut the thought out and keep going.

Not so long after Carl's passing, I had a personal introduction to death myself. I was riding on the bus home from school with Oscar when I started to get a horrible stomachache. I rushed home and waited for my father to arrive. "Daddy, my stomach hurts so badly. I'm so sick." There was little response, so I had no choice other than to try to ride it out. A short time later, Billy Richards, the cutest boy in the school, came over. I let him only into the hallway. We were both in the Catholic Youth Organization through our church, and we were planning a dance and looking into getting a bus so the kids from Owensboro could also come. Finally I said, "Billy, I'm really sick. You're going to have to go." As soon as he left, I passed out from the pain and collapsed.

To make matters more dramatic, I hit the back of my head hard on the floor and was bleeding.

"What happened, Gal, did you slip up?"

"Daddy, I think I fainted." Such a thing had never happened to me before, but it was a safe assumption.

My father proceeded to do the next worst thing. He went into the cabinet and brought out a bottle of patent medicine, a.k.a. "snake oil." It was some cure-all elixir he had mail-ordered. He gave me a teaspoon of it. I promptly threw up.

"I think we need to go over to Pauline's house," my totally helpless and clueless father concluded, alarmed at seeing my rapidly deteriorating condition. Walking was the only option because we didn't have a car. My sister lived at least a mile away.

"Daddy, I don't think I can make it." But I walked all the way hunched over. By the time we got to Pauline's, I was in sheer agony.

Pauline decided that it was surely something that a good old-fashioned enema could fix. It was a close runner-up to my father's earlier "next worst thing" intervention. They all went to bed after the deed was done. I remained on the sofa writhing in pain. After a few more hours, I called out to Pauline and cried how I couldn't take it anymore. By this time, the pain had moved down to my right side. She finally called the doctor in Rockport. He came and examined me and said she needed to get me to the hospital in Owensboro immediately. Nobody had a car except for Marty's husband, that abusive man who was never pleasant to me to begin with. He was furious that he had to drive from Owensboro to get me, and didn't say a word in the car the whole way.

It got worse. We got to the hospital's emergency room and the doctor took one look at me, a fourteen-year-old girl, and assumed that I was pregnant. Great! Adding insult to injury, or more accurately, embarrassment to agony, the doctor performed a pelvic exam on me. Excruciating! Finally, they decided to operate. The appendix was perforated and ready to burst. I would have ended up like my brother Carl if they hadn't operated. It made sense that part of my father's paralysis in helping me was related to the trauma associated with Carl's death. He was equally troubled about how he was going to pay the hospital bill. At least he was sober at the time.

They kept me in the hospital a bit longer than usual because they probably realized there was nobody at home to take care of me. Reverend Mother Superior Auxilium as well as Ilean, Pauline, Marty, and some other friends came to visit me in the ward I shared with seven other people. So did my friend Ruth Helen. She was the first new friend I made when I started high school in Owensboro.

Ruth Helen was one of those girls who had already become a tall, full-figured woman. And there I was, still a girl, at five feet two inches and flat-chested. She lived in a mansion in Owensboro. Despite our radically different economic backgrounds, we found that we had a lot more in common once we opened up to each other about our problems. My eyes opened to the fact that my family circumstances were not just the domain of the poor. She told me that her mother, a glamorous, wealthy, and well-traveled woman, beat her. Her father was also an alcoholic. I'm getting ahead of the story, but Ruth Helen and her family would soon make a miraculous impact on my destiny.

What I also cannot forget about my stay in the hospital was one old lady in the ward, Mrs. Chancellor.

"I've got to get these fishhooks out of my side," she moaned repeatedly.

I begged her, "Mrs. Chancellor, don't do that!" She kept taking off the metallic clamps that closed the incision after her surgery. Doctors used those as an alternative when problems with the skin tissue made suturing difficult. I had to yell for the nurse more than once.

I went home to Marty's near the hospital for the first few days after I was released. The day I got there, Marty went into the hospital herself for—guess what?—appendicitis. I often wonder if it was a coincidence or inherent symbolism that we all got appendicitis. In my situation, the case could certainly be made that my body and spirit literally couldn't stomach what was going on any longer, and my insides threatened to explode. When I went home to Rockport, I stayed downstairs on a cot for a while to further recuperate. It was not the most pleasant of times.

The more I look at my own children and grandchildren, the more I'm convinced that infants come into the world with a certain wiring. It is probably one good reason why Babby didn't have as easy of a time coping as I did. When we would talk about what we were going through, it was always curious to me why she was more prone to cry and become negative in her thoughts and words and get nightmares, when my first response was always to look for a solution.

The experience of my youth, as challenging as it was much of the time, proved to have many tangible and positive by-products. For example, I learned how to read people extremely well (most of the time!), something that was put to good use once I started acting. With the few who protected me not always there to shield my eyes, cover my ears, or lead me away from harm, I saw too much. I could easily pick up lies. I had to grow up fast.

I realized very early on that the choice was mine how I was going to respond to my circumstances. I never wanted to be perceived as a victim. And I never wanted people to feel sorry for me. When you come from a disadvantaged and deprived situation you have a tendency to either become hateful and mean or end up as a type of person who is more giving in nature—giving, in fact, in compensation for what you didn't receive yourself. I chose the latter. I also made another conscious decision: to be in the company of achievers rather than losers. I was attracted to role models like my teachers and Ruth Helen, people whom I wanted to be like or whose achievement I felt could be within my grasp someday.

CHAPTER 4

Wide-Eyed and Confident

༖

The burning question on the lips of all of my classmates the last year of high school was, "Where are you going to college?" The girls I knew best were mostly from affluent families, and having the financial wherewithal to go to college was a non-issue. The very fact that they asked me about my plans was proof that none of them knew of my impoverished reality. It also helped that we all wore uniforms. What little they did know was that I lived in another town on the other side of the river. I had never invited anyone to visit because I was ashamed of my house and my father's condition. The only exceptions on both counts, of course, were Oscar and Ruth Helen. Ruth Helen came to my home on a few occasions to pick me up or drop me off. But even she respected my situation. She didn't ask to come in but stayed in the car.

There was more to it than just saving face when I told them

with assurance, "I'm going to the American Academy of Dramatic Arts in New York City." I had first learned about the school while leafing through the thick college guidebook in the school library. "Founded in 1884, it was the first conservatory for actors in the English-speaking world...its mission is to provide students with the tools needed to make acting their profession." Immediately, I was certain that this was the place for me. But as good of an imagination as I had, I did not see any possible way of getting there. It was more in the category of a wild hope.

Ruth Helen knew of my dream and decided to take initiative on her own. Her family was very wealthy, and she was extra sensitive to my circumstances because of her father's alcoholism. She also loved music, and at her house I had heard a recording of opera for the first time, a performance by a Brazilian soprano named Bidú Sayão. Ruth Helen decided to talk to her family and explain how badly I wanted to go to New York. They knew me, but why would they want to help me? Ruth Helen and I had talked about it, and of course, I felt a little uncomfortable simply because I needed help. But I trusted her (and still do), and I was honored that she believed in me enough to take action.

"She's the lead in the school musical. Please come and hear her," Ruth Helen told them. So her family agreed to come see me in *Jerry of Jericho Road*, a popular operetta in school performance repertory at the time.

"She's good," they said after the performance, but they had another thought in mind. They knew Christine Johnson, a very successful singer who had recently moved back from New York to Owensboro to marry her childhood sweetheart. Christine had created the role of Aunt Nettie in the original Broadway production of *Carousel* and was the first to sing "You'll Never Walk Alone" and "June Is Bustin' Out All Over," which became popular standards. She was also a distinguished operatic singer with the Met. So Ruth Helen's parents took me to sing for her to find out what she thought.

Christine was very tall with a powerful and imposing presence complemented by a very open face. She was also pregnant with her first child at the time. Christine took me through some vocal exercises, a type of training totally new to me that I really enjoyed. She also spent time talking to me and asking me questions. "What do you know about New York?" she inquired. I told her what little I had learned from going to the movies. She listened and set me straight with good advice on what I should expect if I ended up going there. For example, she told me how the streets ran, the avenues from north to south and streets from east to west, and how the subways and buses worked.

But her questions had a more serious purpose. She had heard me sing and was impressed sufficiently enough to want to work further with me and put in the time. She wanted to make sure that I wasn't just some silly girl with unreasonable expectations. "And what are your goals?" I told her that I wanted to be an entertainer, a good singer, and a good actress. From the time we spent together, about ten sessions or so in total, she saw that my desire and dedication were rock solid.

I remember how Christine always smelled so good, an impression made stronger by the fact that perfume and cologne were luxuries that had not existed in my world. The other delightful smell in her house came from the kitchen. She loved to bake and made sure I had a piece of her apple pie or anything else she might have on hand.

On one occasion, I came to her door in the cold pouring rain with neither raincoat nor scarf to protect my throat, which in her world was unthinkable. "If you want to be a singer, you can't go out like this," she admonished me. I did not volunteer that I owned no raincoat, scarf, nor umbrella.

During our visits, she would sing with me. She had a magnificent voice, a beautiful and unforgettable mezzo-soprano. William Hawkins, a distinguished critic at the time and a friend of hers, told me that she had so much talent but that her voice was even more beautiful when he heard her sing in the kitchen rather than on the stage. This same writer—who became a good friend of mine as well—in an otherwise glowing review later made a comment about how he had first met me when I was a student. Hearing my thick country accent at the time, he had felt sure I would soon be back on the farm taking care of the pigs. Oink, oink.

One day, Christine called Ruth Helen's family and gave her verdict. "I think this child has talent, and her head is screwed on straight. She deserves a break." If Christine had said no, things would have been very different. She remained a mentor and an inspiration to me because she was such an incredibly positive person. Through the years, she came to see me in various shows, and even in her nineties she still wrote me long handwritten letters. She passed away in 2010 at the age of ninety-seven.

I do not remember squealing, jumping up and down, or yelling, "Oh my gosh" when I got the news. Don't get me wrong, I was extremely grateful and very happy. But my mind was already focused on the concrete tasks ahead, no different than I am today when a new project comes my way. This was really happening! There was much to do to prepare over the next few weeks before moving in September. What to pack? Would I have enough clothes for the winter?

Since the time I had walked home singing the songs from the movie musicals I saw in the local theater, I had always felt it as a kind of destiny, a calling, a vocation. I never wavered in my desire to entertain people and make them feel happier. When I was very young, I thought for a while that I would enter a convent to become a nun. But when I found out that nuns in those days were not allowed to drive a car and couldn't go out on dates, I changed my mind. However, getting the sponsorship from Ruth Helen's family reinforced that deep faith I had as a child. Miracles did happen. Prayers were answered.

There was also the matter that I had the lead in a local musical in Owensboro. I had to tell the director that I was going to New York. He was very excited for me. Everything was set except for one important step: I was not officially enrolled at the American Academy of Dramatic Arts until I passed their audition. Being so busy helped dampen any fear and anxiety as my departure for New York neared.

Suitcase packed with some new clothes that Babby had bought me, I said goodbye to my father and my sister. Although Babby was three years older, I felt like I was the big sister as she started crying. I knew that I was leaving her alone with our father, who by this time was becoming noticeably ill with the swelling on his face. But nobody said, "Oh, I wish you wouldn't do that," or "Please, don't go." I reassured my sister, telling her, "Don't worry, I'll come back for you." And I would fulfill that promise in the coming months.

"Be careful, Gal," my father said to me. "Remember your character." He was always cautioning me to look out for a certain suspicious person and how he or she was up to no good. He was usually right. Despite his limited experience, he could read people fairly well. He wanted me to be safe, but truthfully, I was more concerned about his well-being. I had some guilt about leaving my father and Babby, since abandonment had been such a high-impact issue in my life.

I can imagine I was a funny sight, the look of astonishment on my face staring out the window at the skyline of New York City as the airplane made its approach for landing. It was a strange mix of emotions, excitement, and terror, but at the same time absurdly familiar, as if I were coming home. I must have been in such a state of shock, because I cannot recall the slightest memory of how I made it from the airport to the Barbizon Hotel for Women where I was booked to stay for just the first night.

As I rode up higher and higher in the hotel elevator with the bellman, I remembered Christine's advice that I should be sure to give him a tip. When we got to the room and I went to give him the money, he reached out his hand but asked for a little something more. He put his arm around me. I thought, "Uh-oh, this is going to be terrible." He was being overfriendly, to put it mildly. My self-protective mechanism kicked in, but it was still disturbing and made me feel all the more vulnerable as I was newly arrived in this big city. Because of my experiences with my father, there has always been a disturbing ambiguity when someone is overly attentive or inappropriate to me. On one side, it is an obvious and clear violation that feels awful. On the other side, it is hard for me to say, "No, don't do that," or "How dare you!" It is a strange combination of not wanting to hurt someone's feelings and also not being totally confident and experienced in knowing what to do.

The next morning I visited the school for the first time. It was not your traditional ivy-covered brick edifice or a classroom building of any sort, but rather was housed in the Carnegie Hall building. The school occupied rooms on different floors.

I reported for my audition to the office of Charles Jehlinger, a distinguished-looking man with a mane of gray hair, who was sitting behind his desk waiting for me to show what I could do. Dr. Jehlinger was a noted expert in the Stanislavski system, an intricate way of creating highly realistic characters, which was a precursor to the "Method acting" that actors like Marlon Brando, Paul Newman, and James Dean under teacher Lee Strasberg made commonplace later in the 1950s. Such a background makes the degree of patience and kindness Dr. Jehlinger must have summoned during my audition all the more remarkable.

The school had sent me a book before I left Rockport of short scenes culled from contemporary plays. For some reason, I chose an excerpt from *The Subway* by Elmer Rice. I had never seen nor ridden on a subway, much less had any way of knowing how its barreling locomotive was expressionist symbolism for a cold and inhumane new age of technology. My character, Sophie, was seduced and pregnant, betrayed and abandoned by her lover, who was going off to Europe. "Eugene! Eugene!" I wailed with all the dramatic effect I could muster before pretending to throw myself down on the tracks of the oncoming subway train.

It could have just as well been over right there. Dr. Jehlinger could have said, "Sorry, Miss Henderson, you are not material for us." Jump a train back to Rockport and go to Plan B. Become a nurse. Or Plan Z—oink. But failure was not an option that day. I had set a goal: I had come to New York, and I was going to give it three years. "If I don't land a job in my chosen profession in that time period, then maybe it's not for me," I rationalized. Deep down, I didn't think it was going to take me that long, and ultimately, it didn't. But now when I talk to people about this time of my life, I tell them that once I was in it, there was no way Dr. Jehlinger or anybody could have stopped me short of throwing me down on those tracks and running me over. I was hypercritical of myself even as a beginner, in the kind of insecurity that drives artists not to rest on their laurels. So I thought I was awful as the distraught and suicidal Sophie. But fortunately, Dr. Jehlinger saw some potential in me, or perhaps he was influenced by Christine Johnson's letter of recommendation. At best, Dr. Jehlinger must have admired the guts of a kid from the country choosing such a scene. I made the cut. One remarkable postscript to this story happened when I appeared on a recent talk show. One of the hosts had somehow located a copy of Dr. Jehlinger's hand-scribbled evaluation form from that audition and presented it to me. At the bottom, he wrote, "This girl has some promising qualities. Possible to become a promising actress."

The next order of business was finding affordable housing and right away, since my one night budgeted at the Barbizon was history. The school arranged for a room at the Three Arts Club for Women on West 85th Street. It was established in 1906 to provide women pursuing careers in music, drama, and the fine arts with a place to stay. It had eighty-seven rooms in total and a supportive and safe social environment.

My room was the size of a walk-in closet. There was no window, the only light coming from a light bulb on the ceiling. There was a linoleum floor, a tiny closet, and a desk. The bathroom and communal shower were down the hall. And even though the bed was little and narrow, it was the first one in my life that I didn't have to share. The place was clean, with not a cockroach to be found. Back in Rockport, I'd get up at night to go to the bathroom and the floor would be covered with them. It was not pleasant to have creepy-crawlies on you. The chiggers, mosquitoes, head lice, and you-name-it were also great motivation to leave home. So I loved the Three Arts Club. It felt good and safe.

Most of the tenants were older and only one was a fellow student at the academy, Sonya Benke. Sonya and I very quickly became wonderful friends. We'd often bring back a quart of ice cream to share from a shop called Rikers down the block on the corner of Broadway. Once we took out a Ouija board. We took turns asking questions while holding the divination planchette. I asked the spirits whether I would ever get the chance to work with the great Rodgers and Hammerstein. It was the kind of innocent and childlike wild dream aspiration akin to a hapless Cinderella wondering if her prince would ever come. Rodgers and Hammerstein were the pinnacle of success on Broadway and the theater's most famous duo. I think I had recently seen a performance of *The King and I* and loved it so much. I thought, "Oh, what a thrill it would be to one day play Anna and sing those songs." But what remote chance did I have, a million to one perhaps? Not according to the board. It said "yes."

One of my ice cream/Ouija friends was a woman across the hall. She was big and tall and funny as all get out. One night she came in and had a white stain on her dark dress, and it didn't look like anything from Rikers.

"What's that?" Miss Innocent wanted to know.

"Oh, this guy tried to, you know…" She explained nonchalantly that it was semen. My brother Joe was the first one to talk to me in any graphic detail about sexuality. Before I went to New York, he gave me a book to read and said I could ask any questions. So I knew a little, but was still very curious.

"What did you do then?" I asked.

"I took care of him. I beat him up." That was about the extent of any sexual education from my peers.

For the first couple of weeks, I was terrified to look up at the skyscrapers from the sidewalk below, having never seen a building higher than two stories in Owensboro and vicinity. It had also been frightening in the beginning to walk the couple of blocks to church for daily mass in the predawn winter darkness. Guys driving by in cars would pull over and try to proposition me. But that feeling of fear, too, was fleeting. Since then, I have never felt a lot of danger being in New York. Even in the most difficult times of my childhood, I sensed the presence of a kind of guardian angel around me. Given my situation and how I was raised, I was (and still am) very hypervigilant. I was always very aware of people. I could read their vibrations and sense danger. I was able to follow my intuition long before I knew what the word meant. If I was in a building and I saw a strange and scary person in the elevator when the doors opened, I knew to wait for the next one. Don't tempt fate!

I began to adapt fairly quickly to life in New York, ensconced at the Three Arts, having met some of the students and the teachers and settled into a routine at school. Attitude is important, and what was expressed deep in my core was how thrilled I was to be at the American Academy. From the start, it was a supportive environment. And with few exceptions in my career, the spirit in that school has carried over to theater productions and studio sets. I never felt any jealousy. We recognized that each of us came with our own distinctive talents and our particular strengths and weaknesses. For example, when word spread that I was one of the few students who could sing, people went out of their way to include me in any activity where music was involved. The feedback from both teachers and students was encouraging, whether it was praise that bolstered your confidence or critical guidance to help you step through your fears and grow. If you were serious, focused, worked hard, listened well, and tried to be a good friend, you found a strong extended family grounded in love, mutual respect, and shared purpose.

With all the hard work, this was also a time of liberation, and I made sure to also have a lot of fun despite living on very little. My friend Sonya and I would go to the Horn & Hardart automat, the early- to mid-twentieth century's idea of a fast food chain. We would go up to a wall of little windows displaying ready-made food. You put a coin into a slot that unlocked the little door so you could take out your fruit cup. When Sonya's mother came up to visit from Washington, D.C., she took us to dinner at my first fancy eatery, Jack Dempsey's Broadway Restaurant (owned by the famous heavyweight boxer). "Whoa, this is something!" I said. There were lots of people, white tablecloths, and things on the menu I had never been able to afford, such as a steak.

It was also an exciting perk going to school in the Carnegie Hall building. We found a way to sneak into the upstairs portion of its famous performance hall. One day, I saw the legendary cellist Gregor Piatigorski rehearsing with the symphony, his long fingers caressing the neck of his instrument and the other hand smoothly guiding the bow back and forth. As he finished his solo and rested his bow, he looked up with his intense Russian profile accentuated by dark raised eyebrows toward the conductor, Dimitri Mitropoulos. He suddenly started shaking his head back and forth in a cadence as if saying, "No, no, no, no." I whispered to my friends with firm conviction, "He's not happy." But no one else besides me seemed to take notice of his displeasure. As the rehearsal went on, I realized that I had jumped to a conclusion. It was just his mannerism to follow and feel the music and no sign of discontent. Here I was worried that somehow Dimitri was not doing it right.

While at the academy I also decided, "I'm going to have a boyfriend, and it's going to be great." Jerry Sanyour, a classmate, came along to fill that role nicely. He loved to dance, and so did I. We would go to Greenwich Village on a Saturday night with Sonya and another boy. There's a first time for everything, and my true inexperience came out (literally) as he held me on the dance floor. Hmm, what's that? Oh, so that's an erection.

One of the establishments in the Village we went to as part of my continuing education about life was the Rainbow Club. On the stage, there was this beautiful girl with a great figure. For her last move, the girl took off her bra and she was suddenly a flat-chested he. To my knowledge, I had never seen nor met a homosexual or a cross-dresser, but the Rainbow would change all of that. That same night, a great big burly blonde with long hair spotted me from the stage and walked over. Titanic was her name. She had a cigarette and gently blew the smoke in my face as she imparted a short but succinct nugget of wisdom: "Don't worry, honey, I was young once." It would take a little while before I fully understood what she meant. She had seen the somewhat disturbed look on my face. She saw that I had so much to live through to truly understand. When I was young, I could be very judgmental, something that my oldest brother, Joe, worked with me to temper. The compassion was not quite there, because I had not had much opportunity to make many mistakes up to that point (but I sure made up for it later). Titanic's quip helped me truly step forward and remove any remaining hesitation.

The intensity with Jerry ramped up as well. One day, we sat in a little park area on Riverside Drive. "I have to tell you something," he said in that tone that could only mean something heavy and serious was about to be delivered. My mind raced in the pause. What could he possibly say? He was a bit dark-skinned and had curly hair. Was he going to tell me he was black? It was a good guess but not right. "I'm Middle Eastern," was the big revelation he wanted to get off his chest.

"Yeah. So? I don't understand." He wanted me to know his background and his religion. I told him that it didn't matter to me. He must have experienced some prejudice and wanted to get it out in the open and cleared out of the way on the front end of our relationship.

A bigger issue was that he wanted to get serious and have sex. We made out, but it was nothing compared to today's standards. As a token of his affection, he had given me a small gold football charm he had been awarded in high school. But I said, "No, we can't." I was getting more and more confident in my career, and I didn't want to get embroiled in something that could take me off track. And I was only seventeen going on eighteen. Also, I still went to confession!

He started dating someone else because I wasn't putting out, but he never asked for his gold charm back. We remained friends and continued socializing for a while. Many years later, when I was appearing in Toronto I got a letter from a woman who lived there. She had been a very close friend of Jerry's and sadly informed me that he had died much too young. "He always talked about you and what a great time of life that was." A couple of years later, I got another letter, this time from his mother. She knew that he had given me the little football, and would I mind sending it to her? I did, along with a heartfelt note.

Speaking of prejudice, there was a matter I had to take care of regarding myself. To most of my fellow students, I must have sounded very amusing with my charming combination of southern drawl and midwestern twang. Whenever Teresa Gnassi from the Bronx and I got up to speak in class, we were made fun of, but in a nice way. "The accent you have is one of the most difficult to lose," my wonderful speech teacher Aristide D'Angelo said. "It's almost more difficult than a foreign accent." Before I could get totally discouraged, he added, "But if you really follow my advice and really practice the exercises I will give you, pretty soon your ears are going to hear what you're doing and you're going to be able to correct it."

Seeing my accent as a huge obstacle to my goal, I was an eager and motivated student in his class. We took the bull by the horns. The girl fresh out of Rockport would say, "Aiiiiice creeeeem," stretching out those vowels as if I had all the time in the world. "No, it's 'ice,' like 'eye,' not 'aiiiiiii.'" I'd go home and practice, practice. "It's 'down town,' not 'daauuun tauuuuun.'" "Repeat— down…town…down…town." Another tough one was "that." My version seemed to go on twice too long—"tha-eeeeet." Mr.

D'Angelo wanted me to talk more in clipped Middle Atlantic syllables.

Just before I went home to Rockport during a break to visit for the first time, I went to Mr. D'Angelo. "The people back there are going to make fun of me, too. They'll think I've gotten all snooty."

He replied, "It doesn't matter. Practice. Use it. Hear the difference." That's exactly what I did. It worked. I brought with me my new Mid-Atlantic accent, but when I was with family, I would revert back. Mr. D'Angelo was brilliant, and I owe him a debt of gratitude for his patience with me.

While I was getting rid of my accent, the other teachers got to work to take whatever raw talent I had in me up to a higher level. One day, one of the acting teachers, Ed Goodman, asked me in class to do something to demonstrate a point about human behavior. "All right, Florence, you look out the window. Just start looking out the window." So I went over to the window and that's what I did. I kept looking out the window, keeping quite still and concentrating on the task. I thought to myself, "This is not so difficult. I could stay still like this for hours." Nothing broke my attention for a few minutes until the teacher's voice broke the silence.

"Now, that is *not* human behavior," he said in critique of my performance.

"But you told me to just look out the window," I shot back, wondering what I could have possibly done wrong on something so simple.

"Well, that's all well and good," he explained. "But a normal person would change their posture, fold their arms, shift their weight, or do something." The devil was in the details.

Another kid was doing a scene, and Mr. Goodman lashed out: "For God's sake, why are you sitting like that? Do you have a problem with your entrails?" The word "entrails" threw me for a moment, especially said with his British-sounding inflection. "Oh, he means intestines," I realized. Mr. Goodman was not the only teacher who could be tough. Perhaps it was their way of helping us develop a thick skin in preparation for the certainty of a critic's bad review. Being judged was never easy and nothing new to someone with a Catholic upbringing. You get used to it, and just try to find a way to get through it.

Mr. Goodman also said something that I immediately took to heart and have passed along to others countless times: "Keep a cool head and a warm heart." It's so important in this business.

We learned in the acting classes that it was more than just rehearsing your lines. You had to dissect them and be able to answer anything about your character, the "who, what, when, where, and why." We learned how to do our own stage makeup, and how to make ourselves look older. One of the first important tips I learned was that you didn't have to make up your face for the whole theater. You only had to concern yourself with how you looked to the people in the first ten rows. Beyond that, they would need binoculars to see your face in any detail. An actor who doesn't do this will look pretty grotesque to those up front.

The key thing is to learn your flaws and find a way to correct them. When I started doing television, my education took a greater leap forward. I learned more techniques and asked a lot of questions. Soon I was doing my own makeup because I didn't like being fussed over, and still do to this day. I start with a base and then apply different tones from there. You need to be very careful to blend so your rouge doesn't make you look like a circus clown. With putting on eye shadow, try not to go too light in the shade. It will give you a big flap when you close your eye. My biggest pet peeve is reserved for those who do a great job on their face but neglect to also do their ears. You see it a lot on television newscasters—lovely faces framed by big white ears. Drives me crazy! Last but not least, if you care about your skin's long-term health and appearance, make sure you clean your face extremely well before you go to bed. Don't slack on this one. I don't care how tired (and/or drunk) you are.

Body movement and how you carried yourself on the stage was also an art like choreography. We trained how to faint without killing ourselves in the process. There was a specific way you could gently go down so as to not crack your head open. In another class, we trained on how to look like you were straining to push against something very heavy like a huge rock. Anytime I find myself standing with my shoulders slumped and my posture looking more like a question mark than an exclamation point, I still hear Sarah Mildred Strauss barking at me with her aristo-cratic rolling R's, "Rrrrribs up!" I will also never forget a comment she made to the class that I think she did for my specific bene-fit: "Remember that the boy you think you love at eighteen is the same one you won't spit on at twenty-one."

On the singing and comedy front, the instruction at the academy didn't add all that much to my skill set. George Burns used to say that you can't teach comedic timing; you can improve upon it with practice, but you either have it or you don't. I think the same goes for having a good sense of humor. You can't teach it if it's not already there. Looking at some of my earliest child-hood photographs, you can see in my face that I was born with the desire to make people laugh. And all those times I got in trou-ble for mimicking my teachers at St. Francis were now being put to good use.

What was more challenging was learning how to work with the sadder spectrum of feelings. They taught us about sense memories—how to go back in time to mine your own experi-ences to bring forth in your performance a desired emotional state. I got depressed in one of the classes because I started thinking too much about my father. "I don't want to do that again, it's too hard," I thought.

Learning how to cry was harder. It too was about getting in touch with your feelings, specifically about something that made you very sad. You would think that I had a reservoir that could unleash a torrent of tears. Just flick the switch. There was one problem, though, and it is a reason why I still have trouble crying today. As a child, it was not permitted. "Don't you cry, don't cry," my mother would warn me, with the unspoken threat that if I did, then she'd give me a real reason to cry by whipping the gizzard out of me. So I'd suck in whatever was bothering me, take a deep breath, and say, "Oh, all right." In fact, I had only seen my mother cry once, when I was a little girl and had accompanied her to church on Mother's Day. The priest gave a sermon apropos of mothers. Whatever the priest said penetrated the barrier she constructed to help her get through her hard life. She was quietly crying and trying to hide her face. It made me so sad. I put my little arm through hers and tried to comfort her.

There was also much to learn from watching the other students. They may have come from all parts of the country and diverse ethnic and socioeconomic backgrounds, but there was great camaraderie. We were all striving for success, yet despite the competitive climate, fellow students were generous in helping one another. Thanks to that quality, my studies at the American Academy of Dramatic Arts would soon come to a sudden and abrupt end.

CHAPTER 5

Wish You Were Here

It was my first audition, a cattle call at the Alvin Theater for a part in the chorus in the original cast of the musical *Wish You Were Here*. "You can sing, so you should go," my fellow students encouraged me. Some of them had already auditioned for the show, but nobody had gotten a job. I was told to bring a bathing suit, but of course I didn't have one. One of the students, Candy Parsons, who was in *South Pacific* with me years later at Lincoln Center, lent me hers. Another student gave me a piece of sheet music to take with me and told me how to get to the theater.

Ask any successful actor and each will have his or her own version of this rite of passage. For example, when Martin Sheen and Zalman King were starving young actors in New York, they actually shared the same suit for an audition. When the first finished, they went into the restroom so the other could change into it. Luckily, they were the same size. Unfortunately, Candy and I were not.

I arrived with my long blonde hair and simple clothes, bathing suit in tow, and took my place in line. When it was my turn, I handed the sheet music for "Only Make Believe" from *Showboat* to the pianist and sang to the darkened audience. When I finished, the director and cowriter Josh Logan and composer Harold Rome emerged from the shadows and addressed me from their seats below: "Did you bring a bathing suit?" I told them that I had. "Go down to the basement and put it on and come back."

Downstairs, an old stagehand named Charlie Bauer heard me in distress.

"What's the matter?"

"This bathing suit doesn't fit," I told him. It was both too wide and too low-cut over the breasts. I was struggling to hold the back end and the top part up at the same time.

"Hold on. I'll get some safety pins," Charlie offered.

It is one thing to be terrified about going to your first audition, but the added worry about accidental nudity (displaying more of your talents) did not help. The bathing suit was required because there was a real, fully functioning swimming pool in the middle of the stage. The musical was based on a play, *Having Wonderful Time*, by Arthur Kober, about a Jewish summer camp for young people in the Catskills.

I went on the stage, but the safety pins were not doing the job. Everyone must have laughed as I sang and tried to hold myself together and keep the suit from falling down. "Are you okay?" they asked.

"No. This isn't my bathing suit. I borrowed it." They laughed again. Luckily, I did not panic during the performance, and was spared the nightmare of a wardrobe malfunction.

"Will you come back in a week and sing for us again? And bring a bathing suit that fits!" More laughter.

So that is what I did. I came back. I had purchased a bathing suit that fit. There is a lot that can go wrong during a live performance. Who knows? Perhaps the fact that I showed some fearlessness and spontaneity under that pressure and turned the negative situation into an advantage gave me the decisive edge. I got in the show. I won the role of the New Girl. I would sing in the chorus. I would also be given one line: "Can I still see the game?" I will never forget that line!

After the audition, I went back to the head of the school to get his advice. I had only completed a year, but had been invited back for the second year and was loath to quit. I explained to him that I had been offered the job and asked him if I should take it or stay in school.

"What, are you crazy? That's why you're here!"

Out of school and starting off in the play, I was so eager and exuberant that some of the older chorus girls said some mean things, trying to put me down for my desire to be good and get better. It was ironic in this new phase of my life how the deprivation of my childhood proved to be an unexpected ally, not just in this situation, but other times when things could feel threatening or overwhelming. It maybe also helps explain why the bathing suit debacle did not take me off my game.

It was a consequence of that law of the jungle, how only the fit survive, mixed in with another axiom—how what doesn't kill you makes you stronger. I had learned the hard way as a small child to not be dependent on other people. Away from my immediate family and close friends back home, I had no one I could count on. It forced me to become very resilient. When things were especially tough, I had to somehow find a way to sustain enough courage to keep going every day. With that life experience, I was not going to let the chorus girls' comments affect me or take me down to that level. I was prepared with a good stockpile of fortitude, something that would prove very useful as my career soon began a rapid upward trajectory.

Being on my own without much cushion of support, I had another resource that kicked into high gear. I put my faith into action, that tremendous faith that I retained since childhood, and it did not disappoint. I had seen how God would help you, but it wasn't for the lazy. You had to pitch in and do the work too. I went to church almost every morning. I knelt down every night and said my prayers. I asked for guidance. I asked for success. It was not a hollow, naïve, or egotistical mental concept or fantasy, but a mystical presence that I felt deep in my core. I did not feel alone, even back during the hardest moments of my childhood. Honestly, I felt that I was protected, and that I had a special pipeline to a greater force that could help me, assuming that I had talent. And by this time, judging by the reactions of people, it appeared that I did have something to offer.

Although my formal schooling ended when I joined the cast of *Wish You Were Here*, the real education began when I entered the stage door and began learning from the great masters, the best of the best. Josh Logan was one of them, a very brilliant but also a troubled man who suffered from a bipolar disorder. After the play finished its run, he had a total breakdown. Some people were afraid of him, but I never was. You could learn a lot if you just listened and watched how he worked.

The girl who was the lead was fired. She was apparently a malcontent from the start. "He's putting his tongue in my mouth," she complained about the guy with whom she was doing the kissing scene. Josh put up with that for the time being, but soon his patience ran out. When she was onstage in full rehearsal and failed to step into her spotlight he had had enough. "If you can't find the light on the stage, then you don't belong on that stage," he told her as she was let go.

I may have only had that one spoken line in the play, but Josh taught me a valuable thing: "Make sure the audience can understand you. If they can't hear you or don't understand what you're saying, they immediately dislike you." That's true in life as well. Similarly, I learned that whoever had the strongest intention on the stage is whom the audience would find most compelling. Having performed in one way or another since I was a small child, I knew how to get attention, and I loved it when I did. But advice like this and practice applying it took things to a more refined level.

I also learned that when you entered that stage door, whether you were in the chorus or were the leading lady, it was a responsibility and a privilege not to be taken for granted but cherished with the highest respect. My first stage manager, Bobby Griffith, who went on to produce some big Broadway shows like *The Pajama Game*, ran the theater in a no-nonsense manner. One evening I was running downstairs to change for the new scene for my "New Girl at Camp" line, singing at the top of my lungs from excitement about being in the show. There was an opening downstairs leading to the orchestra pit for the musicians to enter, and my voice was floating out through that opening. "Who in the hell is down there singing?" Bobby screamed wrathfully. "Jack Cassidy [the male lead in the show] sounds like a soprano!" He was so strict that it could be terrifying, but working with people like that sets you up and teaches you discipline. If you didn't get to the theater on time, you had better have been hit by a car on the way. For that reason, I always make it a point to show up early.

When *Wish You Were Here* opened, it was one of the hottest nights on record in New York City and the air-conditioning in the theater broke. The reviews were mixed. Josh called the cast and crew together after the first few performances and stood up on a chair. "Don't worry, I will make this a hit," he said. And he did. The show went on to sell out performances for the next two years.

What also made a difference was a segment on Ed Sullivan's television show, then entitled *Toast of the Town*. Sullivan had been a very powerful newspaper columnist in New York when he made the move to hosting a variety program on this emerging new medium. For our performance, Sullivan went to the trouble of having a replica of the swimming pool built on his stage. It was only a foot or two deep, with mirrors placed on the bottom to create the illusion of deeper water. It was my first TV appearance, although only in voice singing off camera. Lines formed at the ticket office the next morning after the broadcast.

Television was just starting to emerge out of the novelty stage and become the major communications medium of the masses. It is funny to admit that I was on television a few times before I ever owned one. But that wouldn't be for long. And for what he would do for Elvis and the Beatles and hundreds of other acts that he helped launch, Ed Sullivan became the king of Sunday night in America for the next two decades.

In the meantime, Broadway was in its golden age from the post–World War II era well into the late 1950s, and its cultural influence was at its apex until Elvis and the Beatles took over. Although there are still packed houses today and just about every able-bodied actor wishes they could do Broadway, it was truly in the stratosphere back then. The biggest hit songs most often came out of the productions. If you opened on a Wednesday, you would be in the recording studio on Sunday doing the cast album, and within weeks it would be up at the top of the pop charts. Eddie Fisher would later have a number one hit with the title song, "Wish You Were Here."

When I got the play, I moved out of the Three Arts. One of the girls in the chorus, Margaret Ann Cooper, who was also from Kentucky, told me that two other friends and she were going to get an apartment and asked me if I wanted to share. Sounded like a good idea at the time—a fifth-story walk-up on East 61st Street near Bloomingdale's. It could be fun, I thought. And I didn't mind being around a lot of people. There was a fairly large bedroom that could accommodate a bed for each of us. There was a bathroom we shared that could only be accessed by walking through the living room. That proved to be a problem. If one of the girls was seriously dating, she and the guy would take over the living room. You hoped and prayed during those times, "Lord, please get me through the night." You tried to visualize desert sandstorms instead of cascading waterfalls if you felt your bladder reaching capacity. There was no way you wanted to interrupt the festivities on your way to the toilet.

Jerry and I were at the tail end of our dating at the time, but safe passage through the living room was guaranteed whenever we were there. I also dated the noted writer William Safire for a little while, and went out with Tim Murphy, an acquaintance of a cousin who studied with him at Georgetown Law School. He was in the military and a strict Catholic. He was not one to cross a street against a red light, so it figures that he went on to become an important judge, and we still correspond to this day. But most of my energy was concentrated on learning my craft and building a career. My personal life took a backseat, at least for the moment.

CHAPTER 6

Hitting the Road

ᘒ

My one little line of dialogue in *Wish You Were Here* quickly opened some doors. A top agent suddenly wanted to represent me. The production company also started sending me out to do publicity for the show (including that off-camera Ed Sullivan performance with the chorus). Don't ask me why—maybe they saw something refreshing in a young face getting a big break, since the show was openly giving that chance to a few newcomers. It was something to see my name in ink for the first time in newspaper columns. Television talk shows were just getting started and Tex McCrary and Jinx Falkenburg, who pretty much invented the genre, had me on theirs. They thought the country accent that I had worked so hard to lose was the funniest thing and wanted me to demonstrate it. That was easy enough.

There was no videotape in television's infancy and no retakes, although some programs were recorded in kinescope for rebroad-

cast in earlier time zones (by literally pointing a film camera at a
TV monitor). Everything was live, which some performers found
absolutely terrifying. But it did not bother me. Instead, I learned
quickly through necessity that you had to be prepared when you
went on television, not just with stories to tell but also to expect
the unexpected. It helped that I had that early-acquired sense of
what it took to make people laugh. You also had to be flexible
and roll with the punches because the host might go off on a tangent and other things might not come off as planned. Once I was
on a radio show hosted by Barry Gray broadcast live on WMCA
from a restaurant. If memory serves me right, it must have been
my birthday, because they brought out a birthday cake to the table on the raised platform where we did the interview. But the
cake never made it to me. It got diverted at the last second onto
the nicely dressed and very stunned businessman seated at the table below. Too bad it wasn't captured on television, but I'm sure
the way I was laughing must have left little to the imagination for
those listening at home. It was uncanny how in the blink of an
eye the cake had jumped off the table and deposited itself on his
shoulders, plastering his hair and face.

When not at the theater or doing interviews, I was studying. I
had met a wonderful voice teacher named Dolf Swing and took
lessons with him. Twice a week, I had a three-hour acting class
with Mary Tarcai (Charlotte Rae was in my class). I was also going out on auditions, including for the part of the leading lady in
Wish You Were Here when the actress was suddenly fired. I didn't
get that part because they told me I didn't look Jewish enough. A
beautiful dark-haired actress named Patricia Marand got it. Jack
Cassidy remained the leading man.

When you went out on an audition, the decision-makers sat in
the shadows in the seats below.

"Can you come back in the afternoon and sing for my partner?" asked one of the strangers in the audience after I finished one tryout.

"Who's your partner?" I asked.

"Oscar Hammerstein," the man replied. That probably meant that the man I was speaking to was Richard Rodgers. So it was. The Ouija board back at the Three Arts wasn't lying. I found out I was up for the lead as the farm girl Laurey in the last national touring company of the musical *Oklahoma!* I was the right age and had the right accent—again, the one I had just gotten rid of!—so they must have sensed how easily Laurey came to me. They offered me the role that afternoon. I had been in *Wish You Were Here* for two months by this time.

Here I was, suddenly elevated from the chorus to the chance to play a leading role in a major production for my idols, Rodgers and Hammerstein, a dream that came true so quickly it was almost ridiculous. But I had some serious doubts about taking the job. My goal was Broadway, to be on the stage in New York. I thought that if I went out on the road I would be out of sight, out of mind, out of the mix, and unavailable if any other big roles came up. Nor would I be able to continue with my studies and keep learning and growing. I was still very much a teenager, so this display of impatience and chutzpah could be chalked up to that. I was also not worried that if I said no to this part I wouldn't get another big shot. But it was a big decision, and to hedge my bets I still went out on other auditions, one of which was for *Guys and Dolls*.

The casting director for the musical, Ira Bernstein, knew that I had already been offered the role in *Oklahoma!* He strongly recommended that I take the job and have the experience of playing a leading role on the road. "You can really learn your craft." My voice teacher Dolf concurred, emphasizing that doing eight shows a week on tour would be an invaluable education. So I took the job.

In the interim weeks before rehearsals for *Oklahoma!* began, I still appeared in *Wish You Were Here*. I walked each afternoon the twenty blocks from my apartment on the East Side to the theater on the West Side with blisters on my heels. The stage door to our theater was right next door to the one for *Guys and Dolls*. I saw Ira standing outside that door, and I went over to thank him for his advice and told him that I had made my decision. "Maybe we could discuss it over dinner," he suggested. He was a very charming and handsome man, but we just kept it on a platonic level. We dated a few times, but that came to a temporary stop out of necessity when I went out on the road.

We rehearsed in New York for three weeks before the opening night in New Haven, Connecticut. Jerry White, the director, was tough and demanding, but it was something I really liked and never found intimidating. The thought of going from the chorus in one play to the lead in the next, one might assume, would be stressful. The leads in the one high school operetta and the community theater piece I did before leaving for New York were not comparable. But my ignorance proved a great blessing. I had no idea what I was getting myself into. Since playing Laurey was like second nature to me, I hardly fretted.

However, that stress-free experience was short-lived. I didn't realize all the reality checks that would quickly be coming my way. It was on the last days of these rehearsals and right before we were to open in New Haven that I found out my father had died. My understudy was not yet prepared, so the trip home for the funeral was out of the question. It was incredibly hard, but like so many other times of adversity, when faced with little other choice, I stoically barreled through it. Only this time it proved to be a lot more complicated. Cause and effect created a spiraling outcome.

On top of dealing with my father's death and all the stress of opening night in New Haven, I caught a cold. The show must go on. When you are the lead, you bear extra responsibility, and you do what is necessary. I went to a doctor and he gave me an injection. It killed the cold all right, but came close to taking the rest of me along with it. The first thing I noticed was that my fingers swelled up. Then the same thing happened to my legs and to my feet, which looked like piano legs. When I couldn't get the Mary Janes on my swollen feet, the wardrobe person improvised and cut up a pair of black house slippers. Every night I would go to sleep with my legs propped up on the hotel bed headboard to cut down on the swelling. I was in so much agony with the pain. I prayed that it would be gone by the morning, but when I woke up it was just as bad.

I prayed more and said my rosary but also questioned God why He wasn't helping me. Onstage, the pain in my knees and all my joints made each movement a torture, and I did everything I could to minimize my limping. I had to dance during the "Many a New Day" number, and it hurt like hell. Adrenaline kicks in and you find a way to tough your way through it. The cast and crew were very supportive, but looking back, I wonder how I made it and whether any performers today would have gone on under such circumstances. "What did I do to deserve this?" I questioned God in my prayers. Was this some kind of divine retribution because I didn't go to my father's funeral? Was it payback for when I told him I'd rather see him dead than in that condition? With my upbringing, it was so easy to go there.

When we left New Haven, the next stop was Asbury Park, New Jersey. A group of us went to the beach during the day, and I noticed that people started looking at me funny. It turns out that I was getting hives on my face and lips from being out in the sunlight. My tongue had also begun to swell up. They took me back to the hotel, and the front desk called a doctor. He came and looked at me. "My God, child, don't let anybody ever give you penicillin." No one else had thought to question that, but Dr. Alvin Weinstein, who would become a lifelong friend, recognized it immediately. He told me that he was in the Army during the war and quarantined a whole group of men, thinking that it was an outbreak of measles. But on further investigation, it turned out it was a toxic reaction to penicillin. The antibiotic was still relatively new, only in widespread use since the end of World War II. As an antidote, he gave me a shot of adrenaline and cortisone.

"Will it be okay?" I asked him. "I have a show to do tonight."

"You can't. You can't sing like this," he answered. I told him I had to, so he came to the show and gave me another shot just before I went onstage. He treated me for the whole week we were there and never charged me a dime. We had a nurse with the show, and she continued to give me the injections for a few more weeks as we traveled onward, until the poison finally got out of my system. I was lucky that I hadn't dropped dead.

Once I was feeling better, I settled into the routine. On average, we spent about five days in each city, the tour lasting from September through May. I thought it was the most exciting thing in the world to travel. I was given the stateroom on the train because I was the leading lady, but I gave it instead to Mary Marlowe, a veteran actress who played Aunt Eller. I took the berth instead—after all, that's what they did in those movie musicals. Sometimes we would end up on a bus if the trains didn't run. It sounds romantic, but when you're in a blizzard in Minnesota and the driver is lost, it wears thin.

"What's the best way to Duluth?" he asked a passerby.

"Oh, that's right up next to Bemidji."

"Where in the hell is Bemidji?"

The first year, I had a roommate, a fellow cast member who was supposed to look after me, since I was still just eighteen years old. But it turned out to be the other way around. She was a few years older, and she was wild. She would frequently get bombed, and it was a nightmare to try to get her up to catch the train when we were leaving town. When she was drunk, she would tell me all sorts of tragic stories that had happened to her, about abortions and other traumas, and it would keep me awake at night thinking about it. If she had a boyfriend in that town, she would show me the hickeys she got from the night before. It was a baptism by fire and a teachable moment for what I did not want to become when I grew up.

Another ritual of the road was the brainchild of Owen Martin, a wonderful man who played the Sheriff. He explained it when I was first invited to dinner with the others.

"Okay, we're going to say it's my birthday. They'll know we're from the show. That way, we'll get something extra to drink or a dessert on the house." Per the plan, we sang "Happy Birthday" to him. And sure enough, we would get it. Once we did it at a very fancy and expensive place. Owen said after that meal, "All that service, white gloves, and eighteen-karat gold plates, and the food stunk!" Maybe that was payback for all the freebies, but we did have fun. A lot of laughs were also to be had hanging out with the male dancers, most of whom were homosexual. I was further educated in the diverse ways of the world. All of that proved to be a helpful diversion from my own little melodrama. I had a crush on my leading man, who was married. That, of course, was a nonstarter and the end of the story, but I sure loved kissing him onstage!

I trust that the statute of limitations has run out on this accidental crime I committed during the second season in *Oklahoma!* No fingers were pointed at the time, but here, for the first time, you have my confession. Barbara Cook (who played Ado Annie in the second year) and I had our dressing room together backstage in the theater in Pittsburgh. In those days, we had a very neat trick for thickening our eyelashes. We had these little containers of wax with a small candle underneath. We'd melt the wax and put it on our eyelashes. After we would finish at night, we'd cover the makeup on the table with a towel and leave. That's what I did one Friday night. The next day, we came in to do the Saturday matinee and learned that there had been a fire in the theater backstage. My costume, which was a little white dress, was an absolute mess with black soot on it. Pittsburgh was known in those days for having a lot of soot from all the coal-burning steel mills, but this was ridiculous. I paid no attention to it. The show had to go on. When Barbara Cook came out on-stage dressed as Ado Annie, she not only had soot on her dress but also on her face, on the rose on her head, and all over. A little more and she could have done the show in blackface. I took one look at her and became hysterical. So did she, and we fell into each other's arms. The stage manager was yelling at us from the wings to get on with the show, but it took a while before we finally stopped laughing. It didn't take an arson expert to notice that my makeup table was more severely burned than anything else around it. Hmm, someone must have forgotten to blow out that candle. It was pathetic, and I felt bad about it. But now I've finally gotten it off my chest.

All throughout this time, I kept up the friendship with Ira Bernstein from afar despite being out on tour. We exchanged letters, and he came out to see me a couple of times on the road. He said to me after he saw me for the first time, "You just make love to the audience." Part of that probably was due to the fact that I am always very grateful to the audience, what Oscar Hammerstein called the Big Black Giant. When you come from that place of gratitude, I think it opens up the potential of what can happen, some of which can almost seem supernatural. When you listen to actors talk about their experiences on the stage, some remark about their ability to see all around them onstage as if they truly had eyes in the backs of their heads. For me, there were two sensations. First, I had the sensation that I could reach out and touch the person in the last row of the balcony. And second, I felt like I physically grew larger on the stage. To this day, people come backstage after a show and comment how they were certain I was a half a foot taller when performing than in reality.

Being on tour in a long run introduced me to another challenge—doing the same show over and over night after night and keeping it fresh every time. I learned very quickly to say to myself, "This is a new audience. They haven't seen it. I want it to be as good for them as it was for the audience the night before."

Sometimes, circumstances onstage intervened to break the routine in horrifying, hilarious, and unforgettable ways. For example, it does not matter how perfectly well you know all your lines. All it takes is a momentary lapse in concentration. You're singing a song, everything is going fine, and all of a sudden the lyrics are gone! It is not the same as if you are just speaking lines and someone whispers to you the cue to get back on track after a few seconds of uncomfortable fumbling. No, the music doesn't stop for you when your memory hits a glitch. Instead, the only thing you can do is vamp a little, make up some lyrics, and grab back your place a bar or so later or as quickly as you can. It is the strangest sensation, and it scared the heck out of me the first time it happened.

One little incident I found fascinating came as the result of meeting a blind woman and her guide dog on one of those train rides on the tour. I talked to her for a while and got to know the dog a little as well. As we were both getting off, I invited her to the show. There is a scene in *Oklahoma!* where Jud tries to grab Laurey and kiss her. She pushes him away and makes a strong speech to him. When I got to that part, struggling to push him away, the woman's dog started whining from the audience. He was worried about me.

Some years later, I was doing *The King and I*, playing Anna opposite Ricardo Montalban. In a very dramatic scene as the King lay on his deathbed, Ricardo began to whistle "Whenever I Feel Afraid" as the scene required. But that day, his whistle didn't wet. The blowing from his puckered lips was barely audible to me and certainly not to the audience. So I had little other choice than to take over. I leaned over him, my shoulders shaking, lamenting over the dying king. To the audience, it looked like I was crying. But in truth, this outpouring of grief was my attempt to hold back an attack of laughter. And Ricardo, who was supposed to be on death's doorstep, had to harness all the self-control and acting ability he could muster to keep from cracking up too.

Sometimes the spontaneity came from malfunctions of some otherwise brilliantly fabricated sets. Many years later, I was portraying the answering service switchboard operator Ella Peterson in *Bells Are Ringing* in a scene together with another girl. I looked around and noticed that the set was moving, heading east toward me. I signaled to the other girl. We both got up from the switchboard and started to hold the scenery back from closing in on us until the stagehands jumped in to save us. We milked that one for a big laugh. When you slip out of character for a moment, it is called "breaking the fourth wall"—the one that separates the actor from the audience. In this case, all four walls were breaking.

The same thing happened to me another time, but this one was hardly a laughing matter. "It's all so wonderful, wonderful, wonderful." I was singing the lyrics in the lovely coronation scene from Noël Coward's *The Girl Who Came to Supper*. The set was a cathedral. I was supposed to be in the center box surrounded by royalty, adorned with the ermine fur, jewels, and crowns, when suddenly the fantasy dissolves. The girl is left on a stool, the trappings stripped from her, and the cathedral backdrop splits in two and is pulled off to the sides of the stage. But one evening, things took a decidedly different direction. Someone put the contraption into reverse, and the shell of the cathedral started to collapse on me. I had to jump out of the way quickly before the winching mechanism that held the set onto its tracks literally cut my feet off. I looked like a flamenco dancer. The demolished stool that I had sat on seconds before left little to the imagination of what could have been my fate. A few moments later, after they got the set moving back in the right direction, I went over and picked up a couple pieces of the former stool and waved them to the audience's cheer. Survived again!

Sometimes a problem onstage would be more personal in nature. God forbid you should get the runs when the curtain rises. It happens often enough that most theaters have a toilet within easy reach of the stage. I was doing *The Sound of Music* and had an attack of acute food poisoning in Chicago. Everyone in the cast and crew knew I was sick, so when I would finish a scene, I made a dash to the bathroom and rushed to be ready for the next scene. John Meyers was my leading man, the Captain. In one of the scenes, the Captain asks Maria to stay for dinner. At first she says, "No, I couldn't," but then changes her mind. As I was going up the stairs on the set to exit the stage, just about overdue for my next pit stop, John said his next lines, "You'll have to hurry. You'll have to change." I gave him the most pathetic, most sarcastic of all looks. The audience was certainly not in on the joke as he doubled up laughing.

The other thing that could mess with an actor's mind during the performance was if they knew that someone important was in the audience. Thinking about that tough critic or one of your peers or idols sitting out there could drive you crazy. However, nothing came close to playing Maria in the aforementioned

Sound of Music with the real Maria von Trapp watching me play her from the front row below. Yikes!

Perhaps the most special guest in the audience was during the first year of the tour of *Oklahoma!*—my mother. When we hit Cleveland, I got in contact and invited her to come see the show. We had corresponded throughout the years, but this would be the first time I would have face time with her since she left Rockport. When I saw her it was clear that she was little changed in physical appearance outside of a few extra pounds around the middle. Some hours later, I could safely say that nothing was radically different about her personality either. She carried on in her inimitable spirit of forthrightness and frankness, doing what she wanted to do and fairly oblivious to the feelings of those around her.

After the show, she went out with us to a restaurant, ordering her usual can of beer. She got on like fire with my wild former roommate, kindred spirits.

"You must be very proud of Florence," someone said. Her reply was always the same and very protective.

"I'm proud of all my children." She was not one to gleam with satisfaction. "I loved you. You were wonderful." I knew she was happy for me, but she never made a big deal out of it. But one other side of it was no doubt the frustration that such success did not happen to her in her lifetime. I think she would have loved to be there onstage herself and command all that attention.

That night after the Cleveland show, she did get a different sort of attention. We went back to the hotel, where in the room there was a jump rope that we used for exercise. My mother grabbed it and demonstrated her prowess. The people on the floor below complained about the noise from the ceiling. When the front desk called, she responded, "Tell them not to worry about it. Think nothing of it!"

I think I inherited some of my mother's forthrightness. I can also be very frank and spontaneously carefree in what I say and do, but I think it has served me better because I learned to temper it with a little more awareness and sensitivity. A few years later, I invited my mother to see *The Sound of Music* in Chicago. I didn't want to be embarrassed, so I told John Meyers preemptively, "Please do not ask my mother anything about my childhood." We went to dinner after the show, and the first thing John did was turn to my mother. "Elizabeth, tell us what Flo was like as a child."

My mother looked up and didn't miss a beat. "Just like a fart in a whirlwind!"

CHAPTER 7

The Big Break

∿

The chance to star in the motion picture version was all part of the deal for signing on to go back out on the road for the second season of *Oklahoma!* The actual filming would be done several months later once the tour came off the road. It was all very rushed, and I was clearly feeling uncomfortable. I had flown out from New York and booked into the Studio Club in Hollywood for the quick one-night stay before having to fly back the next day. The Studio Club was the West Coast equivalent of the Three Arts, a chaperoned dorm where Marilyn Monroe and dozens of other leading ladies passed through in the early part of their careers. The next morning, I reported to the studio at the appointed hour for a screen test.

After makeup and wardrobe, I took my place on the mark on the set indicated by the gaffer's tape and waited as the crew made the last adjustments. The director was Fred Zinnemann, a four-time Oscar recipient who helmed such classics as *High Noon, From Here to Eternity,* and later *A Man for All Seasons.* The man walking around and giving instructions about the lighting was no slouch either, the legendary Academy Award–winning cine-matographer Harry Stradling. He filmed virtually all the great leading ladies of Hollywood in the 130 films to his credit, includ-ing *Easter Parade* and many others that I had seen as a child at the movie house in Rockport. And there I stood on the threshold of fulfilling that little girl's wildest fantasy.

But I didn't get the part of Laurey in the movie. When I got back to New York to rehearse for the second season of *Oklahoma!* I discussed the bad news with Jerry White. He told me, "Don't be depressed about this. In the scheme of things, you'll see that it's going to be all right."

"I'm not depressed," I told him, although my eyes could not hide the fact that I had been crying. It was the first time in my young career that I did not get something that I wanted. "I'm a little discouraged." But I assured the director that I would do the second season as I had promised and told him I would make it even better than the first one.

Although the screen test was hurried, they had treated me fairly. I was probably awful. With no experience working in film, I sang with too much intensity, projecting as I normally did to be heard live by hundreds of people. Preparing for this screen test with an acting coach would have been a good idea had I pos-sessed the insight at that age and the luxury of time. But as often was the case, perceived negatives sooner or later turned into posi-tives, as Jerry had promised. One of those pluses was getting back in front of New York audiences for a run at City Center, which generated great reviews. And while the film was not my fate when the season concluded, another dream come true would take its place—the chance to headline a smash Broadway show.

Leaving the touring company after the second season was bittersweet. The experience of being on the road that so many had thought would be a good education for me felt fairly complete. I learned the true meaning of "the show must go on." You were expected to be there and perform at one hundred percent every night whether you felt sick or had a broken toe, cracked rib, or whatever. Gone were the crazy roommates. And the chapter was closed on the crush on my leading man. The fact that I got to kiss him every night onstage wasn't so bad. As I mentioned, he was married, but he was very obviously still a player with the ladies. I thought he was great, but my upbringing kicked in to save me many times. Nevertheless, when you are in a long engagement, the crew and your fellow actors become your family. One of the hardest things in our business is always saying goodbye. But then, if we're lucky, we get to say hello to a whole new group.

Fortunately, leaving *Oklahoma!* was not the end of my personal relationship with Richard Rodgers and Oscar Hammerstein. I was willingly on call to sing whenever they had special events and performances. At one such occasion, they asked me to perform at a private event at the Waldorf for Aly Khan and a big group. Two memories stand out the most. First, it was the first time I ever saw Marilyn Monroe in person, and her beauty more than lived up to the hype. More important, when I was singing "When I Marry Mr. Snow" from *Carousel*, I knew right away that I had goofed and inverted a couple of lyrics. I also was certain that my transgression would not go by unnoticed. Afterwards, Oscar, that great big teddy bear of a man with the trademark crew cut and the lovely smile, came up to me.

"You sang very beautifully, but—"

I cut Oscar off. "Don't say it, I knew the second I did it that you'd get on me for it!" We had a great laugh.

Oscar had a shy quality about him. He was a big man, while

Dick Rodgers was shorter, and both had wives named Dorothy. Whenever we were together, they were all incredibly kind to me. I had the chance to spend the weekend at the Rodgers home in Fairfield, Connecticut, right after doing a concert for them in the area. I took the opportunity to ask Dick a question about how he worked with Oscar.

"Do you write to Oscar's lyrics or does he write them to your music?" I was curious to know.

He walked me through the process. "I'm very disciplined. I get up in the morning and write. I write the music first, then Oscar does the lyrics." He mentioned that sometimes Oscar would write a dummy melody to his lyrics, but the music, according to Dick's opinion, was not that memorable. Whatever dynamic they had, it created unquestionably the greatest catalog of theatrical music and some of the most beloved and timeless songs in history.

Unfortunately, my time with Oscar was limited. He passed away in 1960 shortly after the opening of *The Sound of Music* on Broadway. I continued to work and sing with Dick all the way until the end when his health deteriorated in the late 1970s. I will never forget the time in 1962 when he asked me to come over to his home to sing a song. Some big producer from Hollywood was interested in doing a remake of *State Fair* and wanted to hear some of the music Dick had written. I sang "I Love a Pig." Despite all of his great accomplishments, I could see that Dick was nervous about this "audition." To make matters worse, he threw his back out when he sneezed the wrong way. But the deal was done, and the film got made.

Off the road from *Oklahoma!* and back in New York, I sublet a lovely apartment on 58th Street from a singer named Genevieve that had a living room with a wonderful view of Central Park. The transition was hard in the beginning. It was a time of loneliness and insomnia. After a couple of months, I brought Babby to live with me. I also started seeing more of Ira. He lived with his parents at the Gorham Hotel, occupying a small apartment. "How do you manage?" I asked him. His family had lived in a lovely home in Brooklyn, but when his brother was killed in the war, things were difficult for his mother, so they moved to the city. His father was one of the biggest press agents on Broadway.

I went and auditioned for *West Side Story* for Leonard Bernstein. He was lovely. I sang well, and they were pretty serious about me. But there was one problem—I didn't look very Puerto Rican. Next up, I was called in to audition for the lead in the musical *Fanny* with a high recommendation from Rodgers and Hammerstein. It was for Josh Logan and composer Harold Rome, who certainly remembered me from *Wish You Were Here*. It was a dramatic role, playing a young woman whose childhood love goes to sea for five years. Right after his departure, she finds out she is pregnant and is pressured by her mother to marry an older man. It was certainly a big departure from Laurey in *Oklahoma!* to say the least. I had the chance to play a serious love scene, taking a guy to bed and getting pregnant. Hmm, would I be setting a bad example from a religious standpoint? I ultimately decided to not let that stand in the way.

I felt fairly confident, despite having my slip fall down in the middle of the audition. (Yes, we wore underslips in the 1950s.) I discreetly crouched behind a sofa on the stage to pick it up. I had not been home to Rockport for quite a while and would be leaving town right away, I told them, as I finished the final audition. "We'll let you know," they said.

The minute I got to Rockport, there was a telegram waiting for me. It read, "Congratulations, Fanny. Come back." It was unbelievable. After a hello and goodbye to my family, I returned immediately to New York.

Becoming a leading lady on Broadway for the first time felt a bit like Alice entering Wonderland. Walking through that doorway, I was suddenly working with the best of the best. We started rehearsals in August 1954 and worked out the kinks in Boston and Philadelphia in advance of the premiere that November. The Italian opera singer Ezio Pinza and Austrian-born actor Walter Slezak were my costars. Lehman Engel was the musical conductor. Trude Rittman wrote the dance music. Everybody in the crew was also at the top of their craft.

Fanny was my introduction to the legendary producer David Merrick. The British singer/actor Anthony Newley once said of him, "Hitler didn't die at the end of World War II. He went into show business." Phyllis Diller went even further: "If anybody needs a heart transplant, try to get David Merrick's. It's never been used."

Merrick was the biggest producer of them all, and he had a well-deserved reputation for being strong and tough. He possessed such an intense drive for success that he would kill you if you got in his way. I had a healthy respect and admiration for strong people, so he never really intimidated me.

He said to me once in the break in between two shows in one day, "You should go out and be seen. We need publicity."

I told him getting prepared for the show was my most important priority. I also had to eat something, and he could see that I had a meal waiting for me.

"Don't think that you're not going to do what I tell you, because this is my baby," he barked. "I would kill to keep my baby alive."

"Okay, Mr. Merrick," I replied. "Thanks for the advice. But I've got a show to do. And doing it well is how I'm going to keep *your baby* alive, so you'd better go now."

One other colorful aspect of David Merrick was his showmanship, thought by many to be the second coming of P. T. Barnum.

If the ticket sales began to slack after the show had been running for a long time, Merrick and his wonderful PR guy Jim Moran would come up with some sort of gimmick or publicity stunt. Merrick even hired someone to bring an ostrich he named "Fanny" to the front of the theater. The stunt backfired because I think it bit someone. He wanted me to sit on the back of that big bird for a publicity photograph. Not in this lifetime!

Whether it was with Merrick or anyone else, the ability to stand up for myself was a newly acquired skill at the time. Prior to that point, I was more timid with authority figures like parents, teachers, and priests or nuns. Women of my generation before the women's liberation movement were expected to be more subservient. It was difficult to suddenly realize that I had a voice and I could say to someone like Merrick, "No, I understand, but I know what I'm doing."

Mary Tarcai, the wonderful acting teacher I studied with during *Fanny*, really helped me crack through that reticence. I might have benefited from going to a shrink, but the class worked almost as well. With my upbringing, I didn't even know therapy was an option. Instead, whatever you had weighing on your heart and spirit you could tell it to the priest. But the norm was to keep things inside, where they would sit and stew for the eventual fireworks show later on.

Mary knew how to push me. Chain-smoking cigarettes for the entire three-hour duration of the class, she was extremely wise and homed in on exactly where I needed help both professionally and personally. I was not as forceful as I could be, she recognized. It was very difficult to go into deeper emotions, especially because of my childhood embargo against crying. But that wasn't going to cut it in her acting class. Honesty and courage to delve into these deeper dimensions were demanded.

Thanks to what I learned from Mary, I was so much stronger in my bearing and gained greater confidence to no longer take guff so lightly. As far as I was concerned, if a producer or anybody else did not want to treat me with dignity or respect, they could gladly hire someone else. People tell me stories about how badly they were treated, and often it was because they were women. Luckily, I never felt that, maybe because I wanted to be so good at what I did that people rarely gave me a hard time. That was always my protection. You have to back it up and deliver the goods when the curtain rises or you won't last very long.

I continued to take acting classes for three hours a day and studied voice daily as well. I never missed a show for a year and a half. Regarding my voice, the only time in my whole career that I ever got into any difficulty was during out-of-town tryouts for *Fanny*. Those performances were designed to test audience reactions and work out the kinks at large theaters in outlying cities (usually Boston, Philadelphia, and Toronto) before opening on Broadway. They had wanted me to sing more forcefully. Belting-from-the-chest singing was becoming popular, so they had me work with a Broadway conductor named Herb Greene. He instructed me to hold my jaw down in a certain way and do a number of things that I knew were wrong. It injured my vocal cords. My teacher had me do some exercises that smoothed things over so surgery was averted. I was very blessed to have very good teachers, and I was lucky to avoid those who were not. I saw too many horror stories. The bad ones want to make you so dependent on them that you can't sing without them. Others can criticize to the point that it destroys your confidence. My teacher right before I got *Oklahoma!* had the right spirit. He said, "You can do it. Just remember what I taught you. And warm up your voice."

Performing in a musical comedy requires that you put a lot of care into your voice. Microphones didn't come into general use until much later in the 1960s. Shifting back and forth between singing and speaking can be a challenge, as it was for one of the other leads in the show, Ezio Pinza. He was an Italian opera singer who spent twenty-two seasons with the New York Metropolitan Opera before retiring and making a shift to Broadway. A lot of singers are just fine as long as they are only singing. They are properly trained how to use the diaphragm and upper torso. The challenge is to find that same support when it is time to use the speaking voice. They tend to go back into the throat, which gets them into difficulties finding balance and being heard. Opera singers are also not used to singing eight shows a week. You have to be extra careful to avoid straining the voice.

There are many things I learned about keeping my voice in shape. Don't cough and clear your throat all the time. Don't go out to dinner at a noisy place where you have to shout to be heard. Inhale steam to keep the vocal cords moist. Before going on in the evening, start humming in the afternoon to approximate the range of the chords and get the diaphragm warmed up, working up to more difficult exercises closer to going on. Consideration in the protection and care of your voice depends on your age as well. The voice also does not fully mature until most singers are in their thirties, so you need to take care up to that point to not injure yourself as I had done (a reason why younger opera singers are discouraged from singing certain songs or roles). And as you get older, you need to spend a longer time training and warming up before shows to keep the voice in shape. The muscle memory may still be there, but singing remains a very physically demanding endeavor.

As I was caught up in the whirlwind of preparing for *Fanny*, one little mundane detail fell through the cracks. I realized while we were preparing the show in Philadelphia that I had totally forgotten to retrieve some clothes at the cleaners on Seventh Avenue in New York before leaving town. I called and asked Ira if he could do me a favor and pick them up for me and keep them until I returned. The next day, there was a knock on my door before the matinee, and there was Ira. "I've brought your cleaning." It was a shock, albeit a pleasant one, to see him standing there.

This remarkably thoughtful gesture marked a tipping point. Our friendship suddenly opened up to something much deeper. I was still not old enough to buy a drink in a bar and a novice in the affairs of love, but a hopeless romantic nonetheless. He was very attentive, supportive, very sweet and kind to me, and not very demanding. Unconsciously, I probably surmised that it was also a plus that he knew the business but was not a performer. He would not have a learning curve dealing with the rigors of my career. Over the coming weeks, I grew in my love for this man, but when he asked me to marry him some months after coming to see me in Philadelphia, it scared the heck out of me. He got down on one knee to pop the question at my apartment on 58th Street. My response was, "I don't know."

"You probably need some time to think about this," Ira replied. Whoa, that was an understatement. I told him I would let him know.

Just prior to the opening of *Fanny*, I was profiled in the September 20, 1954, issue of *Life* magazine. "Reunion Before Renown" was the title of the four-page pictorial spread, and a reporter and photographer flew home with me to Rockport. For those not around to witness the heyday of *Life* from the 1930s to the early 1970s, nothing else in the American media world at the time had more impact, clout, or prestige.

The short text accompanying the photos described "a scrawny little blonde girl" who had now returned and how "dozens of people were pleased to see how prettily she had grown up and how close she was to a big success." Everything in the article looks quite idyllic. I'm shown as the fashionable young woman on the airplane from New York to Kentucky, reading the music score from the upcoming play in her seat. A perky version of the same woman wearing shorts and showing a lot of leg does an impromptu backyard recital with her sister Emily for adoring aunts and cousins (and a few supposed relatives whom I can't for the life of me recall—perhaps they were neighbors who crashed the shoot to have their moment in *Life* too). The pious version stands in an old parish church singing. Studious version vocalizes with Christine Johnson accompanying on piano. Celebrity version is fawned over by old boss at soda fountain. Lastly, I'm shown back in New York at Josh Logan's spacious apartment, viewed in profile like a Renaissance painting in chiaroscuro silhouette, kneeling on the floor by the window studying the script.

Truth be told, behind the mask of those smiling and self-confident poses in the lovely black-and-white photographs was another version—the one of a nervous wreck. Since leaving to study in New York, I had only been back two or three times to see my immediate family. I did so because I was determined to keep the connection with my roots. But making this very private and guarded part of my life suddenly public with *Life* scared me to no end and I needed to be hypervigilant. What if my brother-in-law Charlie was drunk or abusive when the reporter and photographer were there?

Of everyone I knew in New York, only Ira knew the true extent of the impoverished conditions of my early life. It was amusing that the people I met in New York just assumed that I was from a privileged background with a great education and all the trappings. Though internally I was completely comfortable and natural about where I came from, old accent and all, I didn't broadcast it.

In the end, everything worked out well, with the exception of my nearly killing the reporter, a delightful young woman who became a friend in the process. I was still a kid and did not have that much driving experience. We hit some loose gravel and the car spun out. She gasped. I felt pretty bad about that, to say the least, but we all got through it without a scratch.

The *Life* article concluded, "Florence's future is anybody's guess. But when her show opens in November, the best guessers, both in New York and home, believe that with her warm voice and spic and span beauty, she will be the freshest, most endearing newcomer on Broadway."

When we opened in New York at the Majestic Theater on November 4, 1954, those best guessers were right. It was still the custom to get the critics' reviews later that night. Such moments become cemented in memory even in the mundane details, like the pink ballerina-length dress I wore to the opening night party at Sardi's that fit me so perfectly and the purse that went with it (which I still have). I loved the telegram sent to Ezio from my idol and friend Mary Martin, who was starring as Peter Pan at the time—"I hope that your Fanny is bigger than my Peter." Other memories you wish you could forget, like the congratulatory kiss ("Why is this man putting his tongue in my mouth?") by the famous writer S. N. Behrman, who cowrote the show with Josh Logan. Most of the reviews were good, while some were mixed, but when all was said and done we knew we had a big hit on our hands. It would go on to run for 888 performances.

About three weeks into the run, I made my first solo on-camera appearance, on *Ed Sullivan*. I had performed live on national television a few times before, but only as part of a duet. The situation exposed a deeper reality about being in the business. I was terrified at the thought that all of a sudden there would be millions of people watching. I thought I was going to pass out minutes before my turn. No doubt the greater pressure of knowing how important this exposure was to the show took me over the top. It was something to get used to, this new feeling of responsibility for the show, because I was in the lead role, a feeling I had been immune to in my beginning days in *Oklahoma!* If I didn't end up fainting first, my next question was—would my voice come out when I opened my mouth to sing? I was still not twenty-one and didn't drink alcohol, but in retrospect, a little slurp of something just before might have helped. Some of the major talk shows put booze in the dressing rooms for that very reason, to encourage guests to loosen up their inhibitions (and tongues) a little before their turn in the hot seat. I was still very much in panic mode during the performance, but mercifully I got through it well enough to be welcomed back for more appearances over the coming years.

Walter Slezak ended up winning the Tony Award for Best Leading Actor in a Musical in the role of Fanny's older husband, Panisse. Walter could be intimidating and frequently such a hog onstage, but I liked him and learned how to deal with him. No one else gave me a more thorough education in the art of upstaging. Upstaging sounds like exactly what it means. Let's say you and I are doing a scene together, looking at each other as we normally would but standing in such a way that we're both facing toward the audience. Suddenly you decide to take a step back toward the back of the stage. In order to continue the conversation and look at you, I am forced to turn my back to the audience. A few moments later, I take a step back in order to reposition myself in the original posture. But guess what? You take another step back, and I am forced to turn my back to the audience again. This dance continues until we're literally about to bump up against the back wall of the stage. That's what Walter liked to do.

Another one of Walter's quirks was that usually he kind of took it nice and easy with his performance on any given night. But if he knew that there was somebody famous or important in the audience (which he always wanted to know), then he truly ramped up the voltage. It was a challenge playing against someone when you were never quite sure whether the performance was going to be on or off. This predicament came to a head over one particular line. Walter complained that he was losing the audience's laugh and blamed me for it.

"You know, you have to do this, because I'm losing my laugh," he told me.

My new assertive and assured self answered back, "Walter, if you did it the same way twice, that wouldn't happen. You're always changing it. That's why it doesn't work." He kept going on like a broken record, until finally I said, "If you have a problem, go to the stage manager, and I'm sure he'll straighten it out for us." That seemed to do the trick. It was nice how a little boundary setting created mutual respect. We never had another problem from that point forward.

The other lead, Ezio Pinza, was a total joy and a wonderful man. There was something so charismatic and irresistibly attractive about him. He loved to tease me. With his wonderful Italian accent, he said, "Oh, Florence, when she gets married, she won't take her husband to bed; she will take him to church." Ezio was having a serious affair with a beautiful young girl in the show. When we caught a glimpse of his wife as she came down the alley toward the stage door after a matinee, we would have to go into high alert to give him the cease-and-desist signal. Years later, I did a *Merv Griffin Show*, and he asked me about my memories of Ezio. I told how wonderful I thought he was, but added in a loving and humorous spirit how you had to protect your backside around him. "Ah, bella," he would exclaim when he pinched "Fanny's" fanny. Well, I got a letter from his wife. "How dare you talk about Ezio that way," blah, blah, blah. Ezio had passed away a few years earlier, but I walked into the middle of live crossfire. I told Julann Griffin, my friend who was married to Merv at the time, about the letter. She said, "You didn't pinch his fanny. He pinched your fanny. And that's the truth."

One other fun thing about doing *Fanny* was you never knew who might be outside knocking on your dressing room door. Josh Logan had directed *Picnic* and brought its star Kim Novak to see the show. I had this preconceived image of her as being this sultry, sexy woman, but in person she was just as beautiful but very sweet. She was easy to talk to, and I found her to be not all that different from myself. We had a lovely visit. Another knock on the door I will never forget was what I had thought was my costar Bill Tabbert playing a trick. Knock, knock. Who's there? "Cary Grant." I wasn't biting on that. Another knock. "It's Cary Grant." When I opened the door, there he was. He apparently loved the show so much that he came back to see it several times. He was a gorgeous man. He would always joke about coming to see me backstage: "I wanted to ask you to marry me, but I didn't think I had a chance." Had he asked, I might have given it some serious thought!

The stage door to the Majestic was right next to the same for the Royale Theater, where Julie Andrews was making her American stage debut in *The Boy Friend*. It was funny how we both got our "big break" at the same time. We became friends and spent a great deal of time together—and we're both still here!

Change and growth during the time of *Fanny* happened in a great spurt. Generally speaking, I was happy emotionally. The relationship with Ira felt right. I was in a very successful show, studying and learning a lot. My sister had come to live with me, and I wanted to make sure she was happy too. But there were undercurrents simmering that would not stay dormant for long.

CHAPTER 8

Yes, I Was a Virgin!

〜

*E*ventually, I said yes to Ira's marriage proposal. The circumstances felt right. I wanted to be married and felt ready to have a family. The fact that we had different faiths was not an issue for either of us. He understood that I was Catholic and very active in my faith. Ira was less so with Judaism and rarely went to temple, although he had great respect for his religion, and so did I. Importantly, he had no concern about my insistence that any children to come would be raised Catholic. We made it a special point to say grace before our meals in both traditions.

I was about to turn twenty when we got engaged. Ira loved practical jokes, so he had quite a laugh when he gave me the ring.

"Oh, it's beautiful," I cried after opening the little box.

"No, no, that's not the real ring," he chortled. Given my background, I could hardly decipher the difference between a piece of glass and a diamond. He took out of his pocket another little box with the real thing, and a gorgeous one at that.

We still took our time before we actually tied the knot, some thirteen months into the run of *Fanny*. It was not easy to get time off in a David Merrick show, but the procrastination was more on my side, the fear of the unknown. It was easy to get hung up in doubts. What was sex going to be like? (Yes, I was a virgin!) It frankly wasn't something I could talk about with my married sisters or close friends. If anything, Ira was the most help in this regard because I didn't know anything about the reality of what I was getting myself into. Such moments are always a test of faith. Either you believe it's going to work out or you don't.

The actual ceremony of getting married in the church proved a little complicated because of our different faiths. In those days, you had to get a special dispensation to marry a non-Catholic. The diocese in New York turned us down, but we got permission across the Hudson in New Jersey. I was friends with a couple of priests there, and they allowed the ceremony to take place, at the altar of the main sanctuary, no less, which was also a big no-no. It is a wonder we did not all get excommunicated.

It was raining and icy that day, January 9, 1956. I paid for the wedding. Afterward, my agent Barron Polan threw a reception for us at his town house in Manhattan. As we were leaving and getting into the car to go off on our honeymoon, the wonderful theatrical photographer Leo Friedman snapped my favorite image of that day. In front of our car was a bakery truck, and on the back of it as if divinely ordained was a sign that read "Long Life" (the name of the company). We then drove off for a week at Barron's house in Redding, Connecticut. An understudy went on in my place, David Merrick's girlfriend. It was the first performance I had missed during the entire run.

One month later, just to make things a little more interesting,

I was pregnant. I was so happy that I was going to have a child. With so many older siblings, I had babysat an assortment of children throughout my youth, but now I was going to have my own. When the reality hit, I also had to take stock about what might happen with my career. Gloria Steinem had not yet arrived on the scene. There were few road maps on how to manage a career and parenthood. Most women heeded the conventional thinking of the time and quit their work. I knew I would have to find another way.

One of the first orders of business was to find an obstetrician. I was referred to one on Fifth Avenue. Ira was very concerned about the cost. The doctor pooh-poohed, "Oh, I wouldn't worry about that. We'll talk." Translation: "You're a big Broadway star, so it ain't going to be cheap." The reality was that we hardly had a lavish lifestyle. Just before we married, we got an apartment at 140 W. 55th Street. My name may have been up in bright lights on the marquee, but remember that I worked for the very un-warm and unfuzzy David Merrick, who held his wallet in a tight fist. And I didn't have a big enough track record to have leverage to demand more. Ira probably made more than I did. Times were different.

Ira said, "We're not going back to him." So I found another doctor who would be covered by insurance. Dr. Myron Steinberg at Mt. Sinai Hospital turned out to be a great choice and would come to be with me through each of my childbirths.

Throughout the pregnancy, I was still in *Fanny*. Morning sickness was hard, especially on matinee days. The whiff of the makeup was enough to nearly make me pass out, but I was determined not to give in to that sort of thing. Any time to go and lay down and rest was taken advantage of until each wave passed.

David Merrick was not thrilled when I left the show seven months pregnant. He would have preferred that I did the matinee, had the baby, and been ready in time for the evening performance.

Barbara was born on November 9, 1956. In those days, they knocked you out as you got into the final stages of labor. You woke up to find a baby in your arms. It was long before the natural childbirth movement, but back where I came from, home delivery without much medical intervention was commonplace, as I had witnessed with my older sister. I felt like a sissy. It wasn't fair. I should have been fully awake and gone through it. A few years later, I bought a record that taught me the Lamaze breathing techniques. So by the time the third and fourth children came along, I did it naturally. Far better!

I felt confident being a new mother...for about a minute and a half. All that so-called experience taking care of my sisters' and other people's kids did not count for much when I was suddenly holding my own in my arms. In fact, I came to realize that I was closer in spirit to being a baby myself. Suddenly I felt like I was back to the beginning. The anxiety started to build, a slow burn at first that quickly became an all-consuming blaze. Would the baby die? And what would happen to the baby if I died? And what was going to happen to my career?

It didn't help that the baby had a stomach problem from the outset. From the time I got her home from the hospital, Barbara was losing weight. She could not hold down food and would projectile-vomit. Following doctor's orders, I had to be up at all hours of the night giving her short feedings, no more than a half ounce at a time, making sure to burp her after every time. Some drops were also prescribed that helped her stomach relax.

Understandably, I was not sleeping very well at night. Speaking from this experience, I advise young women today that you have to sleep when the baby sleeps and let everything else go. Added to the problem was that I was not eating enough. I had watched my nutrition during the pregnancy, but now I had no appetite. Half the time I was probably running on fumes because I was not keeping my blood sugar up. But it was all a symptom of a bigger problem.

Ira was always very supportive of my career, but like many men of his generation, he was not very hands-on when it came to baby care. One day, we drove over to Brooklyn, and when we got back to 55th Street I asked him to hold her for a second while I got some stuff together. In the blink of an eye, she threw up all over him. Was it a bit of payback for all of his wonderful nights of sleep? I had a good laugh about that.

Around this same time, they wanted me to come out to Los Angeles to do *Fanny* with the Civic Light Opera. Despite being a new mother, I was still very career-driven, but I was torn because I felt I needed to be with my child, so I turned down the opportunity. Again, there were no role models around to show me that there was a way I could do both. Ira knew how both family and career were a priority for me, and trying to protect that, he gave everything the benefit of the doubt. My own childhood baggage around my mother ramped up the intensity about being there for my baby. Damned if you do and damned if you don't, it was another no-win situation that I had to tough my way through in the beginning days. In the years to come, it became easier to integrate motherhood with work. Sometimes the children even got small parts in the productions I toured with or in programs or commercials as they got older, which they absolutely loved. They even performed with me in Las Vegas.

Ira went out of town for a show, and I was alone with the baby for a stretch. I had plans to do so many things to fix up our apartment. Clear as a bell, I can remember reaching up in a high cabinet to put away some dishes when—boom!—I was hit with it for the first time, the perfect storm.

Postpartum depression was not a well-known clinical term in the vernacular of the late 1950s, even though the syndrome no doubt affected the same twenty percent of all new mothers then as it does now. Ironically, Ira's uncle was a prominent obstetrician who was speaking out about it at the time. Dr. Ronsheim made the news when he was called in as an expert witness at a woman's trial to explain why she killed her baby. This syndrome can take many forms, but what all sufferers have in common is an inability to think properly. Luckily, I didn't harbor negative feelings about the baby. Instead I was simply mired in a state of profound sadness, stuck in an empty, bottomless pit.

Had I been more knowledgeable about postpartum depression, I might have talked to my doctor about it. Absent that, I was too ashamed to tell anybody about my condition. But the change in me was palpable and disturbing to family and friends who were so used to seeing me always happy and up. Understanding it later as a mix of hormonal imbalance, exhaustion, poor nutrition, and emotional stress, I could have truly been the poster child. Tears of such enormous sadness rolled down my cheeks. I had coped so well with everything in my life up to that point. But now I was overwhelmed, fearful, and sleepless. My appetite for food was supplanted by an emptiness in the pit of my stomach.

When you're depressed with a new baby, everybody tells you that you should be so happy and you should feel so good. Ira, too, felt bad about what I was going through, but he added to the chorus. "You have so much to be happy about." So add guilt to the list, a horrible guilt that I was not happy and joyful when I should have been. I would see other mothers with babies who were on top of it, and it made me feel worse, totally inferior. Oh, and what about the baby? Infants are sensitive to the energy around them, especially coming from their mother. My state of mind was bound to affect her one way or the other. I didn't want her to pick up on my toxic feelings. More guilt.

You wake up every morning and hope that you will discover that the fog has been lifted and the birds will be singing again. Instead, you're locked in hopelessness. "I'll never get out of this," you think. "What's the point?" It is easy to convince yourself that there is no help and no relief.

My brother Joe knew that I was having a tough time and came to New York. I spoke to him about my fears about my death or the death of the baby and how my once steadfast faith had been rocked to the core. He assured me that if I died that he would take care of the baby. When I asked, he told me that he was not afraid of dying. "What do I think about death? I think it's the best experience of life. I think my soul will be in the presence of a great light. I will find perfect peace."

One day, I was feeling really bad. I decided to take Barbara out for a walk, and I noticed all of these people across the street as I left the apartment building. I was curious why they were all there and walked over to see. What the crowd had gathered to witness was utterly horrific. A lady had jumped moments before from the building. I can still see the position of her lifeless body on the pavement and all the blood. I went into the phone booth at the old Ziegfeld Theater magazine stand and immediately called Ira. I did not think that anything could possibly get any worse, but that experience proved otherwise.

On another day, one of those walks with Barbara led to a more helpful development. A producer named Frank Egan saw me with the stroller walking down 55th Street. He put together "industrial shows," corporate concerts, and stage performances for specially invited guests. "Hmm, she must be available," he said to himself, seeing that I was a new mother and consequently not able to work full-time. Unbeknownst to me, Frank and his wife,

Jane, loved *Fanny* and had seen the show six or seven times. He had been a performer himself with a Broadway résumé and had sung with Fred Waring's orchestra. Spotting me on the street, he called my agent, and I went and met with him. Not only did I get the job, but Frank and Jane fast became great friends and remained such for the rest of their lives.

The new friendship also broke through my formidable self-imposed isolation. "Why would I want to be around anybody in that state, and why would anybody want to be around me?" I had thought. It was certainly not helped by a childhood pattern of not imposing myself on anyone harkening back to that appendicitis incident, among others. But Frank and Jane were different. Without imposing a lot on me, they seemed to understand. I confided in them what I was going through. Little by little, I started functioning more and trying harder, but it wasn't easy.

Thanks to Frank's initiative, I gently started going back to work, doing a series of private dates for General Motors' Oldsmobile brand. The performances were lavishly staged but shortened versions of Broadway shows like *Girl Crazy* or *Good News*. GM spent a fortune on these shows, hiring the best choreographers like Bob Fosse or Carol Haney and arrangers like Luther Henderson. The great costumes, dancing, and singing were a big buildup for the grand finale, the presentation of the star of the show: "Ladies and gentlemen, the moment you have all been waiting for—introducing the new Oldsmobile Rocket 88!" The audience was mostly composed of car dealers and their families.

It was great fun, and I continued doing these industrial shows for several more years when the schedule permitted. I also started doing Oldsmobile television commercials. They probably look silly today, dancing and serenading a car, but they were sophisticated production numbers with precise choreography. If it were broadcast on live television, the timing had to be perfect, and it was quite satisfying to nail the two minutes perfectly. Others were put on film, showing me gloating over fins and mufflers while running my finger along a car's top or against its sleek door panels. There were no cue cards or teleprompters either, so everything had to be memorized. Print ads also appeared in magazines: "Broadway star meets road star! That's Florence Henderson admiring the new Olds Starfire."

Returning to New York one night on the GM private plane after a show in Michigan, I looked out the window at the big full moon. I told Frank and Jane of a memory of such a moon when we had a party on the beach when I graduated from high school. My brother Joe had given me the present of a ticket on the Greyhound bus to come visit him in Florida. He knew that I was soon going to New York, and how ill-prepared I was emotionally. I think he saw the situation Babby and I had been in, and in this gesture stepped forward as a surrogate father. He wanted the time for some long talks to make sure I was a little more savvy in the ways of the world before landing in the big city.

That night, as he always did, Joe made me sing. As we looked out at the water and the reflection of the moonbeam on its surface, I sang "Ave Maria" at the top of my lungs. I told Frank and Jane how the light beam on the lake appeared like a magical stairway we could take to walk up to the moon.

When I got home late that night to the apartment on 55th Street, I knelt down to say my prayers at around 2 a.m. I asked for the usual things about taking care of my child and husband, and the rest of the family, including my sisters and brothers. My husband told me just before bed that Joe had called. He worked for the telephone company, and there had been a hurricane in Florida. He had probably been working around the clock and would be exhausted, so I thought it best not to call him back in the middle of the night.

While I was saying my prayers, the phone rang. It was my other brother, Tom. He told me that Joe had died. He had fallen asleep smoking. There were no windows open, so the smoke inhalation from the burning mattress killed him. Ironically, his wisdom from our talk just weeks before about death seemed prophetic when a fireman later told me how smoke inhalation is a very peaceful death. Joe was only thirty-seven years old. I often felt that if I had called him, maybe I would have awakened him and prevented his death. My mother, too, who lived with him at the time, was away and felt horrible knowing that if she had been there it probably would not have happened. It was May 10, 1958. I still think about him every day.

Joe's death brought my situation to a dramatic and unmistakable point of no return. The drive, energy, and inertia that I could always count on now had to take a backseat to something else. Religion and faith, where did you go? It was akin to standing naked and unprotected. With this spiritual crisis along with the physical and emotional factors, my eternal optimism was nowhere to be found. Added to this mix of confronting Joe's passing was that I had never really allowed myself to grieve my father's and my other brother's deaths. I tried to get answers to what all of this meant. I researched and read to find positive explanations but came up empty. Dr. Weinstein advised me to immerse myself in a topic that I had no real interest in to force myself to take my mind away from things. How about reading up on the Civil War? he suggested. I am glad there wasn't a quiz afterwards, because I did not retain much. But it helped a little bit.

It would be a full two years before this pervasive cloud of gloom finally lifted and I would start to feel like myself once again.

CHAPTER 9

The Today Show *Girl*

ᔢ

As I was coming out of my postpartum funk and getting active again, the medium of television stepped up to become an increasingly important part of my life. Some actors are terrified about being on live television, helpless and at the mercy of Murphy's law. More than a few did not thrive on the spontaneity of being unscripted. After my baptism of fire nearly fainting on *The Ed Sullivan Show* during my appearance at the time of *Fanny*, I quickly grew to love it. It was fast and it was live. You had to memorize and be prepared for anything. Here again, my childhood experience proved to be a valuable asset. After all, I had already stared down hell. What's the worst that could happen to me? So when that little red light on top of the TV camera went on, I was fearless. But even if I had been afraid, my psyche would thrust me forward, forcing me to confront whatever it was head-on. Swinging high up on a circus trapeze hanging by the bar? No problem. Just go ahead, dare me! (And it happened.)

For better or for worse, television exposes people, and if you're on long enough and often enough, they are going to learn who you are and what you're like. But the more I developed, the more comfortable I felt. If you're a phony or think you are funny when you really are not, there is no place to hide. It is all going to come out. Thankfully, I was privileged to constantly be around a multitude of very funny and talented people, and I was always trying to learn from them.

Jack Paar and his *Tonight Show* were right up there at the top alongside *Ed Sullivan* in terms of must-see television. Intelligent, witty, emotional, spontaneous, and highly unpredictable, Paar fascinated the public and media alike, and all tuned in with as equal passion to see him as to see his guests. I told my agent that I wanted to do the show. "I don't think you're right for it," he said. Undeterred, I got on through another contact. Bill Hayes (my costar in the industrial shows) and I went on the show and sang a song on January 13, 1960.

The recurrent theme in my life, "turning misfortune into opportunity," struck again, in the same way that ill-fitting bathing suit helped get me my first stage role. It happened when I went to sit on the hot seat to chat with Jack Paar for a few minutes after doing the number. Don't ask me how, but I managed to spill a glass of water all over his desk. Instinctively, I got up and started to wipe up the puddles with his handkerchief. Jack said something like, "I've always wanted a maid like this," and got a huge laugh. And as a consequence of that simple, nonsensical act, our friendship was cemented. I got invited back and soon became a "regular."

I understood that Paar loved good stories, so I made sure to have one or two in hand ready to go each time I went on. Of course, the show could suddenly veer off in another direction. You had to roll with the punches, like the time Paar asked me to sing the same song over again three times. Johnny Carson, who succeeded him, could also throw out whatever was on his card from the pre-interview and talk about something completely off the wall. To hang with them both was a challenge, but always an enjoyable one. These were big personalities, and I had to match them. And because I was fairly successful in holding my own, my reputation grew, and I was in demand a lot on the talk show circuit.

To come up with content to talk about, I would think about things from my life that I considered funny. All of it was based on truth, which is where I believe the greatest comedy comes from. Case in point, Paar loved a story I told one night on the show about Barbara. I related how I would take my little daughter with me to St. Malachy's Church, the actors' chapel, which is on 49th Street between Broadway and Eighth in the heart of the theater district. Purposely, I would take her down front so she would not distract the other parishioners. After a few minutes sitting there, I noticed how her attention was drawn upwards. She was looking up at the crucifix high above the altar and recognized how it was similar to the one we had at home.

"Jesus on the cross," she called out upon making this discovery.

"Yes, that's Jesus on the cross, but don't talk because people are trying to pray," I told her, adding that it was okay for her to quietly whisper if she needed to say something.

"Oh, Jesus on the cross," she repeated a few decibels louder.

"Shhh!"

She paused for a moment and looked thoughtfully up again at the crucifix. "Come here, Jesus, come here."

"Jesus can't come down," I tried to explain to her. "That's there just to remind us of Jesus and that he suffered for us."

She looked up at the cross once again, and I could see the little wheels turning. A couple of seconds later, her little voice seemed to fill the church: "Jump, Jesus!"

I loved television so much that when an audition came up for the job as "the *Today Show* girl," I jumped at the chance. They were testing different people on air for the part. I went on as a "guest host," and they liked what they saw. Conventional wisdom may have questioned why I would want to go in that direction when I was considered a member of that rarefied diva club, a Broadway lead. But from as early as my teenage years, I had a steadfast goal, and within it this move made perfect sense. My plan was to be active as an entertainer at a top level at least until age ninety-five (if God granted me the chance to live that long). I knew that I would need to diversify in order to do that. I thought this challenge would be fun and an opportunity to grow.

Such a challenge came fairly early on. I'm not a conspiracy theorist. I have no idea whether what happened to me in one of my first big interviews was deliberate or accidental—a form of hazing, a lighthearted practical joke gone awry, a malicious prank, or just an innocent and unintended comedy of errors.

My interview subject was a Japanese woman who had written a beautiful book on ikebana, the art of floral arrangement. She was married to an American pilot, and she was wearing a beautiful kimono. We didn't have time to chat before the seven-minute segment was to begin. The segment producer assured me that she did, in fact, speak English.

We went live seated tatami-style on the floor of an area appropriately decorated with a Japanese flourish. We exchanged bows, and I began my questions.

"So, tell me, how did it come about that you got into designing these beautiful floral arrangements?"

"Aaaaaahh aahhaaarrruuuu." (I think she was saying, "Yes, yes, yes.")

Maybe the question was a little too complicated, so I thought I'd go to something a little more basic.

"I understand that your husband is American, and that's how you learned English."

"Aaauuuhhh aahhaaaarruuu."

After two more attempts and the same unintelligible syllabic answers, I realized that I was in quite a fix. The floor manager held up four fingers, meaning four minutes remained to be filled. Funny how time can suddenly stall to a near crawl in these moments. Beads of perspiration were beginning to form. I was desperate. She wouldn't speak. Think fast, Florence!

I held up her book and opened it up to a random page in view of the camera. "Oh, why don't you tell me about this wonderful book with all these incredible pictures? Would you describe this picture for me?" Of course, there was no response.

"Well, let me describe this picture for you." I quickly looked at the caption to the photo. "Oh, here are some daffodils and un-husked *pussy*willows."

The sound of that sexual double entendre unleashed a torrent of laughter on the set. I seized my opportunity for escape. "And now, Dave, over to you!"

Fifty years later, who would have known that it would be commonplace to see commercials for erectile dysfunction on television? Back then, the slightest innuendo that had anything to do with sex or any manner of bodily function related to it were harshly off-limits. On television and in films, there were all sorts of rules about such things as how long a kiss could last. If you happened to be embracing on a bed, better be fully dressed and have one shoe firmly planted on the floor. There was a long list of words, many of which are very tame by today's standards, that could get you into big trouble if you uttered one on air.

On a practical level with a new family, the *Today Show* job was a perfect situation. It was in New York, and for the only time during this show's long history, it was pretaped in the afternoon for airing the next morning. The viewers at home had no idea. The news readers, either Frank Blair or Jack Lescoulie, were the only ones live arriving at the crack of dawn, to give inserts with the latest news and weather.

The accommodation of doing the show the afternoon before was designed for the program's first host and originator, Dave Garroway. Like everyone who has sat in his chair since, nobody enjoys waking up that early every day year in and year out. Dave was a powerful but lovable figure but one with a very big and obvious drug problem. He had this little black leather case where he kept his stash of blue and red pills. "These pep me up, and these calm me down, and I take them together," he told me. He would wash them down with a liquid he called "The Doctor" from a flask he carried in his pocket. When I asked one of the staffers on the show what "The Doctor" was, I was told it was liquid Dexedrine, a powerful amphetamine. That world was all new to me. I had no idea what he was talking about.

The habit was a good reason why his behavior could be quirky at times. One day he came in and all the skin was off his thumb. "Dave, that looks terrible!" I said.

"I was working on my car and got glass fibers in there, so I've been pulling them out," he explained.

"Dave, I don't think those are glass fibers. Why don't you go see the nurse?" There was nothing subtle about it. He had been pulling out the skin fibers.

Dave was the first person I had encountered in the business who was on "prescription" drugs. I knew musicians did it, but it wasn't such an obvious thing to me working in the theater. For most of the actors I knew, alcohol was the poison of preference. For example, if the understudy for Walter Slezak in *Fanny* had to suddenly answer the bell, he would get blasted to self-medicate his anxiety. The other actors would routinely have to turn their backs to the audience to feed him his lines.

Dave would come in sometimes and tell me that he had been up for three days straight, one of the side effects of his habit.

"I really admire you," he said to me one morning. "You have children and you work. My wife…" He was kind of upset and complained that she was not active enough or productive, in his opinion.

"You shouldn't say that," I countered. "Your wife is lovely. She's raising your son." We had developed a nice friendship grounded in mutual admiration. But the pressure of all those years clearly wore on him. He was a very bright and sensitive guy under it all, a very complex man.

As an on-air personality, Dave had a penchant for doing some fairly wacky things, not the least of which concerned his fascination with monkeys. J. Fred Muggs was one of the memorable simian regulars on the show, but one that I would choose to forget. One day, the chimp gently and tenderly put his hairy little hand out toward me and grabbed hold of my cheek like he was ready to rip it from the bone. Guess he didn't know his own strength. That was the beginning and end of our friendship.

But it didn't stop there. "More fun than a barrel of monkeys" was a very common expression of the time, and Dave decided to put it to the test on the program. So he arranged for an actual barrel stuffed with live monkeys to be on the show. When he took the lid off, all hell broke loose. "More *pandemonium* than a barrelful of monkeys" would be more apt. We quickly had a full-scale disaster on our hands. The chimps went completely berserk. In seconds, the set became one big monkey toilet, littered in crap. I quickly leaped up on the desk, adrenaline-boosted gymnastics given the dress I was wearing. Some holdouts were still up in the rafters when I left. Sadly, I was told later that they had to shoot them to get them down. I hoped that wasn't true.

Being the "fart in the whirlwind," as my mother had once called me, life circumstances put me in the center of one particular censorship issue. Not long after the ink dried on the *Today Show* contract, I got pregnant. And yes, the word "pregnant" was on the no-no list. They did everything possible to hide my bulge as it became more visible. A strategically placed potted palm plant worked quite well when I was singing. I never really got that big, but my dresses went up a few sizes as I progressively got larger. Some lady wrote in and referred to me as "sitting up there in my hatching jacket." Now you can almost deliver your child on television!

Don't ask me why my biology always seemed to pick inopportune times in conflict with major career moments. So much for the rhythm method (or "calendar-based contraception"), the only family planning option morally acceptable for strict Catholics! I love my children, but I found out the hard way that there is a good reason why it is called Vatican roulette. Like most forms of gambling, the house almost always finds a way to win in the end.

Some years later, I was appearing on *The Tonight Show* and quite visibly eight months pregnant. Before going on, I was pacing in the hallway outside the green room, which I always did. I never liked to sit down before I worked. The comedian Jack E. Leonard called out to me, "Florence, come in, sit down, sit down."

I said, "That's okay, Jackie. I'm fine out here. I'm just walking, going over lyrics."

"Come on," he said, but I wasn't budging. I kept walking. Finally, he said, "Florence, get in here, sit down. What's the matter with you? Afraid you'll wrinkle the kid?"

In addition to sexual content, if the show ever got into a conversation about religion or anything remotely close to the topic of birth control, Dave did not beat around the bush and told me not to chime in with my opinion. With the term *"Today Show* girl," you get the picture that being a woman on TV in that era left you easily marginalized. Dave Garroway was a powerful force, and I could sometimes feel squelched by him. Maybe I wasn't aware enough to be bothered by it. I was more consumed with trying to be the best I could at my job. Even in a sexist situation, I never felt less because I was a woman. I always tried to hold my own.

Starting out in the theater, I never had the nerve to complain if there was something I didn't like. I'm still very respectful of directors unless they are simply god-awful. In the beginning, I was too busy learning and paying my dues, so it wasn't until much later that I became more assertive. But my attitude was always to make suggestions in the spirit of "let's see how good we can make this." Producers and directors quickly grow tired of bad behavior or people who are difficult to work with. Eventually the word spreads and they stop hiring you. No one will argue with you if you are enjoying your job and doing the best you can, having fun and working harder than anybody. Get there early. Be the last to leave. Be prepared. Know your lines. Move forward with that spirit, and you'll get invited back again and again. I've always enjoyed being a team player.

As I was getting ready to leave *The Today Show* with the baby due, Dave Garroway was also ending his tenure. Hugh Downs was taking over. He knew me from *The Tonight Show*, where he had served as Jack Paar's announcer. He asked me to continue as his *Today* girl. There were good reasons to turn it down. For one thing, they were going back to doing the show live early in the morning. If I had learned anything from my bout of postpartum depression, it was not to willingly invite that kind of stress into my life. It was also time to get back to the theater.

A young woman named Barbara Walters ended up becoming the next *Today Show* girl. The rest is history.

CHAPTER 10

Do Re Mi

❧

*I*t was a totally different experience the second time around with the birth of my son Joseph. The anxiety attacks and debilitating depression I had shortly after giving birth to Barbara thankfully did not recur. It certainly helped that he was a very easy baby, and that I was more confident and experienced as a mother. I was also excited and totally focused about returning to the theater to play the coveted role of Maria in the national tour of *The Sound of Music*. But the most crucial development of all was that I now had the support I needed thanks to the arrival on the scene of Emily Maude Dare, or "Nanny," as we called her.

Nanny joined our household when Joseph was four months old and the tour was about to begin. She was from England, and I had found her through an employment agency in New York. When she first came to be interviewed, I asked her if she minded telling me how old she was. All I could gather from her appear-

Age three going on four. My father
fastened me up with a safety pin
and a Roosevelt button.

My parents, Joseph and
Elizabeth Henderson, on
their wedding day.

My big family: back row (left to
right): Dad, Carl, Mother, me,
Pauline, Joseph; middle row:
Ilean, Marty; front row: Tom,
John, Emily (Babby).

Twelve years old in Rockport, Indiana. I was strong and had a lot of faith and some bravado.

Here's what a cheerleader looked like in 1947.

With my big sister Babby.

Going out with Oscar on Easter Sunday, 1947. Her aunt Hazel gave me the outfit, which is too big for me.

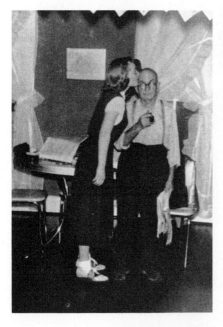

My father at eighty years old, being fussed over by me, then a senior in high school.

Visiting my brother Joe in Florida before the big move to New York City, together with some of his friends.

Playing Laurey and singing "Many a New Day" from the national tour of *Oklahoma!* (Will Rapport/ Rodgers & Hammerstein Organization/ Imagen)

Ira and I leave our wedding reception, our awaiting car parked next to the "Long Life" bakery truck.

Backstage at *Fanny* with costar Ezio Pinza. (Zinn Arthur)

"The *Today Show* Girl" with Dave Garroway. (NBC)

The pretend Maria in *The Sound of Music* with the real Maria, Maria Von Trapp. (Rodgers & Hammerstein Organization/ Imagen)

On the road in Detroit
in 1961 with Joseph and
Barbara. (Ray Glonka/
Detroit Free Press)

Edward G. Robinson and me in costume for *Song of Norway*.

With my mother in later years, backstage at a music festival in Florida.

Playing Nellie Forbush in *South Pacific* in 1967. (Rodgers & Hammerstein Organization/ Imagen)

With Ira in 1967.

In Las Vegas with
my mother when
she told me never to
work with Shelley
Berman again.

There's no fear of
flying when you're
asleep.

Elsie Giorgi, my doc-
tor and great friend.

Cast shot from the beginning days of *The Brady Bunch*. The "bubble" wig was the quick fix for my blond Norwegian look from *Song of Norway*. (CBS Television Distribution)

"The Mother of the Mullet." (CBS Television Distribution)

The 100th *Brady Bunch* episode. (CBS Television Distribution)

"I'll try almost anything once." Practicing with the Philadelphia Eagles for *The Mike Douglas Show.* (Michael Leshnov)

Together with George Burns.

With my brothers
John and Tom.

With my sisters (left to
right) Emily (Babby), Ilean,
Marty, and Pauline.

With Ruth Helen,
my best friend since
high school.

"When You're Good to Momma"—stopping the show with an unexpected performance at the Actor's Fund show in New York.

John and me on our wedding day.

"Team Florky"—Corky Ballas and me on *Dancing with the Stars*. (© Bob D'Amico/American Broadcasting Companies, Inc.)

With my children (left to right) Barbara, Joseph, Robert, and Elizabeth.

My daughter
Elizabeth
and me.

With
my son
Robert.

With my daughter
Barbara.

My son Joseph
and me.

ance was that she was somewhere in amorphous middle age. In the early 1960s, age fifty had not yet become "the new thirty." For whatever reason, people looked older and acted older in the mid-twentieth century than they did in early-twenty-first-century America. She said, "I really don't have to tell you. I could tell you that I am as old as the teeth in my head, but that would be a lie."

Real teeth or not, she was a wonderful woman and an incredible godsend. Going out on tour with a three-year-old daughter and a four-month-old son was a formidable task, but she took so much of the pressure off me as a working mother. Nanny was always kind and supportive, never complaining, and her patience and dedication to my family taught me a lot.

"Nanny, take the weekend off," I told her once when we had been on the road for a while and had settled into a good routine.

"No," she answered back, and the sharp clipped English accent meant that the matter was closed. "You don't take a day off. Nor shall I." When the show was in Chicago, she got up to attend to Joseph in the middle of the night and suffered a fall that hurt her back. Eventually, I insisted that she had to see a doctor. It turned out that she had fractured a vertebra. Talk about "the show must go on." What a trouper.

One afternoon between matinee and evening performances, Nanny was making dinner, and I had invited a couple of the cast members to join us, actresses who played nuns in the show. The conversation got a little bit gossipy as the subject matter turned to a crew member who was having an affair with one of our fellow nuns. I was very fond of this man's wife, and I was blunt in my opinion on the matter.

"I don't know why he's cheating with that girl. She's not even that attractive, and his wife is so beautiful and sweet," I said.

Nanny, who had sat quietly at the table with us the whole time, eating with her knife and fork in that precise European way and not saying a thing, decided to jump in. "Well, my husband always used to say, 'When you're poking in the fireplace, you don't notice the mantelpiece.'" That was Nanny. And that was the end of that conversation.

Nanny was with our family for the important and formative time in most of my children's lives, perhaps twelve years in all. She only took a break to go back to England to take care of a health problem. But as the years flew by, she eventually wanted to spend more time with her daughter and grandchildren. I realized afterwards and quickly by comparison what a gem she was. Nanny was truly a tough act to follow, as some of her successors would painfully demonstrate.

Despite the support from Nanny, things were not always smooth sailing on the road with *The Sound of Music*. To be blunt, it was the first (and hopefully the last) time when my ego got a little out of hand. It was a cumulative effect that mounted as the time I had been out on the road built up.

The show began in the fall of 1960 with a performance in New York on the set of the concurrent Broadway production at the Lunt-Fontanne Theatre starring Mary Martin. Mary and her husband, Richard Halliday, came to watch. The set was identical to the one we would be using on the road, so it was a chance for everyone to get familiar with it. Then off we went for a year and a half, stopping in each city for usually no more than a week or two, with the exception of a several-month engagement in Chicago.

That time in Chicago, as I mentioned before, was eventful on several fronts. There was the food poisoning. There was the "fart in the whirlwind" visit from my mother. There was the visit from the real Maria von Trapp, sitting there right under my nose in the front row, dirndl-clad and all and very striking-looking. When I introduced her to the audience, she stood up and faced them, raising both arms to the heavens to receive their thunderous applause. The moment had the kind of intensity nothing short of the Bible. It was like we had just borne witness to Moses parting the Red Sea or Jesus walking on water. She was very warm and complimentary toward me when we met.

There was a lot of pressure carrying the show. We were always sold out, and with the exception of one week off, I didn't miss a performance. I had the illusion that I had endless reserves and could just keep everything going indefinitely. Working hard all the time, I never learned how to regulate my physical limitations. Mix insomnia with the output of energy required for putting on a great show eight times a week month in and month out, and you have a foolproof recipe for total exhaustion. Despite Nanny's extraordinary help, the demands and responsibilities I still put on myself as a mother and a wife drew from that same rapidly diminishing well.

Ira would fly out on weekends whenever he could, which was true many other times when I was out on the road. One of the weekends in Chicago, there was the worst blizzard in eighty-seven years, so I figured with good reason that he would be a no-show. It was my birthday, and the production threw a dinner party for me at an exclusive club on the top floor of a high-rise. I was in the middle of a conversation when a waiter dressed in a red jacket came over to ask what I wanted to drink. "I think I'll have a little Dubonnet on the rocks." A few moments later, I got my drink, but everyone was staring at me in the strangest way. I turned around. The waiter was Ira. He had found a way to make it in.

In addition to having a great sense of humor about our separations, Ira was very supportive because he knew how important my profession was to me. Of course, keeping myself very busy was my form of coping with all the emotional stuff still unresolved, a highly effective form of sublimation. But during the time in Chicago, some cracks in my usual easygoing and agreeable attitude were beginning to appear.

Under less arduous circumstances, I had always found a way to resolve any issues with cast or production before they became conflicts, but not now. For example, with all the children in the cast, I was very much hands-on, working with them to make sure they came off as naturally as possible. Sometimes one of the mothers would think that she was the director and tell her child to act in a certain way contrary to how they had been instructed. "You can't do that. We're all part of a family here," I would have to tell both the child and the mother. It was not always pretty.

For reasons I cannot remember, I also had a little altercation with the Mother Superior. We had some fairly important and dramatic scenes together, like "My Favorite Things" and "Climb Ev'ry Mountain." Joe Layton, the show's choreographer who had become a friend of mine, came out to take a look at the show and took me out to dinner in order to have a serious talk. He could see that I was wound up too tight. "You've got to back off," he told me. In that state of mind, my response to him was to get upset. I quickly realized that he was right, but that was hardly the end of the story.

Salvatore Dell'Isola was Richard Rodgers's musical director and longtime right-hand man. A fixture in the pit of many Rodgers and Hammerstein musicals, he was a wonderful conductor but quite dictatorial like many in that job can be. It takes two to tango, and I am quite sure that his fuse was short as well, probably because he was not all that enthused about being on the road.

Keeping a consistent tempo to a song was never a problem for me. But when your accompaniment is not being consistent in that regard, it can be a big problem for a singer. I must not have been diplomatic enough when I tried to talk to him about it af-

ter the show. With so little in my tank, I probably said something
to him in a way that he didn't appreciate, and he picked his moment to get back at me with "Do Re Mi."

"Do Re Mi" is one of the show's longest numbers. I played the
guitar, and I would give a nod of the head to the conductor for
the orchestra to come in. Sal refused to take the cue. After a couple of seconds of dead space, I was left no other choice than to
motion to the pit for the whole orchestra to start, overriding his
authority. He went ballistic. He was so furious with me that he
threw his baton down on the floor in disgust.

A few days later, Richard Rodgers called me and said, "I hear
you're having trouble with Sal."

"Yes, he's hostile," I replied.

"You know, he's been around for a long time, but if you're
really, really unhappy, we'll do something about it."

"Lord, no, don't do that," I countered. A conversation was apparently held with Salvatore as well, and the result was that Ira
and I were invited over to the Dell'Isolas' apartment for dinner.

The Italians, as I always say, have a magic pot. His wife's cooking was no different, so much delicious food, so many different
courses, and a seemingly endless supply of each. I was already
tense and uptight, and under the best of circumstances have
never been a big eater. But his wife had made all this food, and I
didn't want to further upset him and his wife by not eating everything on the plate. I bit the bullet because I felt so bad about the
situation and was rewarded with well-deserved indigestion. The
good news was that the end of the tour was in sight, and despite
my struggles, I got through it.

The saving grace with this show (and even more evident in
the show I did a year later) was that no matter how difficult
things were in my personal life, it didn't seem to show when I
was up onstage. The act of performing has always been a love

affair for me, and singing for an audience from the time I was a small child was the best medicine for my soul. You are sending out all this energy, and honestly, you can feel it come back in a tremendous way. When you can create that give-and-take, it is an exciting process. It is very clean and simple, and you can only wish that you could bring that same energy to all aspects of your life. But how I was raised made that more difficult to achieve. Children were not encouraged to express a lot of their feelings. You simply got on with it, stoically riding that galloping horse. If you were a sensitive child, somewhere along the line you have to come to terms with the stored-up feelings— loss, sadness, grief, and anger. So when you're giving so much to please everyone but you're not taking care of yourself in the process, the energy does not recycle like on the stage. Nobody applauds you for giving your all in the real world. Like the title of this book says, life is not a stage. If you are fortunate enough to find a way to get beyond to that place of peace and forgiveness about all that you have suffered in your life, that anger and acting out dissipates instead of lying in wait like a loaded cannon. That's when you start to be more compassionate toward yourself and others.

Recently, my housekeeper Shelley and I had a surprising reminder of how important even the simplest gesture of compassion can be. We were having lunch at a little café called Nichols not far from my house. There was a very pretty young woman sitting by herself right behind us in a booth. She was talking on her phone, and when she hung up, she immediately started sobbing, got up, and ran to the restroom.

"Shelley, my God, I have to talk to her. Maybe we can help her."

When she came back, I said, "I feel so bad that you are sad. Can we help you in any way?"

She thanked us and said, "I just got the news that my mother is dying."

We sat and talked to her for a while, then hugged and said goodbye. I did not tell her who I was, nor do I assume that everyone is going to recognize me. It was not a big deal, just a passing moment. But several weeks later, I got an e-mail out of the blue from the young woman's sister. She told me that her sister had told her about this incident.

"Our mother passed away, but I wanted to tell you how much that meant to us and my sister Kaylee." Some people go through these life traumas and close down in bitterness. Would I have had any positive effect on that young woman had I not experienced losses of my own and worked to find a place of peace in my grief? I don't know.

Just as I had to take a hard look and come to terms with why I had let my ego get the best of me in *The Sound of Music*, I embrace the challenge of understanding what could have caused it. I have also taken solace and gathered strength in times of personal struggle by taking to heart a very simple concept: It is easy to deal with the happy times. It's the adversity that offers up the real test. Could my behavior on the tour have been more of a delayed-onset and milder form of postpartum depression? Were some more of those stored-up and unresolved emotions from childhood coming out of hiding? Certainly some of the same fears came up: commitment, responsibility, expectation, guilt, doubt, and so on.

Regardless of the causes and conditions, they all lead back to the core question: Why are we really here? The only answer that makes any sense for me is to strive to use the gift that has been given me in order to do something in some way to help others.

CHAPTER 11

The Girl Who Came to Supper
Loses Her Appetite

∾

By this time, it may not come as any surprise that I landed a great part in a Broadway musical, and like clockwork promptly became pregnant. In the summer of 1963, I was cast in the lead as "the girl" in *The Girl Who Came to Supper*, music and lyrics by Noël Coward and directed and choreographed by Joe Layton. The musical was set in London in 1911 at the time of King George V's coronation. It was based on a play by Terence Rattigan called *The Sleeping Prince* and was later made into a movie, *The Prince and the Showgirl*, starring Marilyn Monroe and Sir Laurence Olivier. My character was Mary, an American-born chorus girl who becomes involved with a Balkan prince played by the distinguished actor José Ferrer (who is best remembered for the title role in both film and play renditions of *Cyrano de Bergerac*).

The producers surprisingly agreed to hold the show for me until after the baby was born. That moment came just as I was on the set of the game show *Password*. The host, Allen Ludden, was a lovable man, but he was a nervous wreck when I started going into labor in the middle of taping his program. He probably wasn't thinking about the publicity and the incredible ratings potential of an actual childbirth in the middle of "the Lightning Round." However, it was my third pregnancy. As a seasoned veteran, I had my timing down. Only when the contractions moved down into the lower back was it time to get serious. I had such a ball doing game shows that no contraction was going to stop me. Back in the early 1960s, game shows were hugely popular, even in prime time. I loved the competition, having to think fast on my feet and use my imagination. Going to the hospital could wait.

Ten days or so after Robert entered the world, rehearsals for *The Girl Who Came to Supper* started in New York and continued for five weeks total. I felt great in the beginning, but not being with the baby began to wear. As it would be for most mothers, the feeling of separation from my newborn was not healthy. My "tough my way through it" mode kicked in as usual. With rehearsals completed, the show went out of town for tryouts in Boston, Toronto, and Philadelphia. The schedule during this tour was horrendous, rehearsing all day and then performing in the evening. Therefore, the decision was made that the baby and the children would be better off staying in New York under Nanny's care.

Fatigue set in, and so did the loneliness and guilt because of the separation. During my longest absence, Robert had suddenly transformed from an infant to a chubby-cheeked little baby. Oh, how terrible I felt. On top of that, Barbara's first communion was about to happen and missing that would be unforgivable. I rushed to get myself to New York in time for the ceremony and hurried back for the evening performance, producing the kind of stress that adds insult to injury.

Things started out well despite some clear problems with the show. The expectations had been sky-high. We were the second coming of *My Fair Lady*, said the rave reviews. Consequently, Herman Levin, the producer, was overconfident. The show was a smash in Boston but not as warmly received in Toronto. By the time we got to Philadelphia, it was hard to deny that things were not quite right despite the local critics' approval. The problems with the show made me first feel very insecure, then snowballed downhill into outright fright. We got great reviews in Philadelphia again, but I felt intuitively that the show was not ready for New York. When everything is right, there is a pervasive quality of effortlessness. When they're not, things feel forced and unnatural, and consequently miss the mark or wander off track. The audience can feel it too.

One major obstacle was that José Ferrer was definitely miscast in the role. He was a great Shakespearean actor and worthy of the highest respect, but it was clear that singing in a musical comedy was outside his comfort zone. Add two and two together, and it was perhaps no mystery why the audience had difficulty hearing his normally strong voice, which necessitated his use of a new-fangled cordless body microphone. We had a good laugh when I asked him where he hid the device.

"It's in my jockstrap," he told me.

I leaned over in front of him and said, "Testing one, two, three."

Walter Kerr, the powerful critic for the *New York Herald Tribune*, tried to put his finger on the problem with the show, writing, "What [Ferrer] can't do is strike a spark between Miss Henderson and himself...and the lack is serious, behind all the gold braid." Noël Coward admitted to me that he should have played the Prince himself, not Ferrer.

Good reviews aside, things not privy to public view went from bad to worse in Philadelphia. With still so much work left to get the show ready for Broadway, director Joe Layton came down with acute hepatitis. Then came the news that sent me over the edge, spiraling into the worst depression of my life.

I was on an elevator in the hotel when some guy got on and started talking. "It's just awful that he's been shot."

"Who's been shot?" I asked.

"The president."

"Oh my God, you must be kidding." A few seconds later, when we got downstairs to the lobby, we heard that John F. Kennedy had died.

I started to panic. The first thought out of my head was, "I have to go to church." I walked down the street to the nearest one. Others had the same idea, and people were pouring in. I just sat there in prayer.

Herman Levin made us go forward with the show that night because the house was sold out. It was gut-wrenching to perform, especially acute in one scene where my character has a little too much to drink and starts reciting the Bill of Rights. One consolation was that the opening number was cut. "Long Live the King (If He Can)" was just about as inappropriate a message for the moment as you could get. Mercifully, sanity prevailed, and the show was canceled over the next few nights. Everybody was numbed. For once, and rightfully so, the show did not have to go on.

During the immediate aftermath, I refused to watch the non-stop television coverage or read anything about it in the newspapers. Instead, I wrote a long letter to Jacqueline Kennedy, an acquaintance through an exercise class we took together. My son Joseph and her John-John also were in a class together. She was always so nice. When we met, we were both pregnant, she with Patrick, the baby she lost, and I with Robert. My child lived and hers didn't. So with this horrible, violent tragedy, I took it personally. All that promise that the Kennedys symbolized was wiped out so quickly. It was as if I had lost my brothers all over again.

For the first time in my life, I was terrified that I couldn't remember my lines, exasperated by the fact that the production was constantly doing rewrites and changing things. During the out-of-town weeks, I felt guilty being away from the baby. I wasn't sleeping well or eating well. I didn't have anybody with me. Ira stuck with his work in New York. It felt at times like I was in free fall without a parachute. When I really hit bottom, I probably had a nervous breakdown.

When the show was about to open on Broadway, postpartum depression came back with a vengeance. Here I was, doing this role that was so demanding, and failure was not an option. Forget about going on sick leave to give myself time to get over it. There were none of the modern and sophisticated antidepressants available (or if there were any, I didn't know about them), no magic little pill to bring you out of it real fast or, more accurately, at minimum put a temporary Band-Aid on it. Like before, I never told anybody how sick I was, although it had to be noticeable how the weight was dropping from my already slender frame.

Fear carried me through. Commitment, responsibility, and fulfilling expectations put me into some supernatural state of overdrive. It must have been the Holy Spirit working through me. Even though I felt awful, I guess taking pride in what I was doing overrode the fact that I was so utterly terrified.

The Girl Who Came to Supper was something that could have been great, but it missed, lasting only 112 performances. After the opening performance on December 8, 1963, the whole audience, or so it seemed, came backstage and up the flight of stairs to our dressing rooms to congratulate us. I didn't feel deserving that all these people would come to see me and tell me how wonderful I was. Some remarked after shaking my hand how cold I was to the touch. "Yes, I didn't feel all that great tonight," I told them. I took a pass on the usual post-premiere festivities.

To show you how strange our attitudes and perceptions can be, I carried inside of me for decades the thought that the show's short run may have been my fault. The audiences began to dwindle as the weeks went by, so the last curtain came as no surprise. It was easy for my mind to take on that blame because I had felt so awful. There were many times when I was onstage when I thought I was going to completely lose it, forget my lines, and go completely berserk. Somehow or another and miraculously, I did not make any horrible blunders.

Noël Coward sensed what was going on and was wonderful to me. On opening night, he gave me a beautiful amethyst pin that looked like a medal pinned to a ribbon. The note read, "You're first class." With his ever-present cigarette in hand, he was compassionate, understanding, and very aware. And privately, he displayed his wisdom, laced sometimes with a wickedly delightful sense of humor.

We sat together on the plane ride from Toronto to Philadelphia. Only weeks earlier there had been a very serious fire in his apartment, and quite obviously, he had not died. I asked him, "Were you afraid? Afraid of dying?"

Knowing my downcast state, he chirped back, "Oh, no, no, no! I have so many friends waiting for me over there!" He began rattling off the names of all the great people he knew who had passed that he looked forward to seeing again, such as Vivien Leigh and Gertrude Lawrence.

A few years later, Noël came to see me in *South Pacific* at Lincoln Center. If you wanted to go backstage after the show, there was a strict rule that you had to physically exit the theater onto the street and reenter through the stage door. In other words, going through a side door near the stage was forbidden.

Noël came into my dressing room after the show in quite a state of agitation.

"Quick, quick, quick, quick, hide me! I think she's coming after me!"

"What are you talking about?" I shot back.

"Well, I came down the aisle and through this door to see you. This usherette said, 'You can't go there, you have to go outside and through the stage door.'"

"'I beg your pardon,'" Noël said, reenacting the encounter. He drew himself up in an imposing posture (and he was already tall to begin with). "I told her, 'Step aside, dear girl. The day that Noël Coward can't go through any door in the theater, the theater is finished!'" With that he had barged through and came scurrying into my dressing room to find shelter like a puppy with its tail between its legs. Despite all of his accomplishments, he was in many ways a very modest man.

Given my emotional state when the play opened, I didn't even read the reviews. Someone had told me that Walter Kerr wrote some nice things, but that was about all that I registered. An assistant collected a number of the newspaper clippings and pasted them in a scrapbook that was put away on a shelf. Strange as it may sound, it would be almost fifty years before I actually read these articles (in preparation for writing this book), and I was astonished at what I discovered. The reviews were shockingly perhaps the finest I had ever received over my entire career: "Totally captivating." "A joy." "A perfect sweetheart." "A singing-dancing wonder of radiant charm in the title role." "Miss Henderson strengthens her position as one of the loveliest, most spirited and musically gifted young women on the stage today." "Not only a singer of unusual talent and intelligence but a first-rate actress and comedienne." "Miss Henderson's eager Cinderella embraces life with arms wide open." "Miss Henderson has everything a musical comedy star needs—beauty, humor, an exceptionally good singing voice and a spring steel constitution." So read the sepia-tinged fading newsprint in the scrapbook. It is impossible to say whether reading those reviews when they were first published would have eased the emotional burden I was carrying.

I recently got to see some additional graphic evidence of this huge gap between perceptions and appearances during that same time period. Someone sent me a video clip from a Garry Moore variety television show I did to promote the play. Looking at it objectively almost a half century later, none of the fear or deep depression seemed to come across on the screen.

The only possible explanation for my getting through both *The Girl Who Came to Supper* and this TV show had to be that same coping mechanism that insured my survival as a small child. There was a real stigma about depression back then—it was considered an inherent weakness and vulnerability to keep hidden. I just had to close my eyes and the audience would once again disappear. My mother's instructions echoed: "Think nothing of it." In that world, you dealt silently with whatever life threw at you or you got the dickens beat out of you. Depression and any kind of emotional turmoil were not for discussion when I was growing up, and that continued to be the norm through the 1950s and early 1960s.

Given this mentality and the fact that I was not able to dig myself out of this funk, there was little other choice than to just shut down and seal myself off from the world. What made this bout of depression especially sinister was how it threatened my faith. I prayed a lot, but seemingly missing in action was that being who was supposed to be protecting me. The only saving grace was that I was able to hold myself together just enough to keep working. That special energy field of love I experienced being on the stage helped out immensely. In contrast to the bout after Barbara's birth, I was also much more serious about finding out the answers to this dilemma for myself and consumed as many books as I could find on the subject.

Ira and Nanny tried very hard to help, but with little effect. As tears rolled down my cheeks, they took turns trying to comfort me.

"Buck up," Nanny said with that stiff-upper-lip attitude.

Ira tried his best too. "You have everything. You've got three beautiful children. You have nothing to feel bad about." Neither had walked in my shoes with any firsthand experience of what I was going through. Well-meaning and compassionate as they may have intended to be, they only made me feel worse. Just like before, more guilt was piled on for not being happy or feeling the gratitude. It was like adding gasoline to my already blazing inferno.

Slowly but surely, this nightmare of a depression also lifted some months later after the show closed, and I began to feel in balance again. Still in "tough it out" mode, it was a chipping-away process of learning more about what you are feeling and experiencing. You try to keep coping with things, and eventually the coping gets easier, I found. Even if the show had been a hit, I think I still would have found a way out of the postpartum depression. In contrast with the first bout, I was reading a number of self-help books to try to understand the situation better. Also, it helped that close friends like Frank and Jane Egan knew what was going on, and I could talk to them about it. They could make me laugh.

CHAPTER 12

The Pill

The spirit of rebellion, upheaval, and liberation was in full flower in the mid- to late 1960s. With the Kennedy assassination, the Vietnam War, and the civil rights movement stirring the pot, the middle part of the decade was a molten-hot cauldron that frequently boiled over to challenge all our assumptions as a society and as individuals. In Florence Henderson–land, that was quite the understatement.

As this period began, I was the poster child for mid-twentieth-century, good old-fashioned American values, with the major exception that I had rebelled in marrying outside of my faith. I was Little Miss Perfect in my own mind and in the public's perception. My handsome and utterly charming husband and I seemed the perfect couple, with perfect children. Much of this came from the motivation that I so desperately wanted a life with the harmony, stability, and affection that I didn't have as a child.

In fact, this mechanism to compensate for past deficits took on lots of curious forms. For example, I became utterly nonconfrontational when Ira and I got into any kind of disagreement (which was rare). The thought of raising my voice reawakened the trauma of hearing my parents yelling and fighting. So I put a cork in that anger, a quick fix that seeded trouble later down the line.

In the first part of the 1960s, my marriage was unshakable in my pride of righteousness. Constantly surrounded by colleagues who were not faithful to their spouses, I remember believing with all my heart that I would rather die than commit that kind of sin or divorce. My life was devoted to children, marriage, and career, in that order. The heavy load of responsibility and high expectations I set for myself as a working mother gave me the single-minded drive to keep bulldozing through all the rough spots.

My religious upbringing insured that I had plenty of fear and an endless supply of guilt in the offing to keep me in check in case major temptation came my way. That indoctrination began early. Imagine being six or seven years old, and a dour priest comes into the classroom. His lecture for the day is entitled "Introduction to Mortal Sin and Eternal Hell." If you had taken a photograph of all of us at our little desks, I'm sure you'd see nothing but terrified faces, bulging eyes, and mouths wide open.

"When you go to hell, you're in hell for all eternity," he told us as we quaked in our little shoes. "It's like the clock ticking— ever-never, ever-never, ever-never, ever-never." He stretched out the vowel sounds torturously long to make the ticking sound that much more ominous. "That's how long you're in hell." To this day, I don't like to hear a clock ticking!

At home, my mother's frequent use of "the devil is going to get you" kept the fear of that eternal punishment going. It took a long time to outgrow my conviction that it was only a matter of time before the devil was going to show up and snatch me. It had that kind of inevitability that leadfooted drivers face all the time. One of these days, you're going to see those flashing blue-and-red lights in your rearview mirror.

Being Miss Perfect was not necessarily in the spirit of those times and came with a price. "Wholesomeness Is Bad—Singer Suffered from Good Image." So read the headline from one newspaper article about me from 1967. I told the reporter how that image was not to Hollywood's liking. One studio I met with wanted to change my name to Felicity Ford. "I said 'no.' They said, 'How about Jill Jones?' [I snapped back,] 'What's the matter with Florence Henderson?' Do you know what they said? They said that Florence Henderson is too stolid. Too staid. And too long! So I told them that I'd rather be stolid than a flash in the pan. And that was that."

The columnist Earl Wilson added to this chorus. "Florence perpetuates her image as a happy wife and mother of four in her new café act which she's taking around the country after [her debut at the Waldorf]." When I opened for comedian Alan King at the Sands Hotel, he would call me his Catholic yenta. He'd get a good laugh from the audience with the line, "I came to Las Vegas to do some gambling and drinking, and they put me onstage with a Girl Scout den mother."

The 1960s had other surprises in store, most notably in the aftermath of the birth of my fourth and last child, Elizabeth, who arrived blissfully and uneventfully on January 26, 1966. She was conceived during the time I was doing *The King and I* with Ricardo Montalban in Los Angeles, the first performance to open the city's newly christened Music Center in the downtown area. It was a good time for me, and the production was a great success. Critic Cecil Smith of the *Los Angeles Times* had only one negative comment, that I was perhaps too young for the role. "But who can argue with youth and beauty on the stage?" he added.

I had the great delight to call him on it after I read it. "You should have done your homework. The actual Anna was exactly my age." Older actresses had played this coveted role, beginning with Gertrude Lawrence, so that's where he had no doubt gotten the idea. My being a younger Anna gave the romance with the King a little more sizzle. A big part of my joy of being in the play was that Ricardo was truly an unbelievable actor to play against (whistling problem aside). Up to that point in his career, he was often given short shrift because of his name and accent, reduced to Latin lover and ethnic types and always making lemonade out of lemon roles. When finally given other good roles like the King or as Khan in the *Star Trek* movie *The Wrath of Khan*, his remarkable talent really shone in its magnitude.

Despite the pregnancy, I got through the engagement without any unnecessary drama, with the exception of coming down with bronchial pneumonia. I didn't miss a show, but after many a scene I had to rush offstage to cough. When the doctor prescribed an antibiotic, I told him that I didn't want to risk taking it due to the pregnancy. His reply was blunt. "You know, you can die from this, and you won't have a baby." Reluctantly, I took it, and luckily there were no repercussions.

As the due date neared, I was in pretty good shape physically and emotionally and was confident. There was no anxiety nor any hint of negative thinking that I would be automatically doomed after the delivery to another horrible round of the blues. Preparation on the front end was sound prevention—I had time to devote to working out regularly at the gym to build fitness and strength. And I followed through with my promise to myself and learned Lamaze natural childbirth breathing from a record. By the time the ninth month came, when I was back in New York City, a little impatience began to set in. I just wanted to have the baby already. The Fifth Avenue bus had a lot of potholes on its route, so I took it a few times hoping the ride might help induce labor.

I don't think the bus helped, but before long the moment arrived. Awake and aware during the childbirth, I heard Dr. Steinberg ask just before the last push, "What's it supposed to be?"

"It's got to be a girl with dark eyes and dark hair," I said wishfully.

A few seconds later, he said, "Here she is." When she got a little older, Elizabeth saw a picture taken that day of herself as a newborn in a row of similar photos of her older brothers and sister. She was upset. She felt that all the other babies were pretty except for her, pointing specifically to the puckering expression on her face. She chilled out when I explained, "No, no, no, you came out, and you were kissing me." That was her character, a totally sweet and funny baby.

Of course, just when things are going so smoothly, life pushes forward a new challenge. Lizzie's birth brought to a head a problem that had been slowly creeping up on me but suddenly could no longer be denied. Right after labor, I told Dr. Steinberg that I was struggling to hear what he and other people were saying. He arranged for me to immediately see a hearing specialist in New York.

The diagnosis was otosclerosis, a hereditary disorder caused by an abnormal growth of spongy bone in the middle ear that interferes with the transmission of sound. My sisters Babby and Ilean and brother Tom have also had to deal with it, and it can sometimes skip a generation. It is more common in women than men, and, as in my case, is often made worse by childbirth. It is also a misnomer that the problem is due to the bones getting harder. Rather, they get softer and sludgy, so sound cannot get through them to the nerve. If not addressed, it leads to tinnitus and you can eventually go stone deaf.

It probably started manifesting when I was a teenager, but it was so subtle and insidious that it remained under the radar for the most part. But after Barbara's birth, I started to turn up the TV when other people seemed to have no apparent difficulty hearing at a lower volume. Later, when my children progressively began to speak, I had some trouble making out what they were saying and pressed them to enunciate more clearly. It was not their problem but mine, but one positive result is that they all developed such wonderful diction.

As it worsens, you find you're in conversation with people and get increasingly frustrated by not hearing what they're saying when everyone else is. You're always thinking, "What did they say, what did they say?" Around this time, I had an exasperating meeting with the legendary lyricist Alan Jay Lerner, who cowrote musicals such as *My Fair Lady* and *Camelot* with Frederick Loewe, at his home in New York City to talk about his upcoming musical *On a Clear Day You Can See Forever*. I felt so horrible because I missed so much of what he was asking me. I realized that if I wasn't looking directly at people, I'd lose what they had to say. I also would have to get up close, literally into someone's face, which some people may have felt was sexy and others uncomfortable.

If you make your living as a singer, the problem begins to snowball into a nightmare. Certain instruments in the orchestra, especially the strings, begin to gradually fade away out of your hearing range. Are you certain that you're going to hear that special note that is your cue to begin? Staying on pitch had never been a problem before, but all bets were suddenly off.

There was one blessing in disguise. Since the problem was significantly worse on one side, I could roll my head on the pillow over onto the good ear at night if Ira was snoring. Magically, all would be quiet and peaceful.

When Lizzie was a baby, I had successful surgery in New York to correct the problem. The doctor said that I might not feel the need to do anything for the other ear, but a few years later I was having trouble. When performing, I was turning up the volume on the monitors so loudly that everybody else was dying. A fellow performer and good friend, Nanette Fabray, had the same issue and had been in worse shape. She told me about the House Ear Institute in Los Angeles. Dr. Howard House did the second surgery for me, with great results. He put in an implant made of stainless steel and Teflon. You can imagine all the jokes about having a tin ear and being able to cook inside of it without any sticking. I described the difference to one journalist: "After the operation, cars sounded like jets and water from the spigot sounded like a waterfall."

Since that time, I've done charity fundraising work for Dr. House and the House Ear Institute, as well as other institutions that deal with the hearing impaired. I will never forget doing a show with the children at the Lexington School for the Deaf in New York. We performed "Do Re Mi" together, and the children sang along and kept rhythm by feeling the vibrations in the floor. One beautiful girl sang "The Sound of Music" and it was inspiring and uplifting to see how she tried so hard to stay on pitch and quite often succeeded.

Once the problem was identified and healed, I realized that some of the issues that I was beginning to experience with stage fright might have had their origin with my gradually deteriorating ability to hear. It was yet another challenge that life served up to me that fortunately had a lasting solution.

But that was hardly the end of the story. Solving the hearing problem set some gears into motion that would take me far into uncharted terrain and ultimately shatter my carefully ordered world. So much for best-laid plans!

Back in the old days, women of childbearing age with otosclerosis were routinely sterilized to prevent them from further deterioration and becoming completely deaf. Luckily for me there was another option. Father Charles Whelan, a Jesuit priest and a cousin of mine, was worried about my situation. "Look, you've already had four children. Your health and your livelihood are at risk." He granted me special church dispensation to take birth control pills, which had cleared the FDA and become available to the general public only a few years earlier. Needless to say, Father Whelan was on the progressive wing. Around this time, he wrote a highly controversial article for *America*, a Catholic publication he coedited, entitled "Why Does Every Act of Love Have to Be an Act of Life?" You can imagine how that got the fur flying.

For about ten years starting in 1958, the Catholic Church gave permission to use the pill strictly for the treatment of disorders linked to the reproductive system, such as mine. However, Pope Paul VI yanked it away in 1968 with his *Humanae Vitae* encyclical. But if my example was in any way typical, the church had every right to fear the societal change in its wake. They wanted to stuff those pills and the genie back in the bottle pronto!

The pill held the promise to finally give every woman control over her body and give couples like Ira and me the possibility of worry-free sex. In my particular case, yes to the first part, but no to the second. It was a given fact that the rhythm method was a colossal failure for us. Fact number two was that I was obviously very fertile, not such a surprise given my parents' ability to produce babies like a factory production line. But fact number three was that changing longstanding patterns in our relationship instantly by swallowing a little magic potion was sadly not in the cards.

On the surface, the rhythm method's greatest effectiveness is killing any sense of spontaneity in a relationship. Never mind that it also flies in the face of our natural instincts by commanding a woman not to have sex at the time of the month when she's ovulating and hardwired to desire it the most.

We had been married for over a decade before the pill came into my life. Up to that point, the patterns of how we related to each other were all deeply ingrained if not totally locked in. There were no other options. I had married young and so totally inexperienced, unlike young people in later generations who had the opportunity to experiment or try other lifestyle options before settling down. With marriage and immediate pregnancy, I was thrown right away into a whirlwind of responsibility and expectation. Hook, line, and sinker, I bought in to the concept of domestic perfection, i.e., this is about as good as it is going to be, so suck it up. Being the eternal optimist, I always looked at the bright side. I embraced the good and tolerated the bad.

The *Catholic News* painted a rosy picture of our life in an article about ten months after Lizzie's birth. It sounds like one of those picture-perfect family sitcoms of the early 1960s. "With a common sense, matter-of-fact approach to life, the blue-eyed, diminutive singer manages successfully to raise a large family and have an expanding career and has done so for ten years.... 'You have to pray a lot and take vitamin pills,' she quipped....Miss Henderson's busy schedule provides so much variety that no two days are alike, except where her family is concerned. Her household roars from 6:45 a.m. to nine at night—except for the school hours and when she sees them off to school, makes sure the homework is done and eats dinner with the children, as well as puts them to bed. After that, the Bernsteins relax and have a couple hours together, calling it a day around 1 a.m. Even though the pace is fantastic and requires her constant attention, Florence Henderson sparkles and looks like a woman who enjoys the challenge of giving both jobs [as an entertainer and a mother/wife] the best she's got to give."

I loved Ira for all the right reasons. He was a great companion and father, a warm and caring lover, and a supportive partner on so many levels. But he was very worried (and for good cause) that I was going to have a baby every nine months. Not surprisingly, I think this created a deep underlying tension. I felt rejected, and it opened my old wounds around this issue from childhood.

I kept always mindful that Ira's emotional life as a kid was no picnic either. When he was fourteen years old, his older brother was killed in World War II, shot down over the English Channel. Ira answered the door and received the telegram with the news. From that moment, his relatively happy childhood abruptly came crashing down too. Seeing the emotional devastation on his mother, there was a part of him that shut down that spilled over into our relationship just as my reactive programming from my early years did.

Ira and I shared an unspoken compassion for each other because of what we had separately gone through. On the other side of the coin, it bred dysfunction because neither of us wanted to risk going into the scary unknown frontiers beyond our upbringing and conditioning. We were both heavily invested in a carefully constructed façade, one that proved to be more fragile than I could have imagined.

So the pill may not have changed Ira's attitude. But it did mine. I was thirty-four years old. With this single development, I realized how trapped and subservient I had been to a set of hypocritical rules that I could no longer accept. How hard I had struggled for so many years to try to make everything okay.

You come to a point when the talking stops, when you realize that still nothing changes. You realize that the status quo is abhorrent. It exacts a price on your spirit that will attack you at your weakest link—addiction, depression, or mental breakdown, or gradually wearing out your physical body with debilitating and deadly disease.

With the pill, my life went haywire for a while. Little Miss Perfect checked out.

CHAPTER 13

The "No Door Act"

〰

As a sense of liberation began to take hold in my personal life, some boundaries with my work also began to crumble. Some doors that were locked or that I had dared not even attempt to enter, such as working more in Hollywood or doing my own nightclub act, were suddenly flung open. What lay on the other side was certainly beyond my imagination at the time. Before the 1960s would come to an end, both my career and my head would be in a much different place.

Once you've cracked whatever you have been repressing, you suddenly begin to understand the stranglehold guilt, fear, sadness, and anger can exercise over every minute aspect of your existence. It wasn't as easy as simply opening the gate and putting my galloping horse out to permanent pasture. There were still many miles to go before that horse and I would more peacefully coexist. But that incessant drive and control over my life began to slowly loosen, as I gently let go of the reins.

Once the process started, it was almost impossible to stop its forward progress. For the first time, I was much more relaxed, more prone to go with the flow. Other shifts began to take place in that state. Even during my worst periods, I had always loved performing onstage before an audience, but now the enjoyment stepped up to a new level, becoming more aligned with the internal shifts that were starting to happen.

Another message came forward that it was time to stand more powerfully on my own two feet. With that realization, the field began to open up. Opportunities to do variety television shows abounded, while theater work became more sporadic. Someone recently sent me a copy of one of the old *Bell Telephone Hour* summer shows I did regularly during this time period as a singer and host. Talk about a trial by fire. It reminded me just how demanding those programs were. In the course of an hour, you might be doing four or five songs and changing costumes each time. You didn't get much rehearsal time, so you had to step your artistry up a notch if you wanted to be better than just good. Nowhere else but these variety programs did you have the chance to work with and interact with so many varied artists who were at the absolute top of their craft.

One of my lasting memories from *The Bell Telephone Hour* was seeing the incredibly lovely Lena Horne resting backstage with her shoes off and her feet up on a chair.

"Oh, Miss Horne, do your feet hurt?" I asked her.

She looked up at me and smiled. "Oh, you'll find out later." She was about twenty years older, and she was right. Doing two shows a night in high heels catches up with you in the long run.

At their highest form, *The Bell Telephone Hour* and *The U.S. Steel Hour* might feature symphony orchestras, great opera divas,

and ballet companies, extravaganzas that I trust few television en-
tities would attempt to mount as an ongoing regular series today.
In fact, I feel sorry for the younger performers nowadays who
missed out on the opportunity to be exposed to this genre in its
heyday and grow from the experience. In recent years, the only
things that come remotely close are shows like *Dancing with the
Stars, American Idol,* and *Glee.*

Perhaps my very finest acting job was on one of those shows.
I had to do a duet with John Raitt, a period piece for which I
was dressed in a period costume. At one point in the song, I had
to sit down on a chair. Immediately a long and sharp straight
pin pierced through my dress and found its way into the flesh
of my derriere. Somehow and some way, I didn't flinch or use
any profanity when it happened. It sure helped with the high
notes.

You could also get an education just being present and watching the best of the best perform up close, such as the great dancer
Rudolf Nureyev in his prime. I recall how very upset he was
about having to perform on the studio's concrete floor, and rightfully so. That's one major contributor to why so many dancers
from that era developed chronic knee and hip problems.

One summer, I hosted the *Bell* programs out of Studio 8H
at Rockefeller Plaza in New York, the future home of *Saturday
Night Live.* It was the first time that an American television show
was shot in the round with an audience completely surrounding
the stage. They had to get very creative in designing how to keep
the crossfire of cameras hidden from the viewers at home.

The Dean Martin Show was a popular viewing destination on
Thursday nights at 10 p.m. Kate Smith, Lena Horne, and I were
three of Dean's favorites, so we were frequently on the show in
the mid- to late 1960s. He was one of the sweetest and kindest
persons you could have wished for, and I was thrilled to be part of

his enterprise. He was very smart and knew what was funny. He also had a great voice.

Many comedic entertainers of that era adopted a signature character, and Dean's was a debonair, tuxedo-clad drunk with a cigarette in one hand and faux scotch (apple juice) in the other. With a twinkle in his eye, he enjoyed pushing the boundaries of sexual innuendo right up to the censors' limit. The audiences loved it when he frequently lost it laughing in the middle of a sketch. He loved working with people who could be spontaneous and comfortable venturing off script with him.

One day when I was taping Dean's show, Kate Smith called me into her dressing room. She was a major star on radio in the 1940s and in early television, and her iconic version of "God Bless America" took a then obscure song and transformed it into the unofficial national anthem. Yet a generation or so later, ask most young adults who Kate Smith is, and all you'll probably get is a blank stare. (I haven't had that issue myself yet because of a certain television series in perpetual reruns.) She was known almost as much for her beautiful voice as her wide girth, which also made her the sad object of a lot of fat jokes. She made no apologies about her size and it was as much her trademark as Dean's cigarette and drink glass. In her autobiography, she wrote, "I'm big, and I sing, and boy, when I sing, I sing all over!"

In Kate's dressing room that day, she said proudly, "Take a look at my dress," and handed her lavish beaded gown to me. I almost fell over—it was so heavy I could hardly hold it or myself up. Telling Dean something like that was like handing a lamb chop to a wolf.

He said to me, "Did you read the label in that dress?"

I said, "No, what did it say?"

"Everlast," he replied (referring to the brand of shorts and equipment popularized by professional boxers). But he didn't stop there. "Have you ever noticed that Kate ain't got no cleavage?"

"No, Dean, I didn't know that."

"Oh, yeah, she's only got one, and it's the biggggest one!" This was, of course, off camera, but no less terrible and funny all the same. But in many ways Kate set herself up for a lot of it with her divalike ego—and I don't think she minded being the butt of such jokes or had at least gotten used to them decades before.

For a beginner, I was given a generous fifteen-minute performance spot my first time on the show. Among the songs was a ballad, "Hi-Lili Hi-Lo," and for it the stage was decorated with chandeliers. Those details did not escape Kate, and I soon learned that she was oversized not only with her dresses but her persona too. She called the show's director/producer Greg Garrison aside. She had given him his break some years before on her afternoon television program, *The Kate Smith Show*. So Greg was very partial to her.

"Greg, how long have you known Florence Henderson?" she asked him.

"I just met her on the show," he replied.

"Then how come she has all those chandeliers in that number?"

Some years after Kate and I first met on the show, we happened to cross paths at the Philadelphia airport in a VIP waiting room, both having done concerts in the area. She was extra famous in that area because the local NHL hockey team, the Flyers, had a superstition about playing her recording of "God Bless America" before every home game (the team later erected a statue of her outside the arena). In the waiting room, Kate threw down her newspaper and said, "Have you read my reviews?"

"No, Kate, I haven't. I haven't seen a paper."

She said, "Here, read these. They speak it." That was Kate.

Talk about confidence! During the summer of 1966, I officially became the stuff of trivia questions as the first woman to guest host *The Tonight Show*, subbing for Johnny Carson for a whole week. (I would later go on to do it several more times.) They made a pretty big deal about it at the time. The experience interviewing people on *The Today Show* way back when helped out. By hosting talk shows, I learned to never ask a question that could be answered with a simple "yes" or "no." You have to instead prompt the guest to elicit a story. And once you ask the question, shut up and listen. Really listen. The other cardinal rule is to "know your material." It wasn't enough for me to read off the blue index card that the writers would prepare. I did my own reading and research on the people I was interviewing. Lastly, you also have to be a bit of a ringmaster to keep the conversation from veering off track away from key points. The same skill is helpful if you're a guest and the interviewer doesn't want to talk about the book I'm there to promote but goes off on some tangent about *The Brady Bunch*.

When it came to monologues and other parts of the show, it certainly didn't hurt that Johnny had also assembled a great team of writers. It was so easy and comfortable to slip into such a well-oiled machine. On one of the programs that week, I opened the show singing a long medley a cappella accompanied by four male singers for ten minutes instead of the traditional monologue. Risky? Perhaps. There was a musicians' strike at the time, so necessity was the mother of invention. It was a shining example of that sense of unpredictability that has walked along with me like a shadow. Even to this day, I seem to always pop up where I'm least expected. It has kept things interesting to say the least.

The most bizarre Carson appearance I ever made was on December 17, 1969. Over forty million Americans tuned in to the show that night to witness the nuptials of Tiny Tim and Miss

Vicki. For those of you not around during that time period, I'll tell you about him. For those who were, no description is necessary because he was unforgettable. He rose to fame playing his ukulele and singing in his signature falsetto/vibrato "Tiptoe Through the Tulips." I have no doubt that if he had come around thirty years later, he would have fit in and found an audience on a show like *American Idol*, because he was such a quirky performance artist. He was a sweet man to meet him in person, but he had some strange ideas. One day, I was talking on the phone to Babby, who at the time was working for an advertising agency in New York. "You're not going to believe this," she interrupted suddenly. "There's a man here in the lobby with long brown hair and a white face [makeup] going around kissing all the pictures on the wall." That was Tiny Tim. Legend has it that he was so enamored of the fact that he could get free room service when he played Las Vegas that he hoarded the food under his bed. For his wedding to Miss Vicki, I was asked to sing an appropriate song for the occasion. I came out bedecked in a beautiful gown and sang "My Love," Petula Clark's hit song from a few years before. Afterwards, I sat on the panel for the rest of the show. From time to time, Johnny turned his head to make eye contact with me, flashing an expression of disbelief.

Of all the television appearances I did during this time, the one that stands out the most was an appearance on *Ed Sullivan* on September 24, 1967, and for a tragic reason. The day before the show, I was rehearsing with the orchestra a medley from *The Sound of Music* with a conductor I adored and used frequently for live performances named Irving Actman. Irving was a frequent collaborator with lyricist Frank Loesser and had conducted *Guys and Dolls* for him. He was a smoker, and I knew he had a heart condition, so I was on his case about that whenever I saw him light up.

We rehearsed the medley a couple of times and took a break.

"I'm going to run across the street and get some coffee," he said. "Do you want some?"

"Don't worry about it, I'll go get my own." As I crossed the street, he was coming back the opposite way, cigarette dangling from his mouth and in a hurry to get back. I yelled at him, "Irving, throw away that cigarette!"

"Okay, okay, okay," he said.

We started rehearsing again. Irving went up on his podium, and I took my usual position right beside him. He raised his hand as he did normally to start conducting, but the hand suddenly reached up to grab his head. A second later, he collapsed at my feet. One of the musicians rushed over and gave him mouth-to-mouth. Minutes later, the paramedics came and tried everything to bring him back, beating on his chest and almost kicking him to try to get him going. But he was gone. He had grown to become almost like a father figure to me, and just like that he was gone.

I was devastated, and I told my manager at the time, Ken Greengrass, that there was no way I could possibly do the show the next day. He kept talking to me and talking to me. "This would be the best thing for Irving if you would go on," he told me. It was one of the hardest things I ever had to do. The audience knew nothing about what had happened the day before, but they must have felt the outpouring of intensity from both the orchestra and me and were enthusiastic. It was a showstopper. Irving once confided to me when we were out on the road, "I hope I don't die alone in a hotel room." I promised him he wouldn't. I know it is a cliché, but there is something to be said for dying doing exactly what you love doing the most. As shocking as the experience was, I'm so glad I was with him and he wasn't alone in a hotel room.

Irving and I had been on the road together not long before he passed away. Ken Greengrass had told me, "You really need to have an act and go out." Ken was also Steve Lawrence and Eydie Gormé's manager at the time, and he had seen how playing clubs became a whole industry for them. He was surprised I hadn't done it sooner. My agent Sandy Gallin, who would soon succeed Ken as my personal manager, completed the process and got me into the big Las Vegas types of engagements. As Dolly Parton, Mac Davis, and others would soon find out, Sandy was a brilliant manager who really hustled for his clients.

What was the big deal about going out with your own act? It's about the closest thing you can do to going out on the stage completely naked. There is absolutely nowhere to hide. If you're performing a role in the theater, the audience may like you even if they think the rest of the production leaves something to be desired. But headlining your own act, the buck stops with you. It is your opportunity to display all your talents, along with sharing who you are more intimately—your thoughts, your personality, your humor, and your more serious side. But I loved the challenge and the freedom to be totally in charge of my own material. And I was finally ready to take that big step to go out there by myself and see if I could hold an audience and excite them. The good thing, too, is that you find out immediately if you've succeeded or failed. One of the first times I tried out the act was at an exclusive country club in Westchester. Performing for a wealthy and sophisticated audience would be a fair challenge, I thought. It reminded me of John Lennon's famous call-out to a royal benefit concert audience, "People in the cheaper seats, just clap your hands. The rest of you... just rattle your jewelry." I was relieved. The reaction was tremendous, and I thought, "Wow, this is fun."

One of the major reasons why I didn't do it earlier was that I had a legitimate concern that it might endanger my marriage and my family. The club lifestyle was not one that you clocked into and out of like a day job. The environment of Broadway theater was more protected—you sign in, prepare, interact with the other cast members and crew, do the performance, then go home to your husband and kids. The experience with the audience doing clubs was more intense and raw. You had to be good and on top of your game. It also meant being away from home for weeks. The pressure was far more intense on so many fronts. But freed from so much of the obligation and responsibility that had repressed me, I was ready to take it on. Standing there on the club stage was a form of freedom that I had never had before in my life— just to go out there and be my unadulterated self!

The act officially debuted at the Empire Room of the Waldorf-Astoria on February 28, 1967, for a three-week engagement. As people munched on their turbot mousse with lobster and truffle sauce and prime beef with sautéed endive, I ran through a set mixing Broadway and popular tunes, including "My Favorite Things," "I Know a Place," "Gotta Travel On," "Impossible Dream," "Tonight," "Who Can I Turn To," and a *Sound of Music* medley, among several more. There was quite a buzz in the newspaper columns the following day reporting on Mayor John Lindsay's very public "congratulatory" kiss at the reception following the performance (that's a scene in the coming attractions, stay tuned). Otherwise, the evening was a great success and an auspicious beginning. Rave reviews and great crowds at the Empire Room got the buzz going along the club circuit, so the bookings grew. From there I went on to play an engagement at the Shoreham Hotel in Washington, D.C., and continued on to similar venues.

One of the funniest and strangest compliments I ever received happened during this period. I was playing the Concord, the Borscht Belt resort in the Catskill Mountains in upstate New York. "You're a no door act," said Philly Greenwald, the manager of the club at the resort and brother of famed choreographer Michael Kidd. I had absolutely no clue what he meant by that. "There are very few of you," he explained. "Lena Horne is one of them, and so are you." He went on to tell me that the audience had a way to show their appreciation to the artist besides the Concord tradition of banging wooden knockers on the tables in lieu of clapping. (Maybe it was a one-handed way to applaud without having to put down your fork or spoon.) This was a discriminating audience when it came to supper club performance. A "no door act" meant that nobody got up in the middle of the performance to go to the bathroom. They had seen it all, he told me, so it wasn't a big deal for them to suddenly get up if nature called. So I learned that if people went so far as to hold their bladder for you, it was biological proof that you had to have been good.

The Concord unfortunately was the casualty of the ultimate knocker—the wrecking ball. No longer appealing to the younger generations, the hotel went into decline and stood shuttered and abandoned by the late 1990s and was ultimately leveled to the ground in 2008.

As mentioned before, playing clubs was hardly a sheltered environment, and interaction with the audience could be interesting and sometimes intense. One major factor was the booze. I observed quickly into the process how males and females behave differently when they've had a little too much. For the most part, the men became better behaved up to a certain blood alcohol level, more appreciative and definitely more responsive freed of their usual inhibitions. The women, on the other hand, had the tendency to forget their manners and lose sight of the fact that a performer was up there entertaining them. They would turn to their companion and chat away, sometimes with more than enough volume to compete with the singer.

I don't know about other performers, but when I'm on the stage, my senses are heightened. I hear everything and see everything. At a performance with David Brenner in a big tent near Atlantic City, I was singing "Send in the Clowns" when I heard the audience tittering. I immediately checked myself to make sure nothing was falling off of me. I then turned around and saw that there was a big dog just sitting there on the stage and looking at me. Of course, the audience loved it. I stopped everything and engaged the dog in a conversation. "Are you enjoying the show? If you like it, you can stay." When I started again, the dog looked up at me, thought about it for a second, and gave me his answer by promptly walking down the aisle and out the nearest exit. The audience and I had a great laugh.

During this same engagement, there was a terrible rainstorm with thunder and lightning. Being in a tent is not the safest place to start off with, but water began flooding the orchestra pit with all the electrical wiring down there. A lightning bolt struck. I immediately threw the microphone down on the stage floor. Some guy from the audience yelled, "Don't worry, you can't get electrocuted. It's okay." To prove his point, he came up onstage and took the microphone in his hands, and for added emphasis he kissed it during a flurry of thunderclaps.

"Good," I said. "You sing!"

Another time, some years later, I was doing a big production number of Bette Midler's "Do You Want to Dance," which we put together with another song, "Ten Cents a Dance." I had male dancers in the act, and the guys and I played up the drama of the song in the choreography. The dancers leaned on me and weighed me down as I sang the words "ten cents a dance, that's all they pay me." Again, I heard the audience snickering. I looked to the side to discover a guy from the audience on the stage waving cash in his hands. He was obviously very drunk. "I don't think you can pay me enough," I said and made a few other jokes as they escorted him gently off the stage.

The worst example happened when I played the Desert Inn for a month, opening for Milton Berle. One night a member of the audience started heckling him. No one was killed, but this incident was a reason why that month felt more like a year. I liked Milton well enough, but you had to accept him the way he was on his terms. Well-deservedly, he was a legend in the business, but he had a very abundant ego to go along with it. For example, he came to my rehearsal and, unsolicited, gave me a lecture on how I should do my show. If I happened to get a standing ovation when I finished my part, it was uncanny how fast Milton came out there to thank me and start his show.

Milton was no stranger to hecklers, so that evening he did all the putdowns he could think of. But this guy would not shut up and got even more aggressive. The sold-out audience was not happy, Milton realized. So he jumped off the stage and went over to the man. He picked him up with one hand on the guy's shirt collar and the other by the seat of his pants and threw him out of the room. He then went back onstage and tried to pick up where he left off, but it's hard to be funny again and get a stunned audience back to normal. What made the whole thing more bizarre and out of a Fellini movie was that Milton was wearing clown makeup at the time. No wonder some children are terrified of clowns.

There could also be other extenuating factors why you might not click with an audience every night. Someone told me once about a particularly disastrous taping of a sitcom. They had done the first taping earlier without a glitch, but the director in the booth was dumbfounded because the jokes were not getting any laughs in the evening taping. Then a production assistant solved the mystery. He told the director that they had bused in a large

group from a retirement community for an extracurricular out-
ing. The show and most of the jokes were all themed around
death and dying. Timing is everything, and the audience was obviously not amused.

However, it was no fun as a comedian to go out there and not
be your best before a Las Vegas audience. When a comedian is
having a great night, I could be a little envious of them. When I
appeared with Bill Cosby at Harrah's Lake Tahoe, I came off the
stage dripping with sweat from singing and dancing. I watched
for a few moments from the wings as he took his place onstage
after me, sitting down comfortably in his chair, entertaining the
audience like he was having a casual chat from his living room.
"Something is wrong with this picture," I remember thinking to
myself and laughing.

"You don't appreciate me—I'm sweating up here," Shelley
Berman once yelled at the audience when I opened for him. He
was the first stand-up comedian to play Carnegie Hall, and he
won a number of gold records for comedy, so he was and still is a
true master of his craft. But no one is immune from an off night,
especially comedians who stand there alone armed only with a
microphone. Shelley continued moaning about the audience as
he came off, and I hid in my dressing room so I wouldn't have to
say anything.

My mother happened to fly in and was a witness that night.
Back in the 1960s, Las Vegas was fabulous, and I was mesmerized
by it. It was a glamorous place, especially at the Sands, where
everybody dressed up. You never saw people walking around in
T-shirts, sandals, and shorts unless they were going to the pool.
When I was at the Flamingo, I was alone, and it was a hard place
to hang out by myself. So, long story short, I brought my mother
out.

"Don't ever work with him again," she repeated. "He's not that funny." Neither was my mother. It had been a few years since she last made me cry, and I had decided that she would never do that to me again. Years ago, I would have been terrified of getting verbally whacked by standing up to her, but not anymore. "Oh, when you start paying some bills, then you can tell me who I can work with," I said. In response, my mother retired to the casino for a late night and early morning of blackjack.

"Mom, it's five o'clock in the morning!"

"Go to bed if you want to," she yelled back at me. "Go to bed. Leave me alone."

Speaking of gambling, many an entertainer was as big a player as the people they entertained. In this regard, Alan King was no slouch. One night, he went out and dropped $100,000 at the tables. The management wanted to hold him to it. "Hey, I have a bad elbow," he said. "I'm on cortisone and it made me crazy." They relented and let him off the hook. He was a real character. When I first started working with him at the Sands (when he called me his "Catholic yenta and Girl Scout mother"), he took me aside and told me that he was a little uncomfortable and embarrassed having to bring this up, but... The issue was the marquee outside the hotel. We had equal billing, and our names were required by the contract to be the same font size. The only problem was that his name had eight letters and mine had seventeen.

"I feel so bad to ask you this, but would you mind having a smaller name?" he asked me.

"Nobody sees my name," I told him. "You can make it any size you want—I don't care."

We became great friends despite my continual rejection of his sexual advances. I used to say, "Oh, Alan, give me a break!"

One of the other unpleasant aspects of club life that performers had to deal with back then was that everybody smoked in the clubs. There were no laws against it or even a designated section set aside. The term "secondhand smoke" did not yet exist in the dictionary. Your hair reeked, along with your gowns that cost a fortune, not to mention what it was probably doing to your insides, especially the toll on a singer's throat. It could get nasty. Lainie Kazan had been performing at the Plaza Hotel in New York City a week before I was to open. A man sitting right in front by the stage was smoking a big cigar. Lainie asked him very politely to put it out since the smoke was bothering her. He refused. So she went over to him, took the cigar, and put it in a glass of water. It must have been a very good cigar, because the man got up and hit her in the chest. It was a good-sized target, because Lainie was back then and still is quite zaftig. The incident made the newspapers.

Cut to a week later. I was standing there on the same stage and, lo and behold, there was a different man with a big cigar blowing smoke at me. I reminded the audience that just a week before Lainie Kazan had asked a gentleman to put out his cigar and had her ample cleavage accosted. In a premeditated gesture for comic effect, I looked down at my own much lesser-endowed bust and said, "I guess I don't have to worry." A big laugh followed. And the man put out his cigar.

Regardless of drunks or smokers or Alan King trying to hit on me, I wouldn't have traded those times for anything. The same time as I was out there having a blast singing for my supper, there was a bigger story happening inside that was both exhilarating and petrifying. The club scene truly hastened the inevitable. Telling me back then to "be careful what you wish for" would not have stopped caution from blowing away in the wind.

CHAPTER 14

Detours and Other Digressions

✑

No one ever promised that the path was going to be straight and narrow. Sharp curves, detours, and U-turns made things quite adventuresome out on the road during this time of self-awakening. Call it a case of arrested development, immaturity, or a delayed onslaught of teenage rebellion, because in many ways that isn't a stretch.

Deferred for all those years were all the things that young people normally should be experiencing as a rite of passage upon leaving the nest. Branching out and trying different things...Going to college...Having a relationship or two that didn't work out...Experimenting...With the exception of studying that single year at the American Academy, I had leapfrogged headlong from adolescence to adulthood.

As described, there was one side of me that was having the time of my life doing the nightclub tour. But the other side was engrossed in dealing with a real Pandora's box. I was trying to solve all of the things that were going on inside of me that were suddenly freed from the repressed depths. There wasn't the luxury of cherry-picking the issue of the week to focus on. Everything seemed to come up at once, demanding urgent attention like a chorus of crying babies.

There was no depression to smother these feelings as in the past, and the devil and all his threats could go bother someone else for all I cared. Instead, when matters got too intense during this period, I called on that old family friend, alcohol, to help quiet things down. After all, that was how I was raised. If you had trouble, how did you cope? Open the bottle. I can't say that I was happy about my consumption, and Ira was none too thrilled about it either. Thank God that particular crutch to help keep me on the horse was cast aside.

The liquor flowed freely, and often in the culture of the nightclub circuit was the steadfast companion of many a performer. It wasn't a good thing for any of them either, with one possible exception—George Burns. Based on the results, those untold thousands of cocktails and fine cigars probably did a lot more good than harm if you live for a century and have a brilliant career in the process. For years, George had a set routine that the first thing waiting for him when he got off the stage was a double gin martini, one of at least four he imbibed each day. I'm sure it also put him in a good mood. Over the years, whenever I appeared with him on TV or onstage, he never failed to be good-natured and very gracious, especially to all those who came backstage after the shows to visit with him. I was the last performer to work with him in Las Vegas, which happened to be on his ninety-eighth birthday, although he fulfilled his promise that he would live to be a hundred. His famous joke was that he couldn't die before then because he was booked.

For me, however, the alcohol was really just the opening act, warming things up for the main attraction: The Affair. In the twenty-first century, celebrity love affairs and infidelities barely raise an eyebrow, and those who end up staying in a marriage for twenty, thirty, or fifty years are considered almost a freaky curiosity. But for a toe-the-line Catholic in the middle of the twentieth century, "till death do us part" was a serious vow, a one-way ticket. Of course, for those trapped in very unhappy situations, the death part took on a truly long and protracted meaning. Lovelessness, neglect, and abuse can be lethal in the long run. Plan B was resignation to the conditions as they were, another form of death by a thousand cuts, slowly but surely shriveling up, stressed out and diseased. Plan B also offered the optional route of checking out with drugs, alcohol, food, gambling, and other addictions.

I was certainly a prime candidate for Plan B. As gut-wrenching as it was to go against my long-held beliefs and have an affair, so was making the decision to write about it in this book. There was no way that I could truthfully tell my story without disclosing it, since it is at the top of the list of life-changing moments. Before signing the contract, I thought deeply about my ex-husband, whom I still love dearly and cherish as a lifelong friend. We were fortunate to move on over the years with forgiveness and acceptance of personal responsibility. We found a way to stay close and connected despite going our separate ways. I didn't want to do anything now that would jeopardize this. Nor did I want to be a part of anything that might be construed as making myself look good at his expense or in any way pointing a finger of blame.

I thought also of my children, now all adults with families of their own. One of my sons even took me aside because he was understandably concerned about just how graphic I was going to be in talking about this period of my life.

In the end, the same answer applies to my ex-husband, my

children, and the prospective reader. The ultimate love I can share is to offer up my experiences, warts and all, with the intention that it will in some way be helpful to others. For my family, would it have ultimately served them well had I followed the likely pathway of Plan B? Or will they read these pages and view their mother and grandmother as someone who made hard choices (and often mistakes), but modeled for them in her actions something helpful in the final tally? If I am honest and forthright in telling how I dealt with my problems instead of sweeping everything under the carpet, maybe they will avoid the possibility of carrying on the family legacy of riding galloping horses. For Ira, I hope that he will see a more enlightened purpose behind the retelling of what happened between us and not some ridiculous attempt to settle old scores. I hope it will be an inspiration to all of those who are out there today struggling to forgive each other and themselves. As difficult as it was at times, it worked out well in the end for both of us. Ira is happily married to a lovely woman who is a friend to my children and me.

The affair was with a man who was one of my musicians. I think he was in the same place as I was in his marriage. There was enormous chemistry between us, and we were crazy about each other. It is a gross understatement to say that I was in conflict about the whole thing. I didn't know where in the hell I was, or what I was thinking. Everything was turned upside down. But there was one thing for sure: I was ready. I felt I wanted to seize the opportunity. Who knew if it would ever come again?

When people step outside, there's usually a good reason for it. If you are in a union that is functioning well from both a spiritual and a physical standpoint, you are going to think twice about violating that. I enjoyed sex with Ira, but the stress over the whole family planning issue, as mentioned before, was a heavy burden to overcome. That healthy sexual desire and drive hardwired into all humans that can be a continuous source of joy and rejuvenation was not working in our relationship. Instead, we grew accustomed to the static, low-grade tension to the point where the dysfunction was tolerated as normal.

I told him once, "Ira, I know you love me, but I don't think you like me very much." He was by nature not the jealous type, but given the emotional constraints of his childhood, I think he resented my freedom and my persona. I often felt he would have been happier had he married a nice Jewish girl from Brooklyn. I, on the other hand, brought my own special baggage to the mix. The expectations I had about romance and happiness were unrealistic and naïve in so many ways, a tangible by-product of my upbringing that also put strain on the relationship. All those newspaper and magazine articles about being the perfect wife and mother in the perfect home were not a public relations exercise but something I deeply believed. It was like that concept that if you repeat something enough times, it can turn an illusion into a perception that you start to believe and regard as fact.

The affair with the musician ended after several months. He didn't want to leave his wife, and I didn't want to risk losing my children. Ira found out about it, which I probably wanted him to do, and needless to say, he was very upset about it. I told him, "It's not that I don't love you. I will always love you. It was something I had to do." I am sure there was a part of Ira that was equally frustrated, but whether or not he ever went outside the marriage, I don't know. I never asked him. After the initial trauma subsided, the matter seemed to fade into the woodwork on his part. There were attempts to heal the rift. We tried. He tried. I even delicately bought a few books to try to spice things up.

I would like to be able to make it a nice and tidy story and say that when the affair was over it was also the end of my infidelity. But that was not to be the case. None of the affairs were really meaningful and all were short-lived. I guess I had to give it a little more research to be able to say with conviction that sex for the sake of sex did not prove very satisfying for me. One of the incidents in particular demonstrated convincingly that it wasn't the kind of life I wanted.

PARENTAL ADVISORY: To my son or anybody else potentially allergic to TMI (too much information), please stop here and skip over these next few pages. I will indicate with a row of asterisks when it is safe to resume reading.

I had alluded earlier that the much-ballyhooed kiss from John Lindsay at the premiere party for my nightclub act was just a prelude. What I am about to share is the kind of fodder for the tabloid press that I truly wanted to avoid in this book. I can hear and see it now as I go out to do interviews after its publication. I'm on a network morning show. The host says to me, "Florence, I really enjoyed your book. What a great life and wonderful insights you share, blah, blah, blah...But I can't stop thinking about your one-night stand with the late former New York City mayor John Lindsay. Please tell us more about it!" Sixty seconds later, the host says that they're sorry they don't have more time to talk about the rest of the book, about the deeper meaning of life and the profound secrets of happiness I reveal, but how they loved that juicy John Lindsay story!

At the end of the day, I decided to relax my principles and let this story skip by my internal censor despite the future consequences I have just described. One reason is that it is a good cautionary tale for all and a poignant reminder to listen to that little voice called *the intuition*. When it says, "No, this isn't the right thing for you to be doing right now," please know that it is usually not blowing smoke. Take heed or that Old Testament form of instant karma will get you, sooner more often than later. In my case, divine providence did not dawdle.

The other reason for sharing it is that I'm still pissed off at him and myself! It may have been over forty years ago, but it seems like yesterday. This story still makes me cringe, so I'll get right to the point and spare you any unnecessary details.

John and his family were casual friends of ours, and throughout his political life I had made a number of appearances for him at benefits and some campaign events. I was out in Los Angeles, and it so happened that he was as well. He called me and invited me to come along with him to a get-together at the home of movie producer Dan Melnick (who had been married to Richard Rodgers's daughter). I accepted. After the party, he invited me back to the Beverly Hills Hotel for a drink, just down the street from the rented house on Rodeo Drive where the kids and I were staying at the time.

From here the story gets blurry and crazy. There was no tremendous sexual attraction from my point of view. I didn't believe in one-night stands and frankly detested the very thought. But he was extremely persuasive. I was lonely. I knew it wasn't the right thing to do. So, what did I do? I did it. I went home later that night.

I woke up the next morning. Something didn't feel right. I pulled off the sheets and looked down my pajama bottoms, and saw that something didn't look right either. What in the hell is this? What are these little things? Terrified, I rushed into the bathroom. I looked at myself in the mirror. Oh my God, one of the little black things I saw below was crawling on my eyelid! I had no idea what they were, but then suddenly it hit me. I remembered my brothers who had been in the Navy talked about guys going to prostitutes and coming back with the crabs. Oh my God! To this day, I've never thoroughly researched crabs. Where in the hell do they come from?!

I got up the courage to call my physician, Dr. Giorgi, and she told me what to go out and buy. I was leaving the next day to go up to San Francisco to open a nightclub engagement at the Fairmont Hotel. When I arrived, there were flowers from John Lindsay and a note of apology. Guess I learned the hard way that crabs do not discriminate but cross over all socioeconomic strata. He must have had quite the active life. What a way to put the kibosh on a relationship.

As promised, here are the asterisks.

* *

My philandering days were over not so long after they started. I hated that life. I decided to give it one more try to salvage my marriage with Ira. But deep down, nothing had radically changed, and I still knew that I wasn't where I was supposed to be. From that day forward, I held out the promise that someday, somehow, I would be in love and share my life with someone equally committed to exploring that exciting and sometimes thorny path of personal growth—speed bumps and U-turns included.

CHAPTER 15

Hollywood...Finally

⁓

By the mid- to late 1960s I was getting a lot of media coverage. An impartial observer leafing through my scrapbook from circa 1966–1970 would be impressed with the hubbub of activity. There were newspaper and magazine articles including notices, column items, and in-depth interviews and photo spreads focused on club appearances, benefit concerts, and bigger splashes for starring roles in larger productions like the first revival of Rodgers and Hammerstein's *South Pacific* at Lincoln Center for a summer run of sold-out performances in 1967.

More than a few of the articles in that scrapbook pointed out how very odd it was that with all the success, Hollywood hadn't really made a place for me. There was certainly no conscious effort on my part to reinforce any dissatisfaction with my career direction. I was perfectly happy with the way things were. The articles wondered with disbelief how it could be that I was still waiting to be noticed or discovered by Hollywood.

My attitude about the whole Hollywood thing was the same as I felt about my encounter with Frank Sinatra on one of my early trips west. I had just finished doing some live Oldsmobile commercials on a Bing Crosby television special and was outside the studio waiting for a cab. A little Karmann Ghia sports car pulled up, and the man inside rolled down the window. "Hey kid, you need a ride?" It was Sinatra. He was smartly garbed in a hat, a black jacket, and black-and-white-checked trousers. He was a guest on the show and had recognized me.

"I'm going to the Hollywood Roosevelt Hotel," I told him.

"Get in."

The younger and more innocent version of me was a little nervous because Frank had quite the reputation. I knew that because I got more than I was asking for when I once questioned a noted film actress rather innocently after a concert we were doing for Richard Rodgers.

"What was it like dating Frank?"

"It's great," she told me. I thought that was the end of her answer, but she added ever so matter-of-factly, "He just can't ever get off. Wears me out."

"Really? Hmm." Not much more you can say after something like that.

Cruising in his sports car, we chatted about some mutual friends, including the choreographer Carol Haney, who taught him how to dance in the movies. Throughout the coming years, I got to know Frank, not well, but he was always very nice to me. But as he dropped me in front of the Hollywood Roosevelt, I was relieved that he didn't hit on me. At the same time, a tiny little part of me felt humorously slighted not to have been asked. It was symbolic on another level about the Hollywood film and television industry. I was very content with my career, but it would be nice if the studios and the networks came a-courting.

I guess it spoke to the power of putting the message out there to the universe. Only a few weeks after those newspaper articles questioned why I wasn't doing a film or a television series, both happened in quick order in 1969.

I went to London to do the screen test for *The Song of Norway*, based on the life of the Norwegian composer Edvard Grieg and adapted from an operetta of the same name. I got the part in what would become my first real film. For purposes of historical accuracy, I have to admit that I had done another film a few months before that, but I am happy to say that not even Google makes any mention of my participation. I was with Ira and friends on vacation in Italy when the call came in to do a cameo role. It sounded good at the time—a film with Dick Van Dyke and directed by Garson Kanin called *Some Kind of Nut*. I can only vaguely remember doing a scene in a swimming pool. What was more memorable was a chance to see my musician friend once again before heading back to Italy, as the affair was still on at that point but beginning to wind down.

The Song of Norway turned out to be a wonderful and totally unforgettable experience for what would turn out to be a totally forgettable movie.

The chance to finally work in film, but also one about classical music, was exhilarating from start to finish. It was a huge thrill that we got to record all the music with the London Symphony. The icing on the cake was the fact that the film would be shot on location in Norway and Denmark for three months. We shot on location in the fjords and mountains and the older sections of very picturesque towns and cities from Lillehammer in the north to Copenhagen and Odense farther south in Denmark. I took my two smallest, Lizzie and Robert, along for a good portion of the production, and they enjoyed the experience too, except for one part. We had to take a seaplane to some location and it was a very bumpy ride. I was sitting next to the pilot and they were behind me. I have a photo of them somewhere showing their sad little faces staring down into the airsickness bags they held at the ready. Poor Robert got the worst of it. Ira brought Barbara and Joseph over for a visit too. I think they enjoyed it.

Hanging out with the legendary actor Edward G. Robinson was an added bonus, and our friendship continued long after the film wrapped. He was short in stature at five feet five, but you wouldn't know it from seeing him on film. Since the time he first appeared in silent movies in the early 1920s and went on to breakthrough stardom as a gangster in *Little Caesar* in 1931, he had a commanding presence. I asked him one evening what it was like to be regarded as a film star of the highest caliber for so many years. His answer pooh-poohed the whole thing. He explained that his secret of longevity in the business was not taking himself or the business too seriously. "Well, my dear, stars are in the heavens, not here on earth. I've just always tried to do my job the best I can and be a real professional. That's what it is all about."

It was also inspiring to work with the European talent, notably the Welsh-born comedian and singer Sir Harry Secombe and the great English character actor Robert Morley. Another Englishman on the production, Ray Holder, taught me how to play the faux piano so that it looked like I knew what I was doing. I can read music, but I'm not a pianist. He showed me the different chords and how to place my hands on the dummy keys, and it came off quite authentic on film.

Unfortunately, my accomplished skill at the fake piano was no help in making the film a success at the box office or with the critics. First and foremost, it was a classic case of bad timing. Musicals like *My Fair Lady* and *The Sound of Music* had been huge successes in the mid-1960s. *The Song of Norway* was designed to follow in their golden footsteps (its title has the same ring as *The Sound of Music*). But you know what they say about the best-laid plans.

When the film premiered shortly before Christmas of 1970, society had made a definitive turn in another direction, and it demonstrably could care less about singing and dancing in beautiful landscapes. Edgy independent films like *Easy Rider* resonated more with the times. Our film was among several other miscalculated musical film casualties that came out at the same time, such as *Mame*, *Paint Your Wagon*, *Lost Horizon* (a remake), and *Darlin' Lili*. It probably also didn't help that the Norwegian actor who played Edvard Grieg was really not a singer.

The production dragged on for two months longer than planned, which created some scheduling difficulties for my next job. Most of the crew caught heavy colds and were ill from the thirty-below freeze in the winter months. Fortunately, Harry Secombe's abundant supply of cognac came to the rescue.

The film was an inspiration to many film critics to get creative with their prose, as my old scrapbook bore witness. "The actors perform as if they were cardboard cutouts in a Christmas display in a department store window," wrote one reviewer. "It would take more than the arrival of a truckload of Nazi storm troopers to save…this year's imitation of 'The Sound of Music.'" Vincent Canby of the *New York Times* echoed a similar sentiment, calling the film a "living postcard." "[It is so] full of waterfalls, blossoms, lambs, glaciers, folk dancers, mountains, children, suns, fjords and churches that it raises kitsch to the status of a kind of art, not without its own peculiar integrity and crazy fascination." He added that this scenery was "so overwhelming that people are reduced to being scenic obstructions." The reviewers were kinder and more compassionate toward me, noting that I had done well despite the circumstances. Joseph Gelmis in *New York Newsday* wrote, "Like Bogart in his worst films, she emerges unscathed because both she and we know that she is better than her material. Yet she is not patronizing, either."

Just as I was preparing to go off to Norway to do the film, another opportunity was knocking at the door. It would come to fulfill the second part of that strange fortune cookie the media served up about why Hollywood hadn't yet found a place for me. Film and now television were manifesting all at once.

"I don't want to do a television series." That's what I told Sandy Gallin when he wanted me to meet with the producers who were putting together a new show called *The Brady Bunch*. First of all, I had four children to take care of and I was working on trying to improve my relationship with Ira. We all lived in New York, and the show would be shot in Hollywood. I also knew that the intense pressures of that lifestyle made divorce an all too common consequence, and my marriage was in such a fragile state. I had also heard about the incredibly long hours it took to do a weekly series. It was no wonder why actors would say how they came to regard the crew like family members since they spent more time with them than with their actual families.

From a professional standpoint, I also questioned my sanity for even considering doing a television series. I was perfectly satisfied with the way things were. After doing the film in Norway, I was prepared to pick up where I had left off. Vegas and club dates beckoned. If a great part in another film or a Broadway play or touring company came up, I had the flexibility to choose. I was also having fun and staying in front of the audience by doing *The Tonight Show*, *Dean Martin*, and other variety and game shows. That lifestyle afforded me that precious balance between being a mom and having a successful career. So when my kids needed me to be there for Back to School Night, a big game, or some other important priority, nine times out of ten I could make it happen. A potential television series in Hollywood would clearly make that more difficult.

"Well, just go down and meet them," Sandy pleaded with me with every ounce of common sense he could muster. When a manager invokes that tone, even very successful actors go into the old insecurity mode of fear-based thinking. Your inner little voice warns, "If I don't at least go and take the meeting, maybe my phone might not ring again. Perhaps my agent will think twice next time about submitting me for something else. Maybe that next time, he won't bother to call about such and such a part that I really want."

Backing down, I told him, "Okay, but I have to be on a plane to Houston tonight." I was scheduled to begin an engagement there at the Shamrock Hotel. The rehearsal was the next day and the opening on the following. But today there was no excuse. The timing was opportune, because I was already in Los Angeles having just guested on *Dean Martin*. So I made the six-mile trip from the Beverly Hills Hotel to Paramount Studios in Hollywood for the meeting.

Entering the gates of Paramount that day (and every time thereafter) gave me goosebumps. I was always aware of the enormity of its history. I had loved movies all of my life. Going to the cinema was and remains to this day a sacred event, and for me, performing is like going to church. On the other side of those gates was where some of the greatest films of all time were shot. In the years to come, I thought of all the legendary stars who had used my dressing room and the parking space I now occupied. I thought about all the classics like Hitchcock's *The Man Who Knew Too Much*, *The Graduate*, and *Rosemary's Baby* that had been filmed on Stage 5, which would soon become my home away from home.

Once at the studio I was shown to an office where three people were waiting to meet me: the show's creator, writer, and producer Sherwood Schwartz, studio production head Doug Cramer, and director John Rich. Sherwood was coming off the success of what would prove to be another all-time TV hit, *Gilligan's Island*. He had worked for decades as a writer on some of the top radio shows of the 1940s and was a pioneer writer on 1950s TV comedy classics like *Ozzie and Harriet*, *Red Skelton*, and *I Married Joan*. His creativity extended to music as well—he cowrote the catchy theme songs for both *Brady* and *Gilligan*. When he was ninety-two years old in 2008, he finally got a Walk of Fame star on Hollywood Boulevard, and I was thrilled to be there to help honor him and participate in the ceremony. Doug oversaw *Mission: Impossible* and *The Odd Couple* for Paramount, but went on to his biggest success with *Dynasty* and *The Love Boat* in the 1980s, partnered with Aaron Spelling. The third person at the table was John Rich, a heavyweight in comedy television for directing *Mister Ed*, *The Dick Van Dyke Show*, *All in the Family*, *Newhart*, *Barney Miller*, and the list goes on.

After chatting for a few minutes, they cut to the chase. "Would you mind doing a scene on film for us?" they asked me. I told them about the plane I had to catch later that evening. No problem, they said.

Immediately, they dispatched me to a makeup trailer to get ready. It belonged to *Star Trek*. William Shatner was in there, and he wasn't terribly friendly. "What is she doing in here?" It was as if I were an enemy Klingon who had invaded his trailer. What was also humorous was that he didn't make the slightest gesture to discreetly lower his volume to avoid my hearing him. He obviously had no clue who I was, perhaps just another extra or a bit player that had wandered by mistake into the stars' makeup room. Years later, I reminded him about the incident, and we had a good laugh about it.

There was more bizarre comedy inside that trailer before I left for the soundstage. The makeup artist happened to put some long eyelashes on me that would be more suitable if I were playing a streetwalker rather than the matriarch of a blended family of six children.

"What the hell is this?" I exclaimed. But I didn't have the confidence yet to speak up and say, "No long fake eyelashes!"

You have to remember that actors are very careful and particular about their "look," especially how their faces appear in makeup and how they're lit. A light hitting you the wrong way will let everyone know how little sleep you had the night before or how the passage of time and hours in the sun have turned your face into cracked leather. It's not about vanity. How the camera likes the actor is a crucial part of his equipment and maybe what got him the job. And often it is the actor himself who has to be vigilant, because if he doesn't care about his appearance, usually no one else will. For that reason, I am so grateful for all I learned from all the talented makeup artists I've worked with over the years.

Before we started the scene, I wanted a clear disclaimer about the eyelashes. "I don't think Carol Brady would wear these," I told them. Doing my standard trick of trying to turn a negative once again into a positive, I got the point across with humor and everyone on the set cracked up. I personally would have chosen to give the character a different look, I told them. This memory is particularly ironic and amusing to me given the iconic fashion influence the show would grow to have. People made an absurdly big deal about how my hairstyles would morph into something new with the beginning of each season.

Anyway, I did the scene together with an actor (not my soon-to-be-costar Robert Reed) who was portraying my husband, and then I made the plane to Houston.

I was about to go onstage two nights later when the phone rang. It was Sandy. "They want you to come back right away to do the pilot," he told me.

"I'm opening," I told him.

"Talk to the promoter."

So I went over to the promoter and told him what happened. He said I could go if I could find someone to fill in for me. Jerry Vale, who had a string of pop hits in the 1950s and 1960s, graciously agreed to step in for me. I gratefully told the promoter I'd be happy to come back for the same salary if my new show became a hit. I would keep that promise.

CHAPTER 16

Brady-monium

༄

The English used to be able to boast, "The sun never sets on the British Empire." Similarly, I can say, "The curtain never falls on *The Brady Bunch*."

At this moment, someone somewhere in the world is watching *The Brady Bunch*. Since the show debuted on September 26, 1969, it has been continuously broadcast in the United States and overseas in over 122 countries as one of the most beloved television series of all time. Full-set compilations of the show sell in steady numbers. You couldn't kill it with a stick. Some people writing fan letters today from former Communist countries go so far as to assume that the shows are brand-new—outmoded clothes and hairstyles and glaring lack of computers or cell phones notwithstanding.

Many people think those few years on *The Brady Bunch* are basically the sum total of my career. In reality, the show was but a small part of my list of credits, but because of its lasting power, it is never going to go away. Such is the enormous power and penetration of the media. Many people would also assume that I could write several books on just the *Brady Bunch* experience alone. Because so much has been written about the history and impact of the show already, I am not going to attempt that. In reality, it was not so chock full of dramatic stories as one might be led to believe. We were a cast and crew that cared about each other like family, and we made sure to have a good measure of fun to balance the drama that life serves up. But it was hard work and long hours that were fairly routine day in and day out. In fact, some of the fondest memories I will share are of the things that deviated from the norm, especially when we shot on location.

Without the chance to play the role of Carol Brady, I don't think the Smithsonian Institution would have honored me as a "cultural icon," nor would *Entertainment Weekly* and TV Land use that same word, ranking me as one of their top 100 TV "icons" of all time. Unbelievable. All this came as the result of an opportunity that I was lukewarm at best about doing at the start.

What in fact excited me most about coming back to Hollywood to do the pilot was the chance to work with John Rich. From the time I was a child, I loved being around people who knew what they were doing and were masters of their profession. John was high up in that category. I've always loved working with strong directors, and John was both strong and tough. Those qualities came to the forefront quickly once we got down to work. And not everyone appreciated it as I did.

From those first scenes together in the pilot, Robert Reed (portraying my husband, Mike) proved himself immediately to be both a terrific actor and a very complex man. Gene Hackman was originally tested for the role, which I would have loved. Most of the time, Bob was a delightful curmudgeon on the set. He was extremely well educated and cultured, having attended North-western University and studied at the Royal Academy of Dramatic Art in London (which also qualified him to be a certified royal pain in the butt!). On top of that, he was a classical pianist. Conflicts and issues that were apparent from the first day of work went fairly unresolved throughout the years we worked together. Behind most of it was his attitude — he wanted the show to be Shakespeare, more worthy of his training and skill. "Bob, it's a sitcom," I'd have to remind him whenever the matter reared its head, which it did regularly.

The tension mounted as we were filming the pilot.

"Cut…Don't do it that way!" John shouted to Bob. As John could be, he was loud and direct, and it was more than obvious that Bob was getting angry. We had been doing a love scene that had gone fine in rehearsal but wasn't working to John's liking the way Bob was doing it. I felt I had to step in and do something.

"Excuse me for a moment," I said to Bob. I had suddenly realized the source of the problem. I left him and walked out of camera range and took John off to the side.

"John, just back off," I told the director. "Don't say anything or make a big deal about this, but Bob's gay. He's nervous about this scene." I told him that I knew how to handle it. I went back on the set and we started up again. I don't remember specifically what I said to Bob, but I took extra care with him to make sure he felt comfortable. In that moment, I tried to love him as hard as I could and make him feel great. I wanted him to feel romantic and sexy as all get out. And perhaps, if he knew that I was comfortable about him and his sexuality, he didn't have to be afraid of playing that role. I don't think the crew caught on to this in the beginning like I had, but most did as the show went on.

Every time we'd do a romantic scene, the same nervousness would come up. We'd laugh as he came on set in his pajamas. I think on those days he would frequently self-medicate by drinking more than usual at lunchtime.

After a few days, we finished the pilot and all went our separate ways. There was nothing so extraordinarily special about it in my mind at that time. Yes, I thought it was a good idea to do a show about a blended family. It really hadn't been done before. The kids were adorable. Bob was great, and the fact that he and I were to be seen sleeping in the same bed together might finally break that antiquated taboo on network television. I felt I could bring something special to the character of Carol Brady given the fact that I was a mother of four in real life. Beyond that, I had absolutely no expectation or attachment to the outcome. I just viewed it as a job, and it was done.

Did I think the pilot would sell? I really wasn't sure, and consequently I moved on to other projects, most notably the filming in Europe. To be totally honest, I promptly forgot about *The Brady Bunch* until I got the phone call several months later with the news that it was a go.

It may sound strange, but I really wasn't so aware during the first years while I was doing *The Brady Bunch* that it was growing into anything that might be considered a cultural phenomenon. It is probably one of my major personality quirks that I get hyperfocused when I'm in the middle of a project, especially one as all-consuming as a weekly television series proved to be. It was quite easy to get cut off from the world in the whirlwind of doing a weekly series. We went to work in the dark. We went home in the dark. The long hours and demanding schedule, plus trying to be a real-life mother, afforded little luxury of time for any distractions. When I did have time off from filming, I was usually off doing club dates or musicals to maintain my musical chops.

My MO has always been to keep my attention on the current job to make it the best it can be. Dwelling on the past has never

been a priority. It is the same reason why my scrapbooks remained virtually unopened, a whole cabinet full of videos were
never watched, and audio recordings were never played. Part of it,
I know, is avoidance, because I am my own harshest critic, echo-
ing my mother's judgmental ways. And luckily, I've kept busy
throughout the years, so there is always a new project that demands my full attention. It's also important to realize that once
it's done and in the can, you can't change anything. Whether you
had a great success or a flop, it is your past. You have to learn
to acknowledge it, and love it, but move beyond it. In my later
years, I am thankfully and usually even pleasantly surprised on
the rare occasions when I do happen to see a tape of something
from the past or find an episode of the Bradys while channel surf-
ing. "Hmm, that wasn't so bad." The show makes me smile.

One of the big reasons I think the show has endured for so
many decades is due to the fact that we really tried to make each
episode seem real and believable to the viewer. There was a commitment to be truthful in the way we interacted and reacted to
each other. Every word in the script had to pass that credibility
test. I am sure the background laughter would have been coming
from that place of truth if we had filmed before a live audience
instead of using a laugh track.

I had done enough television by the time the series began
that the learning curve about doing a sitcom progressed very
swiftly. There were some adjustments I had to make in learning
about the cameras and the lighting. Having cut my teeth in the
days of live television, I was already accustomed to how everything moved at a fast clip. Scripts were constantly going through
changes, and we all had to learn new lines every day, sometimes
a lot.

Doing the show was not the cushier life of sitcom stars of later
years where you did a table read with the cast on Tuesday, re-

hearsed and blocked the cameras on the set on Wednesday and Thursday, and then shot two shows in front of a live audience and four cameras on Friday. Ours was filmed in the traditional way, more like a movie. There were no days of rehearsal. We memorized the script the night before. Usually, there would be last-minute changes to our lines, and sometimes quite a few. We would rehearse before the camera, then go off to the side and talk it through while they arranged the lighting with the stand-ins on the set. This was helpful if someone didn't have the scene down. We'd also try to come up with some added nuances to make it more special. Then we'd shoot the master shot (i.e., the broader view of everyone in the scene), most of the time in one take, sometimes two. If you asked for a retake because you felt something wasn't right in your performance, they'd do it again. Then the scene would be repeated to get all the close-ups, which could take considerable time if all nine of us were featured in the shot.

We didn't get coddled or babied. After John Rich left the show, we had another director named Oscar Rudolph, the father of filmmaker Alan Rudolph. He was a short, bald man, and his direction was always the same, which the kids loved parodying. "Okay, everybody, up, up, up, up!" It was an additional pressure that the child actors could only work so many hours by law. Often they'd run out of time, so Sherwood Schwartz would quickly write another scene for Carol and the housekeeper, played by Ann B. Davis, to fill in the gap. During part of one year, they tried to do two shows in one week. That was insanity. But in the end, I give great credit to the cast that the show has sustained. We believed in it. We worked hard at it. Despite Bob's meltdowns from time to time, both kids and adults were very conscientious and professional. So you can understand how easy it was to get tunnel vision. I don't believe I ever sat down and watched a single episode of the show when it was first broadcast.

Speaking of Ann B., what a tremendous professional she was to work with and what a great friend she became. I probably spent more time together with her off camera than with anyone else in the production, hanging out at her home that overlooked the San Fernando Valley. One day, she took me aside and said, "You have to learn how to conserve your energy." I was constantly moving around and talking. It was hard for me to sit still, but Ann B. had a solution for me. She taught me how to do needlepoint. I loved doing it, and the creations made great gifts for family and friends, usually in the form of pillows with floral designs. I was hardly an expert, however. On one trip back to New York when I went to put my things away for landing, I was slightly embarrassed to discover that I had found a way to sew the needlepoint onto my skirt.

Needlepoint aside, being on a popular television series changes your life, in some fairly absurd ways. You can be a big star on Broadway, but still many people outside of the Great White Way have no idea who you are. Get on a hit series that people really embrace, and your life will never quite be the same.

After the show had been on for a short while, I took Lizzie for a walk in Central Park. Some children recognized me and crowded around us.

"Mrs. Brady, can I have your autograph?"

Lizzie tugged at my coat. "Mommy, tell them you're not Mrs. Brady. Tell them that *we're* your real kids." From that moment forward, I had to think twice about going out in public with them. I was comfortable for myself, but I didn't want them to deal with all that kind of attention and feel diminished by it in any way. So for family outings to Disneyland, they'd have to go without me for the duration—and I always regretted that I couldn't be the one taking them.

Ironically, it was a trip to another amusement park, Kings

Island in Cincinnati, that opened my eyes to just how wildly popular the show had become. The episodes shot on location were for me the most fun and memorable, a nice break from the in-studio daily routine. The park was somehow or another owned by the Paramount conglomerate at the time, so some marketing whiz thought it would be a great cross-promotion and big publicity for the newly opened attraction and their hit television show. We had previously done three-part episodes at the Grand Canyon and in Hawaii, but not among the crowds like at Kings Island. The people there in America's heartland went crazy over us like we were rock stars. Forget about sleep at the hotel in the park. Security, what security? Did such a thing exist in the early 1970s? The kids found out where we were and were banging on our doors at all hours of the night. A similar mob scene happened at Disney World, but I was there solo and sans Bradys as one of the first people to perform at Top of the World when the place first opened.

The excitement of getting out of the studio to film at Kings Island, Hawaii, and the Grand Canyon is the easy answer whenever anyone asks me what my favorite episodes are. However, it could sometimes get a little too exciting outside the comfort zone of the studio. Accidents can happen anywhere, even on our set, as poor little Susan Olsen found out in our pilot episode. She got bonked in the face by a falling light fixture and needed a little extra makeup to mask the black and blue. But each of those location shoots had at least one major hair-raising moment we could have lived without. Stunt doubles, where were you when we needed you?

First, there was the roller-coaster scene at Kings Island. Bob refused to go on it because he was terrified of them. So who was going to go in his place? Me. If you watch that scene, you will see a horror-struck look on my face. It was not acting. Nor was it when Ann B. was thrown on top of me whenever we went around a curve. But what you don't see is the blood running down the cameraman's face. To get the shot, they first strapped him across from us on the back of the car. That didn't work, so they sat him facing us in the seat in front of us. On the first big drop, the camera went flying and hit him in the face. With the bleeding stopped and the camera finally stabilized for everyone's safety, we had to shoot another take. Not fun!

Now, about the Grand Canyon, let me say that the name is well deserved because it is deep, very deep, especially looking down a sheer cliff on a narrow trail while sitting on top of a very large mule. The scene called for all nine of us to ride the trail mules down a bit on the trail. A mule skinner named Al was in front, followed by Bob, Ann B., and the children. I brought up the rear. I am not an animal psychologist, so I do not know if it is possible for mules to have a "bad day." But if one could, this was truly an awful one. In fact, my mule may have been having suicidal thoughts, judging by the way it was leaning over the edge and looking straight down. I didn't want to be dragged along as a part of its death wish. The cameras were rolling.

"Al!" I cried out the mule skinner's name as I saw myself a second or two away from going right over the mule's head, disappearing into the abyss, and landing as a little puff of dust at the bottom à la Wile E. Coyote. "Al, what do I do?"

"Just pull up on the reins. It will be okay." When they took me down from that mule at the end of the scene, my saddle was not dry!

The grand prize for near-death *Brady Bunch* experiences goes to the Hawaii trip. One of the writers came up with the idea of how nice it would be for all of us to be in an outrigger canoe. So there we were on the water, all nine of us, and told to wait to catch the next big wave. The boat with the director, the cameraman, and the other necessary members of the crew was a few yards away. We caught the wave, and everything was going great for about ten seconds until I saw that the man on the rudder of the crew boat had lost control of it. The boat was coming right toward us and our rudder man swamped us. Next thing I know, I'm upside down in the water underneath our capsized canoe. I'm hardly what you would call a fish, but I knew that Susan had good reason to pass on the swimming pool when she came over to our house. So my first thought was to hold on to her for dear life. Barry Williams was a strong swimmer, so at least that was a comforting thought in the moment. They righted the boat, and we all climbed back into it. The director said, "Let's do that again!" Poor Susan was a wreck. And if things were not scary enough, my false eyelashes had come off—how rude! We were all shivering, and probably not just due to being cold. But we did it again. The people on shore were all shook up, and understandably, the parents of the kids were a wreck. Of course, we had not been given life jackets to wear. It could have been a major disaster.

Another surprise that I wasn't quite prepared for was how seriously people took the show. Once they let you into their living rooms via that cathode-ray tube, you become part of their extended family. Accordingly, they had opinions on everything and were only too glad to share. People wrote in about how much they loved my hair or detested it. Part of that was due to the fact that I had to wear a big wig for the first season, the "bubble-do" I called it. My hair had been bleached more blonde to make me look closer to Norwegian for *The Song of Norway*, and it was clearly not right for the show. They had filmed the first six episodes without me, so I rushed back to do all the scenes to be inserted with no time to restore my hair color back to normal. That the hair attracted almost a cultlike interest amuses me to no end. Some tuned in for each season premiere with great anticipation just to see the new style for the year. And no one was indifferent about that poor, much-maligned mullet in the 1973–1974 season. It is quite a dubious honor to be known in some circles as "the Mother of the Mullet."

Paramount conducted research to gauge public attitude beyond the hair when the show first came on the air. Some people resented that Carol Brady had a maid. "No wonder she looks so well!" Others thought the house looked too clean and loved any episode in which I got dirty. A sampling of some Avon ladies at the Plaza Hotel in New York objected to the glamorous way I appeared in the series. "Our kids expect us to look like you." Okay, I grant you that the real Florence Henderson has never worn makeup, eyelashes, or lipstick to bed. I did always insist that Carol Brady would be in a beautiful nightgown when Bob and I had scenes in bed, even though that was far from my practice in real life. But it was part of the fantasy, and important to the special warmth and sexual chemistry that Bob and I wanted to project.

A sociologist or a psychologist would have a much better explanation for why *The Brady Bunch* hit a collective nerve and has endured as a global phenomenon for so long. In my opinion, it began with Sherwood Schwartz's ingenious design that worked on so many levels. You know when an idea is truly good because things seem to snowball.

At its heart was the notion of the blended family, a father with three sons and a mother with three daughters coming together to form a new family. Blended families were hardly a new concept, but it probably took on a new significance given what people had gone through in the 1960s in breaking from longstanding traditional mores. (Remember the pill?) Divorce rates were up, and so blended families naturally became an increasingly commonplace occurrence. My widowed cousin had seven children. She married a man who had ten. They became the "Happy

Hanawalts"—an homage to the Brady Bunch. I receive endless stories like that.

Sherwood also had the foresight to keep the show and its subject matter simple and quite universal to the shared experience of children and parents. Entering the Brady world for a half hour each week was designed to provide a gentle refuge. There were plenty of big problems in the real world to go around. Instead, we were a loving family who always tried to find a way to work through its challenges. Mike and Carol Brady were parents who seemed to understand their children and guide them without demeaning them or talking down to them to make them feel worthless. Perhaps the most controversial topic the show took up was Greg getting caught smoking cigarettes at a time when most teenagers were smoking and doing harder stuff. Otherwise, the story lines were grounded in wading through right versus wrong and navigating through a host of everyday moral and ethical issues. There seemed no end to the possible plotlines when mining the rich territory of sibling rivalries, dating, part-time jobs, extracurricular activities at school, and forays into an increasingly adult world.

By having nine cast members that include three children of different ages from each gender, Sherwood also insured that each viewer at home would have at least one character with whom they could identify closely. It was an especially gentle world as seen through the eyes of a child, so all kids could easily relate. That factor, along with the universality of the situations the family dealt with, has much to do with the show's timeless, cross-cultural appeal over the decades. It was strange toward the end that when Sherwood and Lloyd (Sherwood's son) tried to introduce some new dynamics to the show, notably Cousin Oliver (played by Robbie Rist to bring a new younger child to the mix) and the Kelly family next door (as a potential new series spin-off starring Ken Berry), the audience didn't go for it. "Don't mess with a good thing" was their message.

The other part of the equation that is a little less tangible was in the execution, what we as the actors brought to it. First and foremost, Bob and I tried to set the tone for the kids about being professional and doing our jobs the very best we possibly could. The kids learned that they had to come to the set prepared. Nobody gave them any slack in that regard. Since I was not only portraying a mother but was the only cast member who was a mother and a wife in real life, I think the parenting role spilled over into my relationship with the kids. The life of a child actor may sound appealing from the outside, but looking back over the history of the industry, such a large percentage of these children have had difficulties later on as they grew into adults. I tried to impart to the kids on the show a spirit of gratitude. I told them, "Don't ever resent it. Always embrace what you do. Don't talk badly about it. Don't negate it. It is. It's there. You did it. And you did it well. Accept that." And for the most part, that's what they did. Like a real family, we have all remained good friends throughout the years and stay in touch periodically.

Of all the kids, Barry Williams as Greg had the easiest time embracing his role. Barry had a serious interest in becoming a musical performer and he had talent, so I became a mentor to him of sorts. He listened to what I had to say and applied it. He was always a special kid, and I liked him from the start. All right, all right, I know what you're thinking. So let's deal with it once and for all. It is time for me to have the definitive say on our "affair." Get ready for the row of asterisks.

* *

One of the most popular bits of *Brady Bunch* lore that has followed me like a piece of toilet paper stuck to a shoe is my alleged affair with Barry. So juicy is this rumor, some of you readers probably could not wait to purchase the book to leaf through and find this section to learn "the truth."

Those of you who have diligently read this book from the beginning have already come to understand that Florence Henderson has a racy sensibility, in direct contrast to the more staid onscreen image of Carol Brady. Carol would not even give such an idea the dignity of a reply. She would have dismissed it immediately with a bat of a false eyelash. If it happened to be true, she would still deny it until such time as she reached a ripe old age where such things don't really matter anymore. Until then, she would laugh with feigned disdain at why anyone would give credence to such a preposterous rumor.

But Florence Henderson is different.

When Barry published his account of the Brady years in the early 1990s, he put it out there that Florence Henderson and he went out on a date during those halcyon days. It is true. I won't deny it. When the book came out, he asked me to do some interviews with him. Given our close relationship, how could I say no? Our date was a hot topic of conversation during these interviews. We were having fun with the idea. Now, since we're both older, dating the more mature-looking version of Barry doesn't seem like such a bad idea!

Barry asked me to go with him to hear a popular singer perform at the Cocoanut Grove, the famous but long gone Los Angeles nightclub. I didn't give it all that much thought, since I would gladly have done the same for any of the older children if asked. Admittedly, Barry was making his first steps into adulthood at fifteen. But it was innocent enough, and I didn't want to discourage him. At the time, he was not old enough to drive a car by himself. He had a learner's permit, so he drove with his older brother in the car to pick me up. We then ditched the brother, so that we could be alone for our drive to the Grove. We went in and were shown to a lousy table. I whispered sweetly in Barry's ear that the maître d' was expecting a tip. Immediately upon payment, like magic, our host recognized the celebrities we were and showed us to an excellent table. After the concert, Barry was very sweet. We fetched his brother and he gave me a goodnight kiss at my hotel. So from his book, our playful but coy interviews, and the telephone game (where the facts change each time it's retold) that followed, an urban legend was born.

What is very true is that Barry did have a serious crush on me, which I understood and helped him get past. Let us just say that if he had entertained a roll in the hay with me, I would never have done that.

****

Undeniably we had a very special connection—and it goes without saying that I always felt like a surrogate mother to him and the rest of the kids. On a deeper level, I represented something to him that he admired. He loved music and knew that I could sing. He also liked my work ethic, and adopted it then as he still does today. He has remained a dear friend. I saw him together with his son Brandon not long ago. Brandon was about the same age as when I first met Barry, and the striking resemblance to the younger version of his father was almost miraculous.

The camaraderie with Barry and everyone in the production translated in no small measure to the good feeling that people at home felt watching the show. We brought the spirit of family not just to the characters we played but also to how we related to each other in real life. Working together the kind of hours we did, you can't help it. My children would often come to the set, and they developed friendships of their own with their fictional counterparts. Barbara and Joe even acted in a couple of episodes. I got to know everything going on in the personal lives of crew members and their families and vice versa because we were so open with each other. The crew members loved it if you showed interest and respect about their crafts. Jimmy Fields, the head grip (electrician), taught me a lot about lighting. "Why are you using a 10K banger there?" I'd ask him. He made me an honorary member of the lighting guild. John Rich wanted to teach me how to direct because he thought I worked so well helping the kids. I told him that the technology was my Achilles' heel, and I would never know enough about the camera to be good at it. "I'll teach you," he implored. I never took him up on it, and I sometimes feel regret about that.

Laughter and having fun while working was also important to setting the tone. For that purpose I was always doing something crazy. In one of the shows, the famous NFL quarterback Joe Namath guest starred as himself. The plotline was that Bobby lied to his friends, telling them that the football star was coming over for dinner at his house when playing an exhibition game in town. The touching climax of the show is the scene when Joe actually comes to our house. The family goes out to say goodbye to him as he walks down our fake driveway to his car. I whispered to the director, "Keep the camera rolling." When Joe said his farewells and got to me last, I jumped up on him, wrapping my legs around his waist. "Take me away from this family!" I cried. The crew fell down, and it became a favorite on the blooper reel.

If there happened to be a new director working, this fun atmosphere was a little harder for that person to take, since most were probably a little nervous and on edge working on the show for the first time. Jackie Coogan was a guest on one show in which our characters had a car accident and he blamed me. Doing that scene, some gaffe happened and Jackie and I broke up. We got hysterical and could not stop laughing. The director got really annoyed at us. I took him aside. "Excuse me, but when you work this hard, every once in a while it's good to laugh. So please don't talk like that, especially in front of our guest star." But that wasn't the end of the problem. In a courtroom scene in the same episode, Robert Emhardt was playing the judge. He was a great actor. We did the master shot, and then had to do close-ups on everybody, including Jackie, the kids, and me. By the time they got to Robert's close-up, he had done it so many times he couldn't remember the line. The director started yelling at Robert, and the more he yelled the more stressed Robert became. I ran to the phone and called Sherwood. "You have to come down here because it's not right what this director is doing." Much later, I ran into this same director, and he apologized for his behavior, which was big of him. He said it happened during a stressful period of his life. But you can't bring that to work. Be kind, because everybody is struggling with something.

If there was a source of recurring tension on the set, it usually concerned Bob. As mentioned, he wanted *The Brady Bunch* to be Shakespeare. It was the catalyst for terrible fights with Sherwood. We had one show in which there was a role reversal. Mike tells Carol that he thinks she has an easier time of it. She responds, "Well, you take over my job, and I'll take over yours." So the script called for me to teach the boys baseball, and Bob would be in the kitchen baking something. The idea was that he loads up stuff from the refrigerator and manages to drop the eggs. Then he slips and takes a pratfall.

"This is so stupid," Bob complained. "Nobody would ever do that."

"Why don't you try it?" I coaxed him. "I think it's funny. I wish I were doing it." I loved doing physical comedy.

He backed down and tried it, loading his arms up, dropping the eggs, and seeing everything go flying.

"I was wrong," he said, laughing, as he got up.

Another time, Ann B. and I were supposed to be making jam. We had all these pots on the stove, but all we were really stirring was water.

"That's ridiculous," Bob protested. "It's so obvious."

I replied, "It's our scene, and we don't have trouble imagining this is strawberry jam."

A lot of the time, I understood Bob's frustration, but blurting out, "This is crap" didn't win him a lot of sympathy.

As complex and sometimes difficult as Bob could be, it was balanced by his genuine love for the kids. It was fairly obvious to me that he treated the kids as though they were his real family. During a hiatus, he even took them all on a trip to Europe. He did have a real daughter, Karen, from a short-lived marriage, whom he rarely saw. We got to meet her once when she did a small guest role in one of the episodes. It's hard to imagine what it must have been like in that era to be an actor in fear of losing his career if his sexual orientation were to become public. Being in that closet had to be a very stressful place.

I know that he found real solace being around his fictional family. It was something he carried close to his heart to the very end of his life. In 1991, I got a call from Bob. He was teaching Shakespeare at UCLA. He was supposed to give a speech in Little Rock.

"Florence, I'm not feeling well. Could you go for me and give my speech for me?" It was ironically for a cancer research hospital. I told him I'd be happy to go.

"Are you okay?"

"Yes, I have colon cancer, but I'm going to be okay."

When I got back from Arkansas, I called him and asked if we could have lunch together. I told him I'd come out to Pasadena where he had a lovely mansion.

"That would be great," he said enthusiastically. But it didn't happen that time and a few attempts after. We would set something up, and then he'd call and cancel. I waited a few weeks and then called him again to see how he was doing. Everything seemed fine, but he called me one day out of the blue.

"Florence, you know what, I'm not doing well. It's not going to be very long. Can you call the kids for me? Would you tell them?"

I get cold chills and cry every time I think of this conversation. "Oh my God. Of course, Bob. I'll do it." When I did so, each of them was devastated to hear the news. Telling each of the kids was one of the toughest things I've had to do.

I wanted to visit him, but I respected his wish that he didn't want me to see him in his condition because he had lost a tremendous amount of weight. He died very shortly after this last phone call. Along with his real daughter, Karen, the kids and I were just about the only ones there at his private funeral. He was able to keep the veil of privacy and dignity up to that point, but all hell broke loose once one of the tabloid newspapers printed his death certificate on the front page!

AIDS was a new thing in the American public consciousness, a deadly, scary disease that carried a fearmongering stigma. "The father of America has died of AIDS" was picked up and projected like a scandal by the gossip traders. All the newspapers wanted to interview the kids and me. Soon thereafter, Bob's image and likeness started to disappear little by little from Brady Bunch promotional materials and merchandising.

But even from the start, it was evident that Carol and the children were focused on as more the essence of the show. Playing her for me was hardly a stretch. As an actor, you have to draw upon your own feelings and emotions to somehow find a way to relate to the character you are portraying. I think it must have come through in my performance that I understood that character. I drew on my real life as a mother of four children. But there was something else charging the character, as if Carol Brady were some magical antidote to Florence Henderson's childhood. It was as though the trauma and turmoil, the lack of real parental affection or attention, and the material deprivation that happened to me ultimately had a positive purpose once it was channeled into Carol Brady.

It is quite unfathomable to me how this character of Carol Brady could have had the kind of impact she did. To think that a sitcom mother could give comfort and support to children who were parentless, abused, ignored, or unloved. It was almost otherworldly how the latchkey child living in the housing project in some lower-income community or another who writes in a language I don't understand from a place with a name that I cannot pronounce feels a kinship. I've always felt tremendous compassion for children who are lonely and suffering.

It may all be based in illusion, but hopefully one with an overwhelmingly positive impact. Truthfully, I would have played the character a lot stricter and harsher than the TV codes would allow at that time. Situations sometimes dictated a sharp reprimand that wasn't permitted as part of Carol's arsenal. Maybe instead of shrugging my shoulders and being so understanding, I would have given her a little slap on the fanny. I also wanted Carol to be a little more realistic, like have an actual job, for God's sake. But Sherwood wanted her to be always available, and I became akin to those *Father Knows Best* and *Leave It to Beaver* parents who didn't have to work for a living yet somehow kept a nice middle-class life afloat in grand style.

Bob was not alone in having some dissatisfaction with the scripts. After the first season, I went on the record to point out that I thought there were times when I felt that we sometimes came off like a bunch of cardboard characters. "Does the scriptwriter have kids?" I remember questioning. But when the scripts were done right, I thought I came across as a believable mother. After that first year, I decided that I had to be a little more proactive in giving my input. In contrast to Bob, I took a less confrontational approach. "I have an idea how we can make this better" usually worked.

In one scene, one of the kids brought home two friends after school. I had to put my foot down when I learned that these two young actors were not given a line of dialogue in the script. They were just standing there in silence as they were introduced to me. "No kids visiting my house would do that," I told the director. "They would say, 'Hi, Mrs. Brady.'" Then I realized what the problem was. It was going to cost extra if the two kids spoke. I called up to Sherwood and told him that I would pay the additional cost, but he had to give them something to say. He agreed, but I never got the bill.

I know that when I go in public and people stop and want to have a photograph taken with me, it is because of a heartfelt relationship they have with Carol Brady. I make the time for that, as well for answering each and every e-mail and letter that I have received over these four decades, for one big reason: I have the deepest gratitude that I was given this opportunity.

Late into what proved to be our last season of shooting *The Brady Bunch*, Bob started to get into one of his usual arguments with Sherwood, but it soon heated up. "I won't do this," he complained about something that was obviously highly objectionable to him in the script. The discussion was futile, and Bob was asked to leave the set. Sherwood asked Ann B. and me if we would stay and do a couple of extra scenes to effectively write Bob out of that episode. We said sure, and we stayed late to get it done. They asked Bob to go home, but he refused and got very testy. He stayed in the back, observing. It was such a bizarre situation.

As we left the studio late that night, none of us knew that we had just finished the 117th and final episode of *The Brady Bunch*. The show was canceled. But it was hardly the end of the story.

CHAPTER 17

Good Help Is Hard to Find...

~

On the home front, things were in a holding pattern during much of the Brady years and the immediate aftermath. There was more than a legitimate excuse to maintain the status quo: an active parent dealing with the demanding schedule of a weekly series, plus performance engagements sandwiched in the downtime. I was running a tight ship, and it was not the time to rock the boat. Unfortunately, the climate had not really changed for the positive in terms of my overall happiness in the marriage over those years. Don't get me wrong, there were some good times mixed in, so it was hardly all doom and gloom.

The first order of business once we knew that *The Brady Bunch* was not going to be a flash in the pan was to make the move to Los Angeles. I can't say that I was thrilled with the prospect of leaving New York at the time. I was a New Yorker as far as I was concerned—it had been my home from the time I was barely seventeen. Admittedly, I shared the somewhat snobbish attitude that L.A. just didn't measure up to what New York had to offer, the cultural life and the quality of the education for the children included.

Woody Allen once said something to the effect that the major cultural advantage to living in L.A. was that you could make a right-hand turn against a red light. Well, maybe he should have included some other advantages about the car-driving lifestyle. Gone were the jostling over cabs and swimming upstream against the sidewalk crowds on Fifth Avenue. Gone was the constant vigilance over who might be walking too closely behind you or breathing down your neck in elevators. Mercifully gone were those layers of winter clothes, the constant taking on and off. The change for the better in the weather was a good cure for homesickness.

My sister Pauline, who was living with us and helping out with child care, took charge of the move. The kids were a little upset because she gave away a number of things they wished she hadn't. She was very organized, and I, on the other hand, probably would have brought out far too much stuff.

When we arrived at the new house, we were waiting for the moving van that was running late. It was cold both inside and out, as the heater wasn't working. Leaving a world where the building superintendent took care of everything, I was a duck out of water. I didn't know the first thing about the pilot light on the furnace and how it could have been blown out by the wind. But as the hours, days, and weeks went by, the house on top of the hills of Beverly Hills slowly began to feel like home. Ira purchased any furniture we needed in his usual careful and deliberate manner. Some of the crew from *The Brady Bunch* offered to come and wallpaper a few rooms, which was a wonderful perk.

The Trousdale Estates area where we lived was carved out of the hills of Beverly Hills and offered a panoramic view from downtown Los Angeles to Catalina Island on the occasional smog-free days. It was quite the neighborhood to go trick-or-treating on Halloween, with more show business folk per square mile than anyplace else in the world. But otherwise, without an adult willing to drive them somewhere, a kid growing up atop the steep hills felt imprisoned until that magic day of emancipation—getting a driver's license on the sixteenth birthday.

Many a long day and night, I would feel guilty that I wasn't spending as much time with my children as I would have preferred. On the other hand, I also knew there were a lot of full-time mothers at the high school who didn't work and whose children did not turn out that great despite the quantity of "quality time." I think what made a difference to my children was that I never made a big deal about what I did. It was really just about the work and to make a better life for all of us. They could also see that I loved my job, and I think they always knew how much I loved them.

Whenever possible, I would take the children out on the road with me and incorporate them into what I was doing. From time to time, they would appear in the shows. For example, Joe and Barbara played little Polynesian children in *South Pacific*, and later Lizzie and Barbara worked in another production. They also had roles in *The Sound of Music*. Robert and Lizzie did *Annie Get Your Gun* with me, playing my little brother and sister. I was so proud of them. As adults, they look back on those times as some of their fondest memories from childhood. They each have retained a love and knowledge of music, theater, and television.

If I had to go out on the road while they were at school, I tried to stay on top of what they were doing and what their appointments might be to the degree that they used to always think I had eyes in the back of my head. We would leave notes to each other that we would hide in special places. When I came back, they would always make a big sign to greet me at the door saying "welcome home." I'm sure that they missed me and experienced loneliness and loss just as I did being away from them. I prayed that they were understanding and forgiving about my drive to express myself through my work and why it was so important to me. In the final analysis, your children know it when you genuinely love them. If you don't, they know that too, and it doesn't matter how much you do for them, you won't make up for that.

I am sure there were many parts of the package of being my son or daughter that they would have gladly done without. What a pain it must have been if a classmate wanted to become friends with them so they could get to know me. Even worse, teachers could on occasion be harder on the kids because of my celebrity status. "You think you're so special, blah, blah, blah," one nasty teacher snapped at Lizzie. When she told me about it after school one day, I immediately called for an appointment to meet with this teacher. I called her out on it.

"Look, this is my job. I work, and I don't appreciate that you take it out on my child. So I would really appreciate it if you didn't do that." The teacher was trying to look younger than her years in her pink dress with bleached blonde hair adorned with a big bow. What was also noticeable was a very big chip on her shoulder. She apologized.

To a fault, I was maybe a little too protective of my kids. Sometimes you need to back off a little and let them try to take care of their issues the best they can for their own development's sake. Chalk it up to the fact that I had to take care of so many things on my own as a kid without the intervention of a loving adult. I didn't want them to always have to deal with that sort of thing. Again, it's not always the recommended action. In the final tally, I trust that the good outweighed the bad for my children, and that they came to terms with whatever they felt they might have lacked at times. This feeling came forward for me in a song my son Joseph wrote called "Red River." It's about all the red taillights you see on the highway, and the hope that it is transporting people home to a loving situation.

Ira was commuting back and forth, arriving in L.A. on Friday and leaving to go back to his job in New York on Sunday night. That's the way it was, and on some deeper level I probably preferred it that way and consequently went to a lot of places and events by myself. Otherwise, I might have put my foot down. "Get a job out here, for God's sake. You're well respected in the theater business. It shouldn't be a problem." I never demanded that. Rather late in the game, he did just that, but by then it hardly mattered. They say that absence makes the heart grow fonder. It doesn't. A steady diet of separation for long periods is not constructive on any level.

One Sunday as Ira was preparing to return to New York, all the drains in the sinks, toilets, showers, and bathtubs backed up, and a stinky tide of raw sewage began to flow. Ira had to catch his plane. I gritted my teeth and said to him sarcastically, "Fine. You go. I'll take care of it." Talk about symbolism! Reality is sometimes stranger than fiction.

Pauline was a godsend on many levels during this period because I was worry-free with her in charge as a second mother to the children (and no doubt to me, as well as being my older sister). She was very smart, and as a divorcee, had a chance to reinvent her life. She eventually got a job at Cedars-Sinai hospital and moved into her own apartment. After a while, she felt that she should move back to Kentucky to be closer to her kids, and I encouraged that. She had given a lot of years to me, and it had been good for both of us.

With Pauline's departure began a new adventure, one that

probably deserves a whole separate book by itself. That tome would be entitled *Florence Henderson's Housekeepers*, by Stephen King.

It is an understatement that I was fairly spoiled by the years we had my sister, Nanny, and a few others who set the bar very high for their successors. When you have someone living full-time in your home, slowly but surely the truth begins to emerge. And the stakes are very high as you entrust the most precious things in your life to their care.

We all have quirks, eccentricities, and peculiarities. We all carry some unpleasant baggage. We all have our fair share of drama that comes with the human territory. But most who came to work for us were blessed with a greater abundance of all. It wasn't like they were working for Cinderella's stepmother. They got a nice room with a private bath, salary on the generous side, car, and more. The conditions were fairly laid-back, and beyond the daily tasks and responsibilities of their jobs, they were included in the family and its activities to the degree that they wanted to participate.

"Toot, toot, toot, toot, toot..." That was the constant high-pitched drone from one of our first employees as she went about her tasks. She was highly recommended from a doctor in Beverly Hills. On one of her days off, she left the door to her room open. On her bed I saw a book and opened it up. It was full of spells and incantations. We had a devil-worshipping witch living in our midst. The "toot, toot, toot" she shared with me was an occult chant to conjure money and wealth. She told me that she would put a protective ring of salt around a chair to ward off something. The last straw happened when she wasn't getting along with Barbara. She gave my daughter an envelope. Inside was a swatch taken from a piece of Barbara's clothing. It had been burned. Where's the Exorcist when you need him? Goodbye.

The next was a very heavyset woman. She came very highly recommended. All she wanted to do was make soup. There would be pots going all over the kitchen. She did little more than cook and eat. Joe said she did make good soup. Adieu.

Then we hired a very tall African American woman, about six feet tall and very strong. Very highly recommended, but we soon found out that she was emotionally unstable. We were all scared of her. I said to Ira, "We have to let her go." He was afraid to tell her because she was so big and tough. So guess who got that job?

The very sweet woman from Central America was, of course, highly recommended. She dutifully sent her earnings down to her husband and children. One day, she went into an office to pay one of the utility bills for her apartment where she stayed during her time off. There was a long wait, and the clerk called out names to announce when it was their turn. As she waited, she heard a name she recognized and looked up to see that it was her husband, the one who was supposed to be with the children in her home country. When she went up to the clerk, she told her story and pleaded to get the address on her husband's account. "I can't give you that information, it's confidential," the clerk replied. After she told her about sending all the money, the clerk relented. My housekeeper showed up at the address to discover that her husband was living with another woman. A friend was intercepting the money and sending it back to him in Los Angeles. She moved back to her home country, which soon thereafter had a devastating earthquake. I never heard from her again.

Next was a young couple. Highly recommended. They were great at cooking and cleaning. They were devotees of the Maharaj Ji, the round-faced young guru who had a big estate in Malibu with all the Rolls-Royces. They would borrow our car to go to meetings or do various errands at his bidding. We would get into some spirited discussions. "How come you're giving all your money to him, and he's driving all those Rolls and Mercedes, and you can't afford to buy your own car?" There was always a bit of secrecy about where they were going, and they started, for whatever reason, to fabricate stories. Once they told me one thing, but went off instead to Miami and came back sick with parasites. They even showed me the big ugly worms in a jar. That was hardly a comforting thought since they were preparing our family's food. "Okay, I think maybe this is not going to work," I thought to myself. The young couple was history. Sad, because I really liked them.

Soon after, I found a very sweet Lebanese woman, who was a horrible driver. It didn't help that she had a heart condition that she forgot to disclose. From time to time she would nearly pass out. After that was a woman who was a hard worker but a secret drinker—not the person you want driving your kids to school. Then there was the uptight and rigid British girl who believed that children should be seen but not heard—no, thank you. How about the barefooted one in cutoff shorts who would come and sit on my bed and say, "What are we going to do today, Flo, honey?" Another was working out great, but she called me late one night and said she needed to borrow a lot of money from me. Her husband had just been arrested for running a big illegal alien smuggling operation. The money was for bail. Hey, I'm only skimming the highlights.

Finally, I found a woman who ended up being the keeper for several years (and trained Shelley, my current helper and great friend, who has been a godsend to me for many years). But this person had the most dramatic life. Not long after she started working for me, her soon-to-be-ex-husband almost killed her. After a good run, she decided to quit and cashed out her pension plan to start a restaurant. I told her I thought it was a mistake. She lost everything and came back to work for me again.

Sometime later, she wanted to retire and move back home to her country. Her new husband went ahead. I gave her a big severance. She sent the money down to him and bought him a car. Same old scenario—she went down there to find him shacked up with another woman. I never heard from her again, although recently her granddaughter sent me an e-mail telling me that she was helping take care of her child.

One saving grace was that my older children were very aware and noticed when things were not right and kept me posted. They all survived! It doesn't matter if you hire someone from a bonded employment agency. Talk to others, you'll hear similar stories about people living on the edge or just plain crazy. I learned that "Highly Recommended" was code for "Happy to Get Rid of This Person." It's really the luck of the draw. With Shelley, who has been with me through thick and almost thin for two decades, I hit the jackpot.

There were two others who entered my life during this period who, like Shelley, became an indispensable part of my team and support system. In 1973, I was interviewing candidates for the job of being my personal assistant. I was getting toward the end of the process when in walked this spunky, confident young woman dressed in a little beige cowboy suit. Her name was Kayla Pressman. From the sound of the interview, there wasn't anything that she couldn't do.

"You know you would have to go out on the road. There's a lot of travel."

"Oh, I love that."

"Do you know anything about packing?"

"Oh, yes."

"Do you know how to sew in case I rip a costume?"

"Oh, yes. No problem."

She had a contagious energy about her, and so she got the

job. She didn't know squat about sewing, but that little fib was more than made up by many other strong suits. Some even claim that they had never heard me utter a four-letter word until Kayla trained me in proper usage and syntax.

Being a personal assistant to someone in show business is like having to be a jack-of-all-trades. You're constantly put into problem-solving situations where you need to think quickly on your feet. What she didn't know, Kayla learned very fast, not the least of which was operating the lights for my stage show. When I realized just how bright she was, I told Sandy Gallin that she should be a manager. He took her and trained her and she paid her dues big time. She traveled as well with the Pointer Sisters, Patti LaBelle, and other top acts.

Being on the road as a performing artist may sound like a glamorous lifestyle to those not in it, but being away for extended periods from your family and the familiar comfort of your own bed can wear thin at times. It can also be a lonely existence if you choose to isolate yourself. When you're on the road and in different environments all the time, having the support of a hard worker and great friend (and most important, someone you can trust) like Kayla makes a huge difference. When the traveling group grew larger with musicians, singers, and dancers, we created a teamlike, family atmosphere.

With all the changes going on in my professional and personal life, Kayla also grew to be a close confidante who didn't shy from speaking her mind, especially if she happened to disagree with something I was doing. She had come of age in the 1960s, so she was a freer spirit who loved to push the boundaries, and in the process she got me to loosen up, sometimes perhaps a little too much.

Once when we were driving in Florida to see my friend Ruth Helen, who has a home in the Delray Beach area near Palm

Beach, I suddenly grew concerned. "Kayla, how fast are you going?" The speedometer read 85 mph. "Don't you think you should slow down a little?"

"There's a guy on my tail," she shot back.

Moments later, there were the bright red flashing lights of a state trooper. The officer asked Kayla the same question I had just asked her. I slumped down in my seat. I didn't offer to help, no Florence Henderson card pulled, no nice autograph for his child, no nothing.

"You were going eighty-five," the officer filled in the blank for Kayla.

Kayla pleaded her case. "I know I was going fast, but there was a guy on my tail. I had to keep going."

"That guy was me," he said as he handed her the ticket.

Another time, we were flying from Los Angeles to New York. As I will explain a little later, I had progressively become more fearful of flying. A drink or two could have a positive medicinal effect, but Kayla and I kept laughing and kept drinking. Long story short, I exceeded my limit. When we got off the plane at Kennedy, the woman known to millions around the world as Mrs. Brady was holding tightly on to Kayla's arm and trying to disguise the obvious state of being sloshed. Thank God TMZ didn't exist then. When we got our baggage, Kayla said she needed to go find our driver. She stood me up against a pole. "Here, hold on to this. I'll be back." I wasn't so sure she'd be back, because she wasn't too steady on her feet either.

My lone foray into the drug culture of that time also was in the company of Kayla, who was in the mainstream of her generation in the 1970s as a "recreational user." We were on tour in Australia. One night after a show, a group of us that included Kayla, my conductor Allan Alper, and a wonderful drummer named Evan Diner decided we'd get together for a game of

Scrabble. I don't know if it was passing any judgment on the fun (or lack of it) we were having as the game began, but Evan volunteered that he had some marijuana that he would be only too glad to share.

I asked Evan how he had managed to smuggle it into Australia. "I put it in my jockstrap," he replied. He explained that he had put it into a baggie and "made it the size of my left nut." Sounds sanitary enough, I thought. He then took out an appliance he called a carburetor and placed the joint into a hole on it.

It was my turn at Scrabble.

"Have a puff," Evan suggested.

I told him, "I don't think so."

"Oh, just try one."

"Well," I thought, "why not?"

"Breathe deeply," he instructed.

Yes. I did inhale.

The others around the Scrabble board were clearly starting to get impatient. I knew the word I wanted, but for some reason, the signal from my brain down my arm to my fingers was taking its sweet time getting there. I sat there at the board immobilized for God knows how long. They were laughing at me.

Later, I said I was really hungry. I'm not a sweets eater, but I asked if they could get me some ice cream. That was my first and last puff of marijuana.

All the laughs and fun aside, it is a true testament that nearly forty years after she came to work for me, Kayla is still my manager and my best friend.

The other great friend and confidante who came into my life at the same time was Elsie Giorgi, my doctor. She was the one I called when I woke up that morning after to find out what to do with all the little creepy-crawlies on me. My doctor in New York had referred me to her when I came out to live in California. She had a thriving practice in New York but moved out to California, where she attracted a big following too. She had a super intellect, the first woman to graduate from Columbia University's medical school and the one who diagnosed John F. Kennedy with Addison's disease. She wrote health-care legislation for the Veterans Administration. She was way ahead of the times in recognizing the dangers of AIDS early on, and helped so many of her gay patients avoid the devastation of that epidemic in its early years.

When I first contacted Elsie, she barked back with her Bronx accent, "I'm not taking any new patients." Click.

"Okay, jeez." I told my doctor back in New York what happened.

"Yeah, she's kind of tough." But before long, she showed up at my house anyway, as if nothing were out of the ordinary, on call for the doctor I found in her place when one of my kids was sick. We clicked from the first second, and she became an immediate part of our family. She knew what I was going through.

"Dearie, you're the glue," she surmised after seeing the dynamics of my marriage on display.

If you came to her office for an exam, chances were that she'd give you something to eat first. It was her trick to get her patients to relax and open up more if they had a nice snack. She spoke with perfect diction, but if you got her started her Bronx side would come out.

"Dearie, oh please, he's so full of shit." Italian by birth but more Jewish in personality, Elsie told it like it was. That hybrid came forth with her exclamation "Oy Vey Maria." She told wonderful stories about her life in New York. For example, she worked for a trucking company in New York to put herself through medical school.

"You must have known the Mafia?" I asked her. Did she! Her

stories about big figures like Johnny Dio and others were price-less. She was pretty proud of her Mafia connections.

Everyone comes into your life for a good reason, and Elsie her-self would prove to be the very glue that helped keep me together through some turbulent times to come.

CHAPTER 18

Days of Wine and Roses...
and Clam Chowder and Chicken

ᢒ

When *The Brady Bunch* ended its network run on March 8, 1974, things hardly slowed down. On the contrary, I was busier and in more demand than ever. The bounce from a popular television series meant dramatic improvement in the recognition factor and increased the fees I could now command. I was back onstage, a good percentage of the dates in Las Vegas, where I appeared with Shecky Greene for three years at the MGM Grand, plus a host of other performers like Joel Grey, Bill Cosby, Tennessee Ernie Ford, Bob Newhart, Sammy Davis Jr., and, not to forget, Milton Berle.

Being Carol Brady all those years also made Florence Henderson a more viable commodity as a commercial spokesperson. Some actors can be quite condescending about doing ads. It's that "I'm sorry I'm doing this commercial because I'm really a great actress" attitude. I never felt that way. Instead, I approached it

no differently than I did any other performance. I'm there to fulfill the fantasy of the viewer, whether it's about selling tickets or
moving products off the grocery shelf. Look around at almost anyone who has had longevity in the business, and you'll see that
they all did commercials. If the performer's personal image and
the brand come together in a natural way, it's a win-win situation. It is as though you're the star of your own sixty-second movie
that is repeated over and over again. If you pull it off, you have
a great relationship with the public. To this day, people still remember all those Wesson Oil commercials I did for twenty-two
years. I ended up surviving five ad agency changes, which is probably a record, since the new agency almost always cleans house.
If it really works, the brand will look for other ways to support
you—Wesson sponsored the *Country Kitchen* show I did on the
Nashville Network for nine years.

On the other hand, I felt it was important that you had to be
honest about what you did. A few years back, the *Wall Street Jour-
nal* published some public opinion research that showed that Bill
Cosby and I were ranked the two most believable commercial
spokespersons. If you don't believe in what you're saying, don't do
it. I imagined one of my sisters in the Midwest. Would she want
to buy this product? I also had to use it, which proved to be a
problem some years later when I had an offer to do Polident.

"I can't do this—I don't have false teeth," I told them.

"We don't care," they countered.

"I can never say that I use it," I warned them.

"That's okay." We ended up having some fun with those commercials. We did one when I was in the shower. Another was
a song-and-dance number on the moon. People seemed to like
them, and the spots ran for about ten years.

When I first started doing commercials for Wesson Oil and
Tang in the mid-1970s, it was quite different than doing the

Oldsmobile spots in the 1950s. Commercials are not easy. First of all, I wasn't used to all these corporate executives and advertising agency people flying in and hovering in the studio, watching the monitor and dissecting every word. Huge money was involved in these campaigns, and the agencies spent lavishly on the smallest details. To do it well, it's more than just delivering your lines. You have to do all the other things they want, and precisely. Hold the label just right. Don't tilt it so the light reflects poorly. It's not easy to be that precise, but luckily I was good at it.

One particular ad lady was not pleased with my performance during a shoot.

"What is it that you want?" I asked her politely. She tried to explain it to me, but no luck. We did about forty takes (good enough that they printed them all), and it was still not to her satisfaction. The crew was starting to get antsy.

"I want so much to give you what you want, but can you demonstrate it for me?" I asked her, trying to find a constructive solution. She got up and did her version. Both she and everyone else in the studio understood instantaneously that she should keep her day job.

"You know what, I think we have a lot of good takes," she retorted, brushed off her performance like it never had happened, and moved on.

Once I did a demonstration on the *Mike Douglas* talk show to show how complicated shooting a commercial can be. I gave Mike a plate of fried chicken and showed him exactly what he had to do: carry the plate of chicken, walk and talk and take a bite out of it in a highly choreographed way and timed at not an eyelash under or over sixty seconds. He didn't get too far. He fumbled the plate, and the chicken went flying.

Every detail was sweated and every nuance was gone over with a fine-toothed comb. Ad-lib an "um" or an "oh" and you'd hear "cut" because you just put the whole spot a half second over. One spot for Wesson required that I would sing, take a bite out of the chicken so it would audibly crunch, then finish singing the lyric. *This chicken's got a certain... CRUNCH... Wesson-ality.* BING! After the shoot, the great legal minds reviewed the footage and thought the crunch sounded bogus. They were nervous. "We don't want the Federal Trade Commission coming down on us." So I had to go into a recording booth with a bucket of chicken. Take after take, they would play the song and I took my bite on cue. I don't know how many chicken legs I dented that night, but it got to the point where Kayla, Bill Sammeth (who worked with Sandy Gallin), and I got tears we were laughing so hard. The lawyers in the room were not amused. I had to sign an affidavit stating something like, "I, Florence Henderson, do hereby attest that the sound heard is actually yours truly biting with own and intact natural incisors into the said poultry leg." See. Not easy!

Trying to balance the work with family, I took every opportunity to include my kids in commercials just as I did with the shows, which they loved to no end. Lizzie and Robert were in one of the spots I did for Tang. In it, I make the case to a neighbor that one glass of the orange-flavored instant breakfast drink gives children their daily dose of vitamin C.

"You really do drink Tang," the neighbor (ironically holding a basket of vitamin-C-rich tomatoes fresh from her garden to share) is both surprised and happy to see. The pigtailed Lizzie takes a gulp and says convincingly, "It tastes good," smiling at me and then at the neighbor. I poke the tip of Lizzie's nose approvingly with my finger. I remember it like it was yesterday, although YouTube refreshes.

What probably gets more hits on YouTube than the old commercials are some of the selections from *The Brady Bunch Variety Hour.* On the merit of all of the colorful costumes and lavish production numbers, the show has a bit of a cult following. I had mentioned earlier that the cancellation of the original series was hardly the finale for the Bradys. Within about eighteen months of doing that last episode, we were all back together again—well, almost all of us. (Eve Plumb was the lone cast member to opt out, resulting in the "Fake Jan" phenomenon.) Talk about going from the penthouse to the basement—from one of the most beloved television series of all time to what some TV historians regard as one of the all-time worst. Hey, it wasn't all that bad...

To borrow from a famous Bill Cosby quote, the decision to do *The Brady Bunch Variety Hour* was like Napoleon's ill-fated decision to invade Russia: "It seemed like a good idea at the time." In that window of time between the two shows, we had made a group appearance on the Emmy broadcast, and the place went wild. The real catalyst was when producers Sid and Marty Krofft invited the *Brady Bunch* ensemble to appear on their very popular *Donny and Marie* variety show. The ratings went through the roof. The programmers at ABC put two and two together and asked the Kroffts to put together a Brady variety show cloning the *Donny and Marie* formula onto the Brady factor. So, for example, the Osmonds had a real ice rink on their set as a signature piece for their show. After all, they were from Utah. For the Bradys of Southern California, the Kroffts built a swimming pool.

When I heard the idea, my mind went in two different directions. The realist reminded me that some of the kids were not musical at all and wondered how we could possibly pull that off. But the part of me that is a musical performer was excited about the challenge. And that it was. Remember, I am the pathological type to whom you should never say, "I dare you to..."

There was also some comfort level dealing with some of the obvious shortcomings because of the caliber of talent Sid and Marty had assembled. For starters, Rip Taylor as a regular comedic foil and Bruce Vilanch as the head writer were sure to keep things pretty loose and outrageous. Joe Cassini was a wonderful choreographer. Of course, Pete Menefee's spectacular costume designs and the campy über-'70s feel of the show probably drive all those aforementioned YouTube hits. The gowns I wore were fabulous. The coordinated wardrobe of reds, oranges, and other bright rainbow colors seemed to literally scream off the screen, although I have to admit that Bob's big red bow ties looked pretty outrageous then as they do today. When I asked my conductor Glen Roven why he thought that the cult following for the show is particularly strong among the gay community, he didn't hesitate. "All those feather boas, of course!"

My strongest impression looking back on that time was how it was such hard work. To get anything halfway right, the only way is rehearsing over and over again. Among the kids, Barry was very musical and caught on quickly. Geri Reischl, who replaced Eve, was selected for her musicality. Mike Lookinland was pretty good as well. Chris Knight would be the first to admit that he couldn't sing a note and couldn't dance. Variety wasn't Susan's strong suit. Bob was not a natural song-and-dance man, but he cast himself enthusiastically into it and gave it his best shot.

Maureen McCormick had good musical talent, but this was during her drug phase. On any given day, we never knew when she was going to show up. Thank God, she got help and reclaimed her life. Not long after the show went off the air, I took her to lunch. "Tear up your address book," I remember telling her. "These people use you and you use them." She took the advice. She has been happily married for a long time and has a child. We still talk on the phone every once in a while. It is important to me to maintain the bond, and fortunately, my good relationship with all of the kids has endured through the decades.

In *Love to Love You Bradys*, the book dedicated to "the bizarre story of The Brady Bunch Variety Hour," Chris went on record saying that "the idiocy and incompetence of all the people around [Florence] is like working with remedial talent. It's like a school production." Susan summed it up best: "Florence would have been into it, but we were all taking a dump in her church. She's the one with the experience in this field and she's got to lug our sorry asses along with her."

Just like double-knit spandex jumpsuits will only stretch so much, the show could not overcome the obstacles despite the best intentions of most who were involved. All the beautiful Krofftettes and Water Follies girls couldn't do it. Guest stars like Tina Turner, Vincent Price, Milton Berle, Redd Foxx, Farrah Fawcett and Lee Majors, Donny and Marie, Tony Randall, and many others didn't help jump-start the ratings. After nine episodes, the show was put out of its misery. Viewers may have been turned off to *The Brady Bunch Variety Hour,* but it had little diminishing impact on the franchise. There would be more Brady sequels to come and rediscovery by the next generations thanks to the nonstop worldwide syndication of the original series. It's also a DVD best seller.

Since learning how to better handle work-related disappointment when I didn't get the part in the film version of *Oklahoma!* I didn't dawdle long thinking about the cancellation. I thankfully had plenty of other activities to pursue. It's good to push the pause button only so long to digest the lessons from the experience and use it to maintain that healthy sense of humility. But otherwise, you've got to keep fresh. Put on your Teflon armor. If you're going to stay in the business, you have to keep putting your energy forward. Energy begets energy.

During the mid-1970s through early 1980s, I was like a jack-in-the-box. You never knew when and where I would pop up. There were still lots of outlets on variety television shows. That versatility of being able to both sing and act that proved to be such an asset from the beginning at the American Academy, combined with that galloping horse work ethic and the Carol Brady factor, kept the phones ringing with offers.

Perhaps the most fun I had during this time period was being a semiregular on *The Hollywood Squares*. What went on that people saw at home was funny enough, but it did not compare with what happened off camera with such a crazy group of personalities. They taped five shows in one day—three in the afternoon, a break for dinner, and then two more afterward. Wine would be served during the meal, copious amounts and with predictable loosening of tongues on the last two shows. Paul Lynde especially loved to get sloshed. Once, when it was my turn, Peter Marshall asked me, "Would humming help your tennis game?" I was taking tennis lessons at the time from Dick Van Patten's son, and he was always saying, "Keep your eyes on the ball." So I replied, "Yes, because it would take your mind off your balls." I might as well have detonated a bomb on the set. Everybody immediately vacated their little squares in mock protest; even Cliff Arquette, who had recently had a stroke, got up and walked off. It took ten minutes for the hysteria and pandemonium I had caused to subside and to get the show back on track. Peter Marshall still features a video of that segment in his act.

If you happened to sit next to Jonathan Winters, there was a whole other show going on in his brilliant comedic mind. When we'd go to commercial break, he did not sit idly. One of his favorite things to fill the time was to perform his own one-man Civil War or "Cowboys versus Indians" reenactments, complete with sound effects of arrows whizzing by.

Redd Foxx was notorious for his blue comedy routines. If you happened to be the next square over from him, you were in for an earful. Sandy Duncan, the singer and actress, didn't put up with it and asked to be moved. I found that the best thing to do was to just fire back a glib answer to him when he started to talk dirty. He'd respect that and back off. Here's one typical exchange:

> **REDD**: Have you ever had sex with a [black man]? (He had used the N-word instead.)
> **ME**: Oh, yeah.
> **REDD**: Did he ever give it to you in the ass?
> **ME**: No, I wasn't interested. He wasn't that cute.

Redd wasn't that much into the wine with dinner. Instead, he was quite open about his love of cocaine. He would take out his little silver spoon. I'll never forget how Pearl Bailey lit into him. Like many distinguished African American performers of her time, she had worked hard to keep her integrity in a business that had so derogatorily marginalized and stereotyped people of color. In her mind, Redd Foxx was not holding up his part. She had zero tolerance for his behavior. "What's the matter with you? You can't do that! There are children here. Put that away!"

During the evening shows, they would always give the women panelists a rose. I would always twirl mine a little when they'd announce my name at the beginning of the show. Sometimes the stem would break, and I would playfully shrug my shoulders in response. I got a fan letter from a gentleman who wrote how he loved it when I did that with the rose. As I did with every letter, I wrote back and said thank you. Then I got another letter from him and more letters. "I know that you're doing that rose for me and nobody else." This went on and on. I wrote back that I was very happily married, but he totally ignored all of that. He sent me a box full of fake rings, asking me to pick out which one I wanted for my engagement ring and said he'd send me the real one. He showed up a couple of times where I was performing. One of the singers pretended to be my husband, but that didn't faze him. My lawyer got involved and sent him cease-and-desist letters. He sent those back to me with notes in the margin: "They're trying to keep us apart," or "They're working you too hard." He would send me checks. He showed up at my manager's office and made a total of eleven trips to L.A. I had never had a real stalker before, so this was scary. The police got involved, and eventually someone got a hold of the man's son, who was in the diplomatic corps in Italy. The son wrote to me and thanked me for my kindness to his father. He explained that his father had not been well since his mother had died a few years before. After his son got involved, I never heard from the man again.

If you're getting the idea that the path of being a performer is one crazy way to make a living, just wait, there's more. Whether there were good things happening or not, there were few dull moments. Sometimes a voice of sanity would come into my head and question what in the hell I had gotten myself into.

Take, for example, my excursions with the Kennedys in Hyannis Port. These fall into that category of "sounded like a good idea at the time." I was performing with Ben Vereen in Hyannis when I got a call.

"This is Ethel Kennedy. I'd love to have you come out and have a boat ride with us." I told her that I thought it would be wonderful. She picked Ben and me up in a convertible at the hotel. She had packed a lunch, which included a supply of several bottles of wine. We got into her sailboat.

"Hmm, no life jackets," I duly noted, not being a particularly strong swimmer.

The seas were especially rough that day in my novice opinion. For Ethel Kennedy's kids, it was like a walk in the park, jumping into the water and swimming back and forth between boats. I was there holding on to Ben Vereen for dear life, grabbing him in places I don't think he'd ever been grabbed before. The boat pitched and heeled to one side.

"I get ten thousand dollars if the boat topples over," she said, I hoped jokingly.

"Grab the jib," she yelled at me when we hit the next big one.

"I'd do it if I knew what in the hell a jib was!" When the biggest swell hit us, the box with the wine was heading overboard.

"Save the wine, save the wine," she shouted. What about saving the passengers?

She told me about the time she took Sammy Davis Jr. out on the boat. He had the opposite problem. Things were too still. No wind. The boat had no engine, so they were just stuck there in the middle of the ocean. Sammy was nervous about sailing to begin with, so he had a couple of Bloody Marys. He went below-decks and wouldn't come up. They didn't make it back to the theater in time for his concert, not a laughing matter for any performer.

My son Joe was with me and was invited out to sail with the other Kennedy kids, which he loved. Then Teddy called and wanted us to come out on his boat. By this time, my black and blue marks from the first excursion were beginning to heal. I also felt reassured that Teddy had a bigger boat. Ethel had told me, "Before you get on his boat, you should be warned that he doesn't want a mess of any kind. He's very serious about his boat. So just be careful and you'll be okay."

The day arrived, and Kayla and Ira were also coming along. Teddy asked me to sit up next to him at the helm. Regrettably, the waves were rough again. I glanced over at Ira and Kayla. They had already turned pale shades of green. I looked at Teddy and then started to pray that no one was going to barf and create a mess.

"I think everybody needs some wine and clam chowder," Ethel

suddenly suggested. She shook the thermos containing the soup, but evidently someone had accidentally forgotten to tighten the cap. The clam chowder went splashing all over the deck. Misfortune had a silver lining. As delicious as the soup probably was, it took on the exact appearance as if somebody had just thrown up. I started laughing, and Teddy wanted to know what I thought was so funny.

"Because Ethel said that you love a clean boat. Look at this mess." It was harder to explain to him that the real joke was looking at the ever so slightly relieved expressions on Ira's and Kayla's green faces. At least they knew they had one less thing to worry about: If they were going to throw up, they were at least off the hook with Teddy.

Some of the places I got to go might have been beneficial for understanding the ways of the world but given a choice in retrospect I would have done without. Take for example my visit to the Mustang Ranch in Nevada, the famous "legal" brothel. The owner, Joe Comforte, came to my show when I was playing Harrah's in Reno. It was hard not to notice him with the entourage of beautiful young girls, one of whom I was told was the daughter of a high-ranking General Motors executive. Kayla and the boys in the act were curious and wanted to go see the place. The maître d' arranged an invitation for us to visit after our second show.

"It's depressing. I don't want to go," I told the others.

"Oh, c'mon."

So I went along. We stood behind a translucent curtain and could see the scene of a row of girls sitting. An old drunken cowboy came in, and the girls all stood up and made various gestures to say "pick me." We took a tour and saw their rooms that consisted of little more than a bed with a sink. Some of them had stuffed animals. Yikes. It was so sad to me.

Perhaps the worst journey to American society's underbelly

happened some time in the late 1980s. I was appearing at a night-club in Nevada, a jewel of a place where a lot of top acts played. It was a small venue but very tasteful. We arrived in Las Vegas, the closest airport, and a huge white limo came to pick us up. After our arrival at the venue, the owner of the club invited us to dinner. Hollywood could not have done a better job casting someone who looked like a gangster, right down to the rings that adorned each one of his fingers. "I'd like to pay you cash," he said to me that evening at the dinner table.

"Oh, no, you'll have to write a check to my corporation," I told him. Big mistake!

My conductor received a call one afternoon a couple of days later.

"We're going to close the place tonight," said the FBI agent on the line. "There's going to be a raid, so we want to give you the opportunity to come and get your music. We're telling you this because we love Ms. Henderson. We watched her performing while we were undercover."

No one had understood where this man got the money to build this place out in the middle of nowhere. He was no doubt dealing drugs and laundering money. The FBI arrested him that night. Some of the cash was hidden in the walls. When I told my longtime business manager what happened, he made sure I didn't miss the lesson.

"If somebody offers you cash, take the money!" Of course, I never got paid for those performances, but I did pay my musicians. Given the situation, maybe that was all for the best. Oh, and gone too was that big white limo to take us back to the Las Vegas airport.

What continued to drive me through this era was my love of the business and for the opportunity to be there, to listen, to learn, and to contribute. After the kind of fame and success I had with

The Brady Bunch, some performers find it hard to get back to a normal life because they had been living so large. But one of the benefits of my freeform career was that I met and worked with a lot of my peers and had the opportunity to learn from the best. There was no one in show business who knew more about longevity than Bob Hope.

I traveled to Australia to be part of *Bob Hope's All Star Comedy Special* in 1978. We were to do a sketch together and there wasn't much time for us to rehearse before going live in front of a huge audience. So we decided to do it in the car on the way to the venue. I learned from him how comedy was such a precise art. If I added an extra "the," he'd stop me. He said, "You can't do that. It has to be this, or we won't get a laugh. It's the rhythm of what you're saying as well as what you're saying."

But the biggest insight he gave me was from literally watching him do nothing. It was summer in Australia, and it was very hot. I noticed in the backstage area that he was alone, sitting in the corridor quietly, all by himself.

"Bob, are you okay?" I asked him.

He nodded. "I just rest," he explained. "It takes a lot of energy to do what we do. When I was in vaudeville, we'd do fourteen shows a day. The only way we had the energy to do it well was by making sure we had a few moments of rest. Don't be burning up and wasting energy."

That was an important lesson for me to heed. I was someone who never wanted to recognize my physical limitations. The galloping horse syndrome would always make me push myself beyond what anyone else would do, physically, emotionally, and every other way. It was timely information. I heard his voice loudly and clearly because I was obviously not taking care of myself in this regard, and there would soon be some serious consequences arising in its wake.

CHAPTER 19

Cutting Through the Layers to the Truth

⌒♪

Anyone who has logged millions of miles in the air will have a catalog of phobia-inducing close calls (especially from the less technologically sophisticated days of the mid-twentieth century). During the *Sound of Music* tour, I was en route to Dallas when the plane started to vibrate excessively. It was fresh in everyone's minds that another aircraft had recently blown apart due to the same circumstance. There were fire engines on the runway when we landed. I had Nanny and two of my children with me. Not a pleasant scenario.

Another time, I was returning to New York from an industrial show with Bill Hayes on one of the early commercial jets (probably a Boeing 707). JFK was fogged in. The pilot made two attempts to land but had to pull up each time. As the plane went around in circles, the pilot shut off the ventilation system to help conserve fuel and the cabin became stiflingly hot. Just as the fuel was almost at empty, conditions improved enough so we could land at Newark. It is statistically safer to go on a commercial plane than to drive your own car, but that fact fell on deaf ears. It is almost comical how the thought of being trapped inside an airplane that is about to crash was so energetically similar to how I perceived my stagnated personal life had become. All the responsibility with the four children, all the "what ifs," combined with exhaustion and a feeling of being overwhelmed, created the perfect recipe. As this phobia increased in severity in the mid-1970s, I found myself more frequently turning job offers down because I didn't want to fly.

The depletion and exhaustion during *The Sound of Music* caused me to suffer from stage fright as well, which grew progressively more difficult. Insomnia and my general lack of awareness about sound nutrition were also contributing factors that undermined my coping ability. During the *Brady Bunch* years, it was hardly a concern, because acting on film was far less taxing than being out on the road and performing constantly in front of live audiences.

Where this particular fear attached its tentacles was on the act of singing, which is the most demanding and required the most physical control of anything I did. Once I got out there and got the feel of the audience, I was usually fine, but prior to that I would be a wreck. I was a harsh critic of myself, a self-judgment that echoed the voice of my mother. Before going onstage, I concentrated hard to make sure I had command of my breath. Without it, you're really in trouble. For example, when I did *The Tonight Show*, I never wanted to go out and do a slow ballad first. Instead, I'd do a very up-tempo song that would force me to stir up my energy and control my breath. Doing a slower number right after was never a problem.

The mind can be quite insidious in how it constructs coping

mechanisms to make us feel superficially safer in the short term while deflecting or delaying dealing with the true root causes. But there comes a time when the bill has to be paid.

I had noticed the warning signs and beginning stages years before, but now the issues were inescapable. On the deepest level and despite all of my worldly success and hard work was the hardcore fact that my life was essentially tumbling out of control. The resulting fear had to go somewhere, and just to make sure that I'd pay attention, it had attached itself to the things I did the most: flying and performing.

This tremendous loss of confidence was probably rooted in my feeling of being trapped and my lack of courage to do anything about it. The questions I could ask myself were fairly obvious: *You're not happy and haven't been that way for years. What's the big deal? People are getting divorced all the time. Why not be done with it? What's standing in your way?*

The truth, to put it bluntly, was that I didn't have the balls to go through with it. I had plenty of explanations for not doing it. First, there were the restrictions of Catholicism. I had lived my life this way for so long under the same indoctrination. If I should ever choose to remarry, then I wouldn't be allowed to receive the sacraments in the church.

Then, talk about being codependent, I was worried about who was going to take care of Ira and what was going to happen to him without me. Above all, I thought about the effect on the children. Divorce law in New York would not take kindly to my situation, and there was always the possibility that I could lose custody of the children.

Part of the trap was my desire to please everybody and receive the affection from others that had been so lacking from my mother. On the positive side, I knew what rejection felt like, and my caring came across as genuine, whether I was acting through

Carol Brady or stopping a moment to take a picture with someone. I did not want to do anything to hurt someone's feelings.

So I sublimated my deeper-seated emotional needs in work and in living for my children. I was not ready to be honest with myself yet and say, "This isn't working for me, and I know there must be another way." The tools and the confidence needed to get out of the trap I had built for myself were not present...until two major events happened in rapid succession that forced the issue.

When I was forty-eight years old, I had a hysterectomy. There were certainly legitimate medical reasons for it, notably pain, dysplasia, and bleeding. There was also a part of me that naively hoped that it would help our marriage, but that expectation was equally as disappointing as when I went on the pill. From that standpoint, it was a total mistake.

I had grown to be a great believer in the mind-body connection. I thought about my older sister who was so miserable. She had had this operation and that operation. Little by little, they were cutting pieces of her away. "What will be next?" I thought after the hysterectomy. It was a tap on the shoulder that I needed to face some hard facts and seek some answers, and fast.

Just as the organs of my motherhood were removed, my mother suffered a stroke and was dying. I got the phone call from my sister while I was still in the hospital recovering. She was eighty-eight years old and had dementia. My sister Marty told me that my mother had paralysis on her right side as a result of the stroke. She had still been pretty sharp up until age eighty-two. Her second husband (whom she had married when she was seventy-five years old) had recently died, and she had had gallbladder surgery. We had decided that she shouldn't be alone. She would have been a perfect candidate for assisted living and would have thrived in that environment because she loved playing cards, bowling, and other social activities. But at that time, those places were not the norm, so she went to live a more isolated existence with my sister. However, Marty was the only one of us at the time who wasn't tied down, so she went to Florida to live with my mother.

"I can't stand it here anymore," my mother said and repeated again in subsequent phone conversations. I am convinced that she would have lived longer and been healthier had she been in a retirement community, and I always felt bad about that.

I had asked her once about dying. Although she had quite a gruff manner and a rough mouth, she remained a religious woman.

"I just don't ever want to be a burden to anybody," she told me. I prayed that my mother would go peacefully and quickly.

I told my sister, "Just don't let them hook her up to life support. Just let her go."

I could hardly stand up straight with the pain as I got on the plane for Florida to go to her funeral. So much went through my mind, one moment full of emotion and the next remarkably lacking of it. I thought of the time on *The Brady Bunch* when I had to play Carol Brady's own grandmother and how I played that character as tough-talking but funny, modeled on my mother. I thought of her appearing with me on *The Mike Douglas Show* doing exercises on the floor lifting a bowling ball with their fitness expert. She was strong, and if you asked her what she bowled, it was always 250 no matter what. She had boyfriends. She loved those times I invited her to Las Vegas, when she could sit at the blackjack table until all hours of the night. As she got older, I cherished the moments I had to take care of her, brushing her hair and doing her makeup. Her gruff ways softened somewhat around the edges with age. But she still said, "You're not too old to be spanked," and she meant it!

She looked beautiful in the casket. I thought of all the positive lessons from her example. Survival. Independence. Courage. But with recovery from the surgery and everything else brewing, there was little energy left for much outpouring of emotion or grief. I had seen the finality of things so many times before, but now the message was different. On a subconscious level, I knew that I had to do something or I would die. Too many people, including myself, were living lives of quiet desperation. It was time to grow. I also knew that once I truly opened up to that, it would be impossible to turn back. My mother left my father when she was forty-nine years old. My sister Pauline left her husband at forty-nine as well. The way things were appearing, chances were good I would be next in line.

Dr. Giorgi put Ira and me in touch with a wonderful psychiatrist in New York. Ira would go in person, and I would usually do my portion on the phone. Unfortunately, it really didn't go anywhere. It was like hitting an impenetrable brick wall of anger and pride. Many times, I felt worse after the sessions. A lot would get stirred up, but there was very little if any process of where to go with it in the aftermath.

What I came to learn later on is that nothing gets accomplished until you reach a state of surrender. You have to realize that your overwhelming will and desire to fix things and all your best intentions are sometimes not enough. "But I can't fail," your pride has kept saying, locking yourself into a futile battle. Instead, you have to own up to the fact that you're not perfect and that you can't fix this. The act of getting knocked down a few pegs allows your humility to come forward. You accept the fact that you've failed; but in a loving way, you also understand that it is everyone's failure, not just yours alone but a shared one as long as everybody takes responsibility.

The therapy in New York helped me in some ways but did

not get me past the stage fright and fear of flying. A friend of mine suggested that I might try hypnotherapy. She told me about a clinic in Van Nuys, California, the Hypnosis Motivation Institute, founded by Dr. John Kappas, who is generally recognized as the father of modern hypnotherapy. "He's very much in demand, so you'll probably have to go on a waiting list," she told me. I didn't know the first thing about hypnosis, and I was quite frankly a little scared. I saw a newspaper article about a famous athlete who had attributed his success to the help he got from hypnotherapy. I thought, "Well, I've tried everything else. What do I have to lose?" I called, and three weeks later I came in for my first appointment.

From the first moment when I walked into Dr. Kappas's office, I had no other thought than the strongest intuitive conviction that my life was going to change dramatically. The first session with John was wonderful. At the end of it, he said, "I'm sure we'll find out much more, but the first thing we need to do is give you back your confidence. Everyone's adoring you except the one person you want to—yourself—and that is doing a number on you." It was the truth. I had no confidence in myself as a woman, a performer, or anybody. The fears of flying and performing were no doubt coming from that source.

After just a few weeks, I started to see major progress. In each session, John would talk in the beginning. The purpose is to determine what you want to achieve. What are the negative patterns that are causing you to be stuck? Where are the blocks? What are the unresolved conflicts that you have never really settled in your mind? Through the process, you are able to access that unconscious mind that is whirling 24/7 and controlling your thoughts and behaviors stemming from those old programs. *You don't deserve that! You're not that smart! You're poor, and you'll always be poor!* With hypnotherapy, I finally had a highly effective tool to break through all those kinds of negative programming.

Only during the last ten or fifteen minutes of the session would I actually be in a hypnotic state. You're never completely asleep, but you feel afterward a deep state of relaxation just like you've had an incredible night's sleep. Instead, it is your body that is at perfect rest, so still that you hardly breathe. The mind is extremely alert unless the therapist decides that it's in your best interest to take you to a deeper level. The therapist is able to give different sorts of inductions to help achieve the specific depth or breakthrough. Once you understand how it works and how positive it can be (and most important, start experiencing some amazing results), there is certainly nothing to fear. You feel safe and empowered to journey into your past, into those places you once thought were too painful and terrifying to ever visit again.

Hypnotherapy also unlocked the revealing and highly powerful realm of dreams. Since childhood, my dreams have been extremely visual and colorful. What I learned from the work with John was the extent to which we work out a lot of issues in our dreams. The dreams you have right after you go to sleep are wishful-thinking dreams. The ones in the middle of the night are projections. And if you wake up in the morning and say, "Oh, I had the worst dream," that's good, because that time is for venting dreams that help you clear out stored thoughts and emotions. Because I'm so highly suggestible to the point of almost being a somnambulist, this was like finding a gold mine.

One remarkable example is how I carried inside of me such guilt that I didn't say goodbye to my father or get to see him again before he died. After all, the second-to-last time we met, I had told him that I'd rather see him dead than in the drunken state I had found him. Over the many decades since his death, I had never had a dream about him. I don't know what induction or suggestion John had given me in the process, but there was my father on a train. He had his ever-present hat on. I asked him, "Daddy, are you okay?"

"Yeah, Gal, I'm fine. I'm just fine. I'm okay."

"I'm so glad," I yelled back and waved goodbye to him as the train pulled away. I've rarely dreamed about him since, but it was palpable how the emotional burden lifted with that experience.

I had another dream about a little baby. It was sitting all by itself on a curb along a roadside. A short time later, I had another; this time the baby had a little bonnet and dress on and was trying to stand up on her own two feet. Another showed her standing and growing. I realized that I was that small child. The dreams were like watching old home movies that had been locked away in a vault of fear. With the therapist's guidance and support, it was now safe to go back into those devastating feelings of rejection and abandonment. Part of the process was to write out the description of the dream and discuss it at the next session. Reading it out loud to John, I sobbed for that little girl.

The dream work, along with a number of other tools I acquired through hypnotherapy, made it possible to live in a much more honest way. From that grew the confidence to change. I started going to classes at the institute to deepen my understanding about hypnotherapy and the finer nuances of human behavior. Right from the start, it made it much easier to deal with difficult people. Take this one passive-aggressive producer with whom I was working on a major project. He felt that my piano player had done something that wasn't right and wanted to fire him.

I told John, "If he fires Tim, I can't bear the thought of breaking in a new piano player. I have to tell him he can't do that."

"No, no, no," John countered. He suggested another strategy.

Staying very calm, I told the producer, "It will be a real hardship for me if you do that, but I can understand your feelings. If you feel you have to do that, I guess I'll have to deal with it. It will be difficult for me, but I respect your feelings."

"He's going and that's that," the producer replied. But of course, he never acted on that, and the piano player stayed. With all the passive-aggressive people in my life, I would walk around on eggshells wondering when and if they were going to explode. But if you stand up to them and say in a kind or sometimes force-ful way to stop it, they become pussycats. It's like what's really behind their anger is this tiny little compliant monster inside of them that isn't so scary and mean after all.

Here's one other strange insight that came from these sessions. One of the things I regularly did in nightclubs was go out into the audience and sing and sit in a gentleman's lap. The audience would get a big kick out of it. When choosing my victim, I would automatically exclude someone with crossed arms and crossed leg body language. John told me, "No, that's the guy you go to. Try it. You'll see." Sure enough, he was right. Those guys were so much more thrilled than my seemingly more open-looking vic-tims. It was very curious.

Ira went for a while, but to a different hypnotherapist. I think he benefited from it, but it was during this time period that I de-cided to leave. In fact, it was during a therapy session with Ira that I explained to him why I thought it was best to separate.

Hypnotherapy did a lot more than put a stop to my stage fright and fear of flying. It helped unmask the big lies I had been living. If you're lying to yourself, consciously or unconsciously, you're not going to change behavior, both yours and that of the people around you. John always said, "You can't cure anything with a lie!" Understand that lies are not always malevolent or malicious. Sometimes you have to create a fiction in your life to protect yourself from things that had terrified you. But in the long run, if you don't take care of it, those lies will catch up with you and will exact their due one way or another. I did not want to be one of those sick people crippled in their souls and progressively having pieces of their dying bodies cut away.

Working with John, I was unmasking those lies like peeling away one layer of the onion skin at a time. This work was not for the faint of heart. The journey within one's self is the most terrifying of all. It takes tremendous courage. There was no longer any denial or rationalizing belief system to counter the hard truth that I had hung in there for so many years with all those lies and self-protecting illusions. That life of quiet but seething desperation would no longer be tolerated. Finally I had a way to unearth the unresolved grief I had buried. I realized how the fear of flying and the stage fright were symptoms of how I had narrowed down and constricted my existence. With my confidence restored, it was easier to say yes to life again. Finally, there was absolutely no turning back.

CHAPTER 20

D-Day

It was the big no-no. You don't fall in love with your therapist. And your therapist isn't supposed to fall in love with you. That's what conventional wisdom says. And most of the time, conventional wisdom wins—but not in this case. The more time John and I spent together, the deeper our connection grew.

It certainly was not "love at first sight" on my end. On first impression, John was not the most attractive man in the world just to look at him. Neither did I find his hairpiece to be so appealing. But he did have the most beautiful and penetrating blue-gray eyes. So much for the value of appearances...After separating from Ira, I went out on a few dates, but more than anything else, they convinced me by contrast how my feelings for John had grown into something more serious. And that feeling was mutual.

"You can't imagine what a wonderful feeling it is to take off my running shoes," he told me shortly after we became an item. John had a few marriages and tons of relationships in his past, in stark contrast to my life. But he and I shared a strong attribute: Neither of us had truly known what a healthy relationship was like. He had been more prone to be in that category of people who just ran from one affair to the next, taking the course of least resistance. So many of us have the mentality: *Do you want to get married? Yeah, sure. If it doesn't work out, that's okay—just move on to the next.* With all my faults and failings, one thing you can say about me is that I have never been one to take that path.

For the first time, I was open to somebody loving me, and equally, someone whom I could love back. It wasn't the old program of *trying* to get somebody to love me, like forcing blood from a rock. John did love me, and it changed him and me in many profound ways. But it was only the starting point of greater things to come.

A number of people around me were none too happy about this new relationship in my life. Some took the side of the conventional wisdom as earlier stated. Others simply couldn't believe that I could actually make a change and take such a plunge after so many years. Others just "didn't get it" (or didn't want to get it) after meeting John and seeing us together. It had been a daunting time given my history to get up the courage and take my chances. You put so much energy into learning, growing, and trying to solve your major issues. Then, suddenly, you've manifested this major change. You are faced with decision time to stand pat or risk it all. You put it out there with absolutely no guarantee that anything else is going to work out.

You would like to have the support and encouragement of your friends and loved ones at such a fork in the road, but that would have been too easy. Some tried to talk me out of it. Others, many of whom also loved Ira, encouraged me to move forward.

One of the things that oddly enough encouraged me to make

the decision about leaving Ira was a magazine article I had read. It was written by a woman who was almost in the same situation as I was. She had children and a husband, and she wasn't happy. She just felt she needed to move on while she still had some time to experiment and enjoy life and find out who she was. She made the decision to leave, but she paid a price for it. She was judged fairly harshly, but she said it was the best thing she ever did. Her story resonated with me.

Dr. Giorgi was probably the biggest thorn in my side about this. She read me the riot act, replete with her lively Bronx inflection. She did not mince her words, adamantly telling me how I was a fool to leave Ira. It turned into a knock-down, drag-out fight.

I barked at her, "You don't practice the Hippocratic oath—you practice the *hypocritic* oath!" Afterwards, she barked back at me with a note: "Dearie, you must be hurting very badly to say something like that to me."

I countered, "You must be hurting very badly to talk to me like that!" We got through it, and not much longer after that, John and she grew very close. She had broken her hip and was hospitalized and very uncomfortable because she was in pain and couldn't go to the bathroom. John and I visited her, and he hypnotized her to help with her pain and constipation. Before he was even finished with the session, she got up to go to the bathroom.

People who first met John would always remark, "He's so quiet." Some might have regarded him as standoffish because he was so comfortable at gatherings, just sitting and watching and observing. He didn't feel the need to be the life of the party or to fill up the silent space with the noise from his own voice. To those people, I always said, "Just ask him a question." When people would go over and talk to him, I'd just sit back and watch because the same thing would always happen. Once they started to engage him and he began to talk, they simply would not let him go. He had such tremendous confidence, and he knew how to listen (after all, that's what he did for a living). It was a contagious combination.

Finally, I had the courage, trust, and confidence in myself that I could have a different (and happier) life. And I had fallen in love. So it was time to sit with Ira and discuss what we were going to do about formally ending our marriage. We got together at Scandia. The restaurant was an ideal neutral ground and semiprivate, with the kind of ambiance and design that made it a home away from home for the high-profile Hollywood types who frequented it. It was almost eerie how easy and comfortable the conversation went. I had spent nearly a whole lifetime dreading the idea of ever having to confront the D-word, and here it was, virtually painless. When the lawyers got involved a short time later, it got a little more complicated, but not much.

Ira and I truly loved each other. I think he wanted me to be happy. And I deeply prayed for his happiness, which I'm happy to say he found with his wife Carol.

It was all very smooth and amicable. I moved out of the house, and Ira continued to live in it for a couple of years before we decided it was time to sell. Our children were all grown up and on their own. Whatever furniture we didn't need or the kids didn't want, we gave away. Similarly, our financial holdings had been split down the middle. Ira had always been extremely careful with money, so it was an extra pleasant surprise that he had managed to salt away more of my earnings than I thought. Toward the waning days of our marriage, Ira had ironically finally moved out to Los Angeles and became manager of the Shubert Theatre in Century City. By the time we sold the house, he was in a new relationship with Carol. He bought a lovely place in Century Hill on land that was once the back lot of 20th Century–Fox Studios.

The children were not horribly surprised by the outcome. But that didn't make it any easier for them. Their parents had been together for many years, and I don't think they ever witnessed an argument or fight. In some ways, they might have been partially relieved, although I don't want to speak for them. Each needed to try to make sense of it. I took each one aside separately to talk about it. They all told me how sad they were about it. I told them that I was sad too. To Ira's and my relief, the children never really took sides. I think it helped that neither Ira nor I was filled with animosity or blame. Things were more uncomfortable after the separation when the children came to visit me in the house where I had moved. It was hard to acclimate to the fact that their mother had a new home and, consequently, a new life. Seeing my children's difficulty was painful to me, and it was the only time when it felt challenging to stay the course and stick with my decision. There were weak moments when it would have been easy to fall back on old ways.

But this situation was a case in point why John had come into my life. He pushed me to mature. It was truly the first time in my life that I had the backing and support, and finally the courage, to be who I was—and be more of who I was. He challenged me to confront my fears, always pushing me forward. He loved what I did and not only understood my need for self-expression but encouraged me to go further. On one occasion I had an invitation to give a speech. I told John, "I can't do that."

"Of course you can."

So I wrote the draft on the airplane ride to the site. It wasn't as hard as I had thought. The talk was very well received.

He said that any healthy relationship always has to be about mutual ascent, the act of always lifting each other up. It's not about being one-up like "you're down, and I'm up," or vice versa. For the almost twenty years we spent together, we made that reciprocity work on a daily basis. Whenever he gave a speech or taught a class (which was always standing room only), I never missed it. He always went with me everywhere when I worked, too. Being left-brained, he loved all the mechanics and details behind the scenes. He even learned how to work the lights for my show. He watched how it was done and said, "I could do that." And he did it well!

My friends thought I was totally crazy when I told them that I was going to live with John on his sixty-foot motor yacht in Marina del Rey. Before, I would have agreed with them and said forget it. But suddenly my attitude was, "Why not? I'll try that." It was important to him because that boat was his home. He loved the sea. That's where he had chosen to live, and I wanted to support that. The decision turned out to be great, and before long we upgraded to a bigger boat and later a still larger one. We loved taking it out for excursions up and down the coast to Santa Barbara, Newport, and San Diego. Our favorite destination of all was to drop anchor on the ocean-facing side of Catalina Island.

In case you're wondering about the very practical issue of closet space for women, it can be problematic on a boat. Keeping my office/apartment solved that quandary. More important, what about privacy? Aren't you a little bit too much in each other's faces? That was another misconception. Yes, it is intimate, but there's always a place to be alone on a boat if you need quiet time (especially when we upgraded to bigger boats!). You can go up on the deck or find a space in the cabin rooms below.

Making this move to live dockside was another case of opening up and experiencing something completely new and exciting. Where I might have been rigid and all but closed to entertaining the possibility of living that kind of life, I let go and thoroughly enjoyed the process of sharing with John to make that experience comfortable and cozy. In truth, it wasn't so different than living in a triplex in New York City. I truly loved it. It was one huge example of that welcome relief I felt. With John I could finally let go, freed of feeling forced to take charge of all the details like I had for all those years.

Living on the boat, and almost everything we did together, worked so well because we had a process that kept us together. Chemistry may bring you together in the beginning, but process keeps you together. We always found a level of enjoyment no matter what we were doing. It never felt like caretaking, doing something you really weren't interested in out of obligation and hating every minute of it. For example, John liked boxing just like my father, but it wasn't what you would consider my prevailing interest beforehand. However, I watched every fight with him. I knew every fighter and probably ended up more passionate than he was. Likewise, John didn't attend plays or master chorale concerts much before he met me, but he grew to enjoy them just as much as I did. That's why I loved the film *The Fighter* about Micky Ward's life. I watched every one of his fights with John. David O. Russell did such a great job directing that movie.

It wasn't that we didn't have our disagreements from time to time. Unlike my first marriage, where I avoided conflict and kept my mouth shut many times when I shouldn't have, I got the courage to be tough when the situation called for it. Before, I could get a little pushed around by agents and other people I worked with. One day I got very upset with John, and right in the middle of it all he started laughing. "Well, I might have taught you how to be tough, but I didn't mean that you should be that way with me."

After we had lived together for three years, we got married. I was doing a big show in Las Vegas, and we decided on the spot to formalize things. In my heart, I intuitively knew that the amount of time I had left with John would be limited. He had heart problems already by the time we met, and for that reason

I was determined not to waste a second. It turned out in the end that we had nearly twenty wonderful years together. In all probability, I gave him more years than he might have had, just by being there as someone who really cared. "Let's try this," I would suggest. "Maybe if you ate differently." I hired a trainer. He had already had his first bypass surgery. The trainer got him on the treadmill. One day he said, "That's it. I have only so many steps in life. I don't want to waste them on a treadmill." I couldn't argue with that.

My whole attitude about death and impermanence had certainly shifted to a much healthier place, a combination of my inner work and the experience of the passing of two of my dearest friends. The comedienne Totie Fields taught me a lot about courage. She was truly one of the funniest people in the world, and we worked together a lot and became very close. When she went out onstage, she always came out in grand style, wearing the best clothing and her hair done up perfectly. She was very overweight and diabetic, but she wanted cosmetic surgery to lose weight to be in shape for her daughter's wedding. I told her not to do it. Lose weight first, get healthy, and then consider it, I suggested. She was that kind of bullheaded but adorable person who would eat my dessert and say it was okay as long as it wasn't hers. Finally, she found a plastic surgeon in Connecticut who agreed to operate on her, and with predictable results. She went into vascular shock and almost died on the operating table. She was transferred to another hospital and somehow fell out of bed and injured her leg. It had to be amputated.

I came to visit her at the hospital almost every day. "Goddamn phantom pains," she cried out and grabbed on to the bar above her bed. I asked her some questions about the pain, when it came on, how long it lasted, etc. I thought her description was similar to the contractions when you are about to give birth, so I had an idea.

"I'm going to teach you some breathing techniques, so you'll know how to use them when it starts up." I showed her the breathing patterns from natural childbirth. She tried it a few times, and it started to work.

"Oh, you little cunt," she said, using her favorite term of endearment. "Here they give me all this medication and all this physical therapy, and you come in here and teach me a few breaths and I'm cured!"

Totie fought back and learned how to walk with an artificial leg. Even that became a joke with her. She had several different fashion looks on the legs that she used—one had Gucci designs all over it, another was black. A group of us flew up for her first appearance in Las Vegas after her recovery. She walked out on that stage and showed incredible courage coming back and poking fun at herself and her infirmities. She inspired us in the way she persevered despite the devastating effects of diabetes. Her father had the same disease and died at age forty-nine. Her beloved sister also died at the same age from brain cancer.

"I'll never make it past forty-nine," she told me.

"Totie, stop saying that," I warned her, lecturing to her about the power of the mind.

She fulfilled her own prophecy. It was a great loss.

Elsie Giorgi's passing also had a profound impact on my spirit. She had been a great support to me throughout the years, always there to help when something came up. As she got older, it was my turn to take a more active role in taking care of her. But she could be a stubborn patient. After she broke a hip, she started slowing down. Like many transplanted New Yorkers, she loved the freedom of driving in Southern California. She had personalized license plates made up for each new car, the first one with her initials, EAG, followed by the number 1, EAG2 for the second one, and so on.

"Elsie, I told you I'd always tell you the truth," I told her. "You can't drive anymore." I took away the keys to EAG9.

"Noooo!" But after she yelled at me, she quickly acquiesced. Not long afterward she had a stroke and lost the ability to speak, and for someone who loved to talk as much as she did, it was heartbreaking. I had been on the road in Nashville and just returned home when I got the call that she had taken a turn for the worse. I raced to Cedars-Sinai hospital. When I came into the room, a nurse told me that she had just taken her last breath.

"No, she hasn't gone yet," I cried, rushing to her room. She was lying there, and I just picked her up and held her and talked to her. As I was talking to her, her cold body suddenly got hotter and hotter. I looked at her, and one tear rolled down her cheek. It was a very profound experience for me. I removed the jade ring she always wore and gave it to one of the nurses who had cared for her during her illness.

I was in charge of her funeral arrangements. Elsie always wore two dresses that were exactly the same in style, one royal blue and the other shocking pink. Her trademark was this dirty old raincoat. She laughed when we called her Dr. Columbo because she was just as disheveled in appearance as Peter Falk's famous television character. I had her dress and the raincoat cleaned, and people smiled as they viewed her, saying, "That's Elsie." Her ashes were flown back to New York for burial in a jade urn I picked out with a little gold plaque labeled "EAG10" to take her to heaven.

Gaining a better understanding of the nature of love and death was part of the process preparing me for the next big threshold. It is ever fascinating how the universe responds by giving you the tools you need and quickens that process once your heart is truly in a place of trust. To take the leap into both dimensions, it requires a revolution within oneself. Thanks to hypnotherapy and the changes brought about by my life with John, I finally got the upper hand on that lifetime-long resistance, and it brought me to a place of readiness. For the first time, I saw what happens when we finally rise above the fear of going into these places and do so without hesitation or uncertainty. I think it is when the most rewarding transformation begins to unfold.

CHAPTER 21

The Dragonflies

∽

We'll be walking together in San Francisco when you're ninety," John once told me. That would have made him ninety-nine years old, since he was nine years older than I was. John was my best friend and my lover, but in retrospect he was also a father and mother to me. Every day was an adventure even in the simplest and most mundane acts of spontaneity. "Are you free for lunch? I'll meet you at so-and-so." There was never a dull moment, especially when we were out on the boat. He'd always try to get me to do new things, such as guiding the boat out of the dock. It was no problem to back it out. Bringing it back in was another matter. I never mustered the courage. That slip looked awfully small, and the "boat" was almost ninety feet long. But I did learn to drive it and handle it during anchoring.

When bigger career issues came up, he also challenged me to expand my thinking and go beyond self-limiting assumptions. For example, I was offered a cohosting job on *Later Today*, an hour-long morning program added on to *The Today Show*. I wanted to turn it down, only because I didn't see any way I could ask John to live in New York. We had such a great life in California, and John was still seeing clients, although he was semiretired. After his first heart attack and first bypass surgery before we had met, he stopped working fifteen-hour days, but didn't completely give it up. He got so many calls and letters from all the people he had helped: "You saved my life." "You got me off drugs." "You saw me when I didn't have the money to pay you." So he went back on a limited basis, but carved out the time to be with me as much as possible. All the same, it was hard to ask him to make such a sacrifice, and I wasn't sure I really wanted to do it.

"I think you should do it," he urged me. He had good answers for every "but what about..." I offered. It was also hard to argue when he told me that it was a golden opportunity to make his big dream come true: the chance to take our boat through the Panama Canal. That journey would be the longest time we would ever be apart. He parked the boat down in Florida, where we would go on weekends.

Every time he had a health setback, John would fight his way out of it. A second bypass surgery was followed quickly by the death of his beloved younger brother, which crushed him. It was the only time I ever saw him cry. This was heavy on him, but he bounced back again. A short time after, following a bout with pneumonia, he had a CAT scan at Cedars-Sinai. He had been coughing, but the lungs were clear, they told him. A couple of little nodules, but nothing to worry about, they advised.

About two or three months later, he wasn't feeling well and was exhausted. He was also starting to walk funny, a strange kind of shuffling that made it harder for him to get up and down the dock. That difficulty, along with the telltale frozen stare from his beautiful sea-blue eyes were symptoms of his soon-to-be-diagnosed Parkinson's disease. But worse news was in store. His cardiologist Dr. Gerald Bresnahan and heart surgeon Dr. James MacPherson at Centinela Hospital took some contrast X-rays that revealed that those lung nodules had suddenly grown in three short months into two large cancerous tumors. They were the worst kind, small cell and oat cell.

We went to the City of Hope and saw Dr. James Doroshow, a renowned cancer specialist who is now with the National Institutes of Health. "We'll treat it," he told us. "There are some options." John swallowed hard as he heard the devastating diagnosis.

It was undeniable that the cancer and the Parkinson's were exacting a harsh toll on him. The body's various systems work in such remarkable synchronicity in both healthy and diseased states. For example, in the beginning, he was going crazy having to urinate all the time. It was curious to learn how this was caused by the growing tumor drawing all the sodium out of his system. As his situation worsened, his ability to speak weakened, which was especially frustrating for a brilliant teacher. A lovely nurse named Margie Elifano bought him a little chalkboard, but his writing grew progressively smaller and smaller until we could hardly read it at all.

During one chemotherapy session, John got so distraught that he tried to get out of the bed, ripping the tubes out and shouting that he had to get out of there. Dr. Doroshow and the staff came in and were wonderful with him. After another chemo session, he told me that he wanted to go to Vito's in Santa Monica, his favorite restaurant. Despite being in very fragile shape, he was feeling good from the effects of a strong dose of cortisone. But I was worried about taking him there, not the least because of his difficulty swallowing and the high risk for choking.

"It's a little early," I told him as we pulled up outside the restaurant. "You wait here and I'll go in and see." The restaurant wasn't open yet, and all the waiters, kitchen staff, and busboys were sitting at the tables relaxing and playing cards. I explained the situation. Immediately they jumped to their feet and put on their jackets. I got John and we came in a few moments later, and the same ritual played itself out just as it had innumerable times before. Hank the waiter read the specials knowing full well that John was going to order his favorite veal and pasta dish as always. The way they treated him that afternoon is a reason why I love that place to this day. He was choking all through the meal, but it was so important to him.

His hairpiece also figured as a significant symbol of his fighting courage and his hope that something might bring him back. He was worried about his appearance while in the hospital. I love bald men, so it was never an issue for me, but I promised him that his hair would stay in good shape. A stylist came to the City of Hope from the manufacturer and washed his hair and put on a new piece. As sick as he was, it made him feel so good, and I managed to keep that hairpiece on until he died.

"I think you should learn how to hypnotize me," John said to me one day. I was a nervous wreck just at the thought. He had never let anyone hypnotize him *ever*, and even though I had become a certified hypnotherapist, here I was the apprentice suddenly given this sacred responsibility by the master. He knew how beneficial it could be for someone in his situation. If you are a hypnotherapist, you have to have a totally different induction than what you use for your patients, otherwise the therapist would also fall into hypnosis while giving it. So he had me write it all out, along with the specific suggestions that he wanted. It was different than anything I had ever done as a trained therapist myself. Nervously, I tried it the first time on him. He told me that it wasn't bad and there was some hope for me. The second time, it went a little better. And after the third time, he gave me an enthusiastic thumbs-up.

Annette Fields, the patient advocate, took me aside to have "the conversation."

"You have to prepare. We always ask these questions if, God forbid, the treatments don't work, we have to have some arrangements. You're going to have to ask John how he wants to handle it." It's the conversation you never want to have.

"Oh, John, by the way, do you want to be cremated or...?"

"Cremated," he answered back calmly. He was fine with that. That same day, I called Westwood Mortuary and spoke to a very nice man to finalize the plans.

There was a whole practical side of dying of which I had suddenly become hyperaware. There were a few patients I had visited on the floor who passed away during this period. But you never saw them remove the bodies from the room with a sheet over them. I asked Dr. Doroshow about this.

"Is there some kind of hidden compartment underneath, a special gurney?"

"You're pretty smart," he answered. "It's a precaution because they don't want the other patients to become disturbed by it."

It is hard to describe how difficult it was going back into John's room later that day after planning for his cremation and trying to forget about the whole thing. Throughout the whole ordeal, I never allowed myself to get emotional in front of him. Once I stepped outside, it was another matter, and I allowed my emotions to run freely. But I got his strength. I stepped up. Because of John, I met every challenge.

John never talked about the fact that he was dying. He still stayed hopeful that the doctors would find an answer. He thought that perhaps he might be able to get some radiation treatments.

When Dr. Doroshow came in, John asked him about it. "John, you're not a candidate for that, but we'll keep working," Dr. Doroshow said.

Later that same evening, John looked at me and said, "Well, shall we call it a day?"

"Yes, I think we should," I told him.

Per his instructions, I hypnotized him one last time that evening. But in contrast to the other times, I did not count him out to bring him back to waking consciousness, but left him to remain in the hypnotic state for what would be the last two days of his life.

For obvious reasons, I didn't want to leave the hospital, so they arranged a bed first down the hall and later in his room. I desperately wanted to be with him when he was making his transition.

"You don't know when someone is actually going to leave," Dr. Doroshow warned me. "You could be in the bathroom or down the hall visiting other patients. I think he's already there but he keeps coming back and forth. You can't count on being there."

"No, I have to," I told him.

His son, George, and I sat by his bedside.

"That was his last breath," he told me.

"No it wasn't," I assured him. My hand was on John's chest. Right away, I felt one more flutter of his heart and one more breath, and that was it. I know that what I witnessed in the next few seconds was not my imagination but an actual manifestation. The energy started at his feet and came up, up, up and then went out the top of his head. I saw him release and go, the metaphysical and transcendent act of his spirit leaving his body. And just like that, he went into total repose. It was September 26, 2002.

At the memorial, his son spoke and told of his father's great accomplishments in his field as a maverick who broke new ground and created all these new modalities. "But he didn't find true love until he was in his fifties," he revealed of his father's personal side. "It changed him in a very profound way." Those words broke through the veil of sadness and made me very happy.

A man who was the son of the owner of the mortuary came on a motorcycle to the marina to deliver a velvet satchel containing John's ashes. It was all so surreal. We took the boat out to his favorite spot on the back side of Catalina and scattered his ashes there, although I decided to keep a small amount, which I keep in our home. It makes me feel very safe.

The experience of having to deal with all the arrangements for John in my grief-stricken state made me think about sparing my children the same when my time comes. By myself and without telling anyone, I went to Westwood Memorial Park and purchased two spaces for my ashes next to the plaques I had put in a special garden honoring John and Elsie. Westwood is, after all, a famous cemetery for people in show business, so it made sense on that level, too.

Of course, after I made my purchase, the salesperson wanted to offer me a number of additional services. "We can come by and pick you up," the person said. By "you," he meant "the body." At that point in the conversation, I came to the conclusion that I wasn't ready to "go there," in more ways than one. The consideration for my children stopped right there in its tracks. "No," I thought. "They can deal with that!"

Going back to the empty house after John's ceremony was tough. Barbara stayed with me for the first few nights, but then I told her that I would be fine staying on my own. You just can't sit in a chair weeping. I didn't fold my tent. I heard his voice: "Come on! Keep moving forward." He believed that when we kept in motion we kept evolving. Things would keep unfolding. So that's what I tried to do. But it was still very hard for me.

I canceled so many dates during the time of John's illness. I decided to go back to work, but that proved no easy task. There were certain songs that were a struggle to get through. For the nearly twenty years we were together, John had been such an integral part of that artistic expression. "How will I ever do this? I can't do this!" But you just have to suck it up and work through the emotion and try again. There was an audience out there that I didn't want to disappoint. "You can do it," I heard John's voice encouraging me.

I thought about myself as a little girl who persevered in the most vulnerable of circumstances. Nobody could really kill my joy, my optimism, or my smile. I honestly think that you come in with that spirit, and it is your task to keep it alive and not have it get extinguished. And now it was almost paradoxical how my life had completed a full circle. I had once been that frightened but driven young woman who was secretly relieved to be absent for my father's death and funeral. Now I had been a mature woman who stood present and resolute for the soul mate I loved and watched him go.

But the grieving process is not that simple. There were layers of anger and fear still present like scar tissue. One morning, I sat at the breakfast table where John and I always sat, looking out the window. I was sobbing. Before John died, a disgruntled former student embroiled both the Hypnosis Motivation Institute and him in a lawsuit. We learned that the situation with this student was hardly an accident, but something that had happened all too frequently in this person's past. In all the decades of being a therapist and a teacher, John had never been exposed to such nonsense. And because I was also affiliated with the school, I got dragged into it, which upset John to no end in his weakened state. It was a nightmare. It was very costly. And I had inherited it. Added on top of that was the financial stress since I now had to shoulder alone the responsibility of owning a big boat and a big house.

The anger welled up in my sobs. "How could you leave me with all this mess, the lawsuit, the boat, the house! I don't know what to do. You'd better give me a sign that everything is going to be okay."

It was out of nowhere. From the sky came not one, not two, not three, but a whole squadron of dragonflies. They flew down and circled in front of me at the glass door. And then, as quickly as they had appeared, they were gone.

Perhaps I had never paid much attention to them before, but still it all seems so unlikely. For wherever I go and no matter where I turn, I notice the presence of dragonflies everywhere. Not so long after this first incident, Shelley came running in to tell me that dragonflies were surrounding the new car I had just bought after selling John's Cadillac. I can suddenly look down to see them woven into the pattern of a carpet. Or someone is invariably wearing a brooch that brings a smile to my face.

I interpreted what happened that morning as a real sign. I recognized that whether it was from John or from some form of higher power, they could not have sent more powerful messengers than those beautiful winged beings. I suddenly felt a deep gratitude and peace. I knew from that moment that everything was going to be okay.

No matter what form the dragonfly takes on, its appearance strengthens my belief in a realm that is largely unseen but unmistakable in its power. And it is truly uncanny how they often present themselves in one form or another when I need their message the most.

Perhaps the most beautiful manifestation of this happened only a few months after John's death. I was visiting Lizzie and was talking about John. I went outside to her small backyard swimming pool and suddenly felt very lonely. I looked down and saw a dead dragonfly on the ground. The body had split open into two lengthwise halves, as if they had opened to let its spirit depart, leaving behind its body as this exquisite shell. I was awestruck at how perfect that moment was in its clear and articulated message of transcendence.

Part of that message is also about *trust*. When you take the leap into that uncertain void, trust gives you the sense that there will be something better there awaiting you, even in the setbacks, loneliness, and pain that are often the very catalysts to help us acquire life-changing wisdom. So many of us think, "I'm afraid, unhappy, and not feeling well, but I know what I have and it's going to be worse if I step out of it." If you're living life like that, you're not really living. You're doing it because it feels safe, but you're not happy to be there. As you have seen through my adventures in this book, this trust factor requires diligence, courage, and regular maintenance, because it is always being challenged on a daily basis.

Recently, I was filming a commercial for Bausch & Lomb on location on a beach in Malibu. I had become a spokesperson for the company because, once again, adversity had turned into opportunity. I had had cataract surgery in the recent past, so I could speak from personal experience about how their implanted Crystalens worked so wonderfully well. The day was long, with lots of different setups and still photo shoots sandwiched in between the film takes. Despite it being summer, the weather was overcast and the winds blowing onshore were chilling to the bone. I had been working hard nonstop for several weeks, and I had reached a certain point at which I doubted that I would have the physical energy to complete the work that day.

"Come on, I need this energy now," I called out in prayer for help, as I have throughout my life even during the times when my faith was diminished. When we lock into that mind-body-spirit connection and do so with trust, it usually works. It did so that afternoon on the beach. I was able to pull myself together and complete the day.

Dragonflies are the oldest known living insect. In many cultures, they are a symbol of transformation, renewal, wisdom, and enlightenment. They bring about the stripping away of all illusions. They are also the keeper of the dreams that guide us to our potential. What also resonates for me is the Japanese view of the dragonfly as joyous light that reminds us that we are filled with it if we so choose to recognize it. Beyond this symbolism, they brought me something even more important that morning—a reaffirmation of faith.

CHAPTER 22

The Horse Stays in the Game

✺

My life has been very nomadic. Don't get me wrong, I love my time at home, but I still get restless. It's a great feeling to be in demand and still in the game some six decades after taking that first trip to New York City.

One steamy hot summer day in 2010, I landed once again in New York, since it was the closest airport to my concert date. The car trip from Kennedy was brutal, the stifling bumper-to-bumper conditions adding hours to an already long journey that began earlier that morning in Los Angeles.

After such an arduous trip, you can get second thoughts. Once I got to the place where I was staying, I retreated immediately to the powder room to freshen up. Reaching for a towel, I looked up and suddenly noticed the design on the shower curtain. Imprinted on the plastic was a lovely swarm of dragonflies. That I had felt so tired and overwhelmed by the journey suddenly became unimportant. My second thoughts had vanished.

If it is true that your whole life flashes in front of you just before the moment of death, then stepping out onstage to do a one-woman autobiographical show is about the closest thing to that experience. The show I have been doing over the last two years, *All the Lives of Me...A Musical Journey*, takes on many of the same periods detailed in this book and matches them to the appropriate music—from songs my mother taught me, the Broadway hits, and of course, that little sing-along favorite that begins, "Here's the story of a lovely lady who was bringing up three very lovely girls..."

It doesn't matter if I'm about to perform before twenty people or twenty thousand people—I go through the same preparation and ritual as I have done for decades. It doesn't matter how many thousands of times I've performed before, this is a new audience, and I want to be at my best. I am fastidious. I have to be extremely clean—my hair, teeth, makeup, and clothing all have to be perfect. As I've mentioned before, going onstage is a spiritual experience for me. On one side, I go there with the same feeling of respect as I would have going to church. On the other, I go out there with the excitement as though reaching out to a lover in passionate embrace. Once upon a time before hypnotherapy, I would get so nervous before a show that I felt like I would die. Today, I use that same energy for a better purpose. Before walking onto the stage, I go into isolation. I don't like to talk to anyone. I pace. I feel like a racehorse getting into the starting gate. Just open the gate and let me go!

There's always a question-and-answer section in the show, and it is interesting to hear what hits home. Some have questions about Ruth Helen and her family who provided the scholarship for me to go to New York. Were we still in touch? they wanted to know. At one recent show, I shared with them that we had just spent almost a week together on my way to their city. The audience seemed to be in awe that I had maintained that friendship for so many decades. I told them that I couldn't imagine being any other way. It is so important to me to never forget those kindnesses. I think those longstanding relationships go back to that overarching concept of trust. It comes down to meaning what you say and doing what you promise.

Many times, there are also receptions right after a performance. Again, the questions keep coming. It is a humbling phenomenon how people open up to me. Part of it I know must be the comfort they feel because of the persona of Carol Brady, whom they grew to know as if I had become a member of their family. I also know that the brief telling of my life's story through words and music on the stage pushes emotional buttons and hits common chords. Their questions may be directed to me, wanting to know more about my life and experience, but their choice of questions is always fascinating to me in what they reveal about themselves in the asking.

For example, many want to know after learning about my marriage to John whether I'm dating again and believe it's possible to find another soul mate in this lifetime. On this topic, I don't mince my words. There's a lot of loneliness and dashed hopes out there, but even in these short exchanges I want to transmit something to them that may help them to shift into a more positive frame of mind.

I admit to them that I had my dark moments of doubt about this, which I have thankfully overcome. I think a person's tendency is to think, "Oh well, I'll never meet anyone, and I'll never forget about him." I had dinner with some English friends a while back. One of the women said, "Oh, no, I'll never meet anyone. I don't need anyone. It's over for me. But I do have my doggies."

I answer the question by stating that I have not folded my tent to the possibility of having a great companion and partner again. Instead, I've strived to live each day continuing in the same spirit that John and I had together. I often hear his voice: "Come on. Keep moving forward. Things keep opening up. That's the only way we can evolve." So that's what I've tried to do.

I think about the times in our final years together when I'd go pick him up at the boat to go out to dinner after work. I had to drive my car as far out toward the dock as possible because his legs hurt him. He'd see the car. He would jog up the stairs knowing that it would make me laugh. He was pretending to be a misbehaving child because it was really something that he couldn't and wasn't supposed to be doing according to doctor's orders. The real enjoyment was in that spontaneity, a quality I continue to exercise in sharing my life with my friends, children, and grandchildren. I'm so fortunate. If that were it in terms of my allotted ration of soul mates, it would be okay, but I'm not ready to give up.

Dating! That is a different kettle of fish at this phase of my life. For better or for worse, you do get into a set routine as you get older. And what a relief it is to not always feel obligated to unselfishly accommodate someone else and sublimate your own wishes, which I did for a great portion of my life. Once you've reached a state of greater peace and contentment with your life, you're not driven by that same anxiety and grasping need to find someone to fill up some empty spot in your heart. Asking someone else to heal your wounds is a recipe for disappointment. If someone comes along who has a similar spirit and commitment to improving themselves, then you have the foundation for building a meaningful relationship. Above all, once you've had the real thing, it's hard to settle for second best.

Thank God, I've always been a *one-man-at-a-time* woman,

otherwise I'd need a social secretary just to keep track of the in-terested gentleman callers. Please understand that I am grateful for and flattered by all the attention. The investment banker, the former television network press agent, the philanthropist, the chiropractor, the magician, the MD, the mime, the "straight" hairdresser, and the financial advisor have all been hovering around my airspace in recent times. One of them sent me an e-mail that he wanted to come over and cook dinner for me.

"Oh, Kayla, what should I do?"

"You know what that means," she answered with that big-sister kind of tone. In this particular case, I didn't feel like being the dessert.

In this group, I want to especially highlight Dr. Jesse Rogers. He's a great chiropractor, healer, and, best of all, a wonderful friend. I love him dearly. Not only does he dispense great advice on everything from health to spirituality, he's also a great joke teller and always makes me laugh. Here is one sample:

"A guy walks into a psychiatrist's office. He's got a cucumber in one ear, a banana in the other, and a carrot sticking out of each nostril. So he asks the psychiatrist, 'Can you help me? What do you think my problem is?' The doctor says, 'Yes, I think I can di-agnose this . . . You're not eating properly.'"

I do get the most interesting e-mails through my website. It's remarkable how many of the inquiring men who write in to me are in their mid to late forties. Do the math, and I guess it's one of those generational things. They were all probably doing their homework, drinking chocolate milk, and memorizing their mul-tiplication tables while watching *The Brady Bunch* when it was a first-run show.

One guy, who was fifty-eight and a vegetarian, wrote in fre-quently and was sending me pictures of himself. He wanted to meet up. He was quite handsome, but I have not been quite ready to make the leap to online dating. I wrote him back and told him how much I enjoyed his letters, but that I didn't have the time to continue corresponding. He wrote me back a funny and good-natured note: "Oh, I am so sorry that your life is so full. Maybe when your life isn't so full, you can consider me."

For anybody who wants to follow in this person's footsteps, you can certainly feel free to line up and take a number. I will answer all of your e-mails, as I always do.

For a while, I got serious about one of my suitors. But an overseas trip we took together was enlightening, and this once charming and wonderful man turned out to be a certified control freak. Talk about demands. "You can't do that anymore! And while you're at it, give up those friends!" No, thank you. After our last dinner out together, he marched upstairs and got all of his stuff together.

"I think we need a break," he said.

"You're so right," I concurred, and immediately this wonderful feeling of calm came over me as he was carrying his belongings out the door. "Let me help you."

A few days later, I mailed him a nice note thanking him for all the good times, telling him how much I loved his daughter and son-in-law, and wishing him only the best. It was enclosed in the box with a pair of sneakers he had inadvertently left behind.

To get serious for a moment, there's something of a litmus test that you have to think about at this stage, too, beyond whether or not to have sex or get into a serious commitment. After my precious years with John, the issue about being in that place of ultimate trust comes forward. Specifically, it boils down to whether or not you can be there for the other person and take care of him when he needs you. John had so much trust in me when he got sick, that I would be there by his side. On my part, there was no hesitation or question about it. Although it was physically and emotionally demanding at the end, it was such a privilege to be there for him. But a lot of people don't have that in them, or simply don't care enough. So you have to answer in your mind the hardcore question: "Do I care enough about this person that I would be willing to take care of him?" It's not a pleasant thought, but I'm putting it out there because it is a reality and a choice we all have to confront.

"You really inspired me," an older person said to me at one reception after my show. "You have such a sparkle in your eyes. You radiate such an enjoyment of life. I can tell how much you are still excited about your life." This person was only a little bit younger than I was, but it was clear that he recognized a spark in me, something that he had probably lost and wanted to reclaim. Many are curious about why my energy seems far younger than my actual age. Have I discovered some fountain of youth? Or is it because I have a truly great plastic surgeon?

"I've come to this realization the last few years," I tell them. "We can do nothing about the fact that we are getting chronologically older. It does force you to look at things that you really don't want to look at. But once you stop fighting and surrender to that fact, it's liberating. You can't pretend that it's not happening, but your spirit does not have to get old. In fact, when the spirit is truly youthful, the body does a much better job of hanging in there, too."

Part of that liberation has come from the fact that I have confronted and cleared out many of my worst fears. But the one about taking that final big walk into the sky is still definitely a work in progress. On that account, I had a sneak preview a few years back. I was staying with Kayla out in the desert for a few days when suddenly everything shifted into slow motion—walking, breathing, speaking, thinking, and so on. I knew something was dreadfully wrong. She looked at me, and it wasn't too long before I was in the emergency room. One of the major valves in my heart was failing. I was rushed into surgery at Cedars-Sinai. Having been through the process with John's transition, I had fresh in my mind how serious and risky the situation was. Thanks to an incredible surgeon, Dr. Alfredo Trento, the valve was repaired with a minimally invasive surgical technology. Fortunately, it has worked like a charm since, knock on wood.

As a side note, my daughter Barbara was an angel to stay with me in the hospital during the postoperative recovery. It was a wise precaution based on a story Richard Burton told me during a dinner party. The legendary hard-living actor described his time in a rehab clinic where he was sent to dry out from a period of heavy drinking. During the night he saw all these flashing lights, as if there were moving cars in the room with their headlights beaming at him. He glanced toward the window to see if the disturbance was possibly coming from outside, but no, that was not the case. He described the vision to his doctor the next morning, thinking that he must have experienced some hallucinations due to the delirium tremens (the DTs). Again, that was not the case. The sad and bizarre reality was that someone on the night staff had brought some friends into the room as if he were some kind of freak show attraction at the circus. What he thought were headlights were the beams of flashlights from the gawkers. Barbara made sure that no one would get any "celebrity points" at my expense.

The questions I receive during my shows, the letters and e-mails like that little girl who wanted me to pick her up at the crossroads, are moments of grace that I cherish. I hope that in some form or another your experience in reading this book will embody some of that same feeling. I'm a flawed human being like everyone else. I'm no guru and with all certainty my name will not be on any short list for sainthood.

My spirituality has expanded rather than diminished, going beyond the Catholicism of my youth and organized religion as a whole. What has emerged is more of a living faith that encompasses the great wisdom from all faiths. I have always been accepting of other people and their differences. My belief recognizes that everyone is trying to get to that glorious heaven that we all talk about and there are many ways to get there. I still love attending the Catholic mass from time to time. Much of what that upbringing taught me is deeply cherished: about the value of daily prayer, the recognition of the holy spirit each of us carries, and the quality of grace that is ours to share with each other. I also applaud the efforts in the Catholic Church to ease some of its more restrictive policies, but there remains much work to do on that front. The right of priests and nuns to marry if they choose, for women to become priests, and for people especially in poorer and overpopulated regions to avail themselves of birth control, among other critical issues, need to be addressed in a serious way.

I have learned a few shortcuts along this journey that have helped cut through a lot of the nonsense and needless pain and suffering we often inflict on ourselves and those around us. It is why I felt it was important to dredge up the past and chronicle not only my victories, but also so many of my missteps and misfortunes along the way. As the title of this book says, life is not a stage but a series of stages we grow through and learn from. I hope the experiences I've shared have provided convincing proof that all the setbacks and defeats have not deterred me from the path, but continue to teach me valuable lessons and embolden me to want to learn more. I hope that sharing this story will also be a source of encouragement to inspire you to keep moving forward.

I'm still working on my goal to keep working at least until I'm ninety years old. Betty White, look out! Maybe the sequel to this book will tell you how and if I make it.

One thing that erases any doubt in my mind that I'm still up for the challenge was my decision to appear on *Dancing with the Stars* at age seventy-six. I've had good endurance throughout my career, but the demands of preparation, rehearsal, and performance were intense. In the end, I was pleased that I was really able to push myself a lot farther than I thought I could.

I was sensitive about patronizing attitudes about aging, so I made it a point to tell both judges and fellow contestants that I was in this competition just like the rest of them. I didn't want anybody going, "Oh, she did great for her age." I'd rather they judged me on whether I worked hard and did my best to look good. It also didn't hurt that my stamina was just as good as the others'. I never had to breathe hard at the end of the numbers. After the first week, my age was never mentioned again.

Don't ask me why, but there was something about the show that compelled me to want to do it since it began. It made me realize that I am still awfully competitive. I wanted to do well and be out in front with the rest of them as long as I could. That edge was still there just as much as when I was a kid.

I have people stop me in public or write e-mails and letters on how I've inspired them by being on the show. One person wrote in, "I heard you say *stand up straight and hold your stomach in* and it's changed my life." It went back to my old teacher's "rrrrribs up!" advice at the academy. It had also helped that I had done Pilates training for two years with my trainer Kim Smith, so my core muscles were strong. But once you do a new dance, you find out quickly that there are lots of muscles you never knew you had.

I would have loved to have stayed in the competition longer, but it felt good that I met both the challenge and my fears about doing the show. Those fears revolved around the fact that it is a competition, and not being a real dancer, I knew that I would have to work harder. I was also wondering if I could meet the physical and mental challenges. Getting your feet to move is not as simple as being an actor learning your lines. It's a whole different ball game. If I make a mistake in my one-woman show, I always find a way to have fun with it, but when you have a dance partner, it throws everything off. On two occasions the audience was cheering so loudly at the beginning of our number that I couldn't hear the cue to begin the first step.

Luckily, I was blessed to have Corky Ballas as my partner. I knew he was a great teacher and had been a world champion many times. He was very patient. When I'd mess up, he'd say, "Florence *Agnes* Henderson, you know this, now come on!" That's what I get for telling him my middle name. He sounded just like my mother.

Corky was fifty, so he worked intelligently and knew my body well after a short time. He put me through a routine depending on what movements were required in a particular dance. For the rhumba, we did deep knee bends and varied the pace on the treadmill and did sideways and backwards movements too, before the hours of actual rehearsal would begin. "Okay, that's enough for today," he would tell me when it was time to stop.

I never wanted to quit. "Can't we do it one more time?"

"What's the point if you injure yourself?"

There was also pressure because the others had three weeks to learn their routine for the first show, whereas I got started late and only had five days to prepare. It was scary to learn that dance that quickly. I care a lot about what I do. At night, I would lie awake going over the steps because it wasn't something I do all the time. "Oh my God, I don't know this well enough. What am I going to do?" That insecurity made me feel again how it was when I was a young kid starting out in the business. I'm always saying, "I could have done better." I've always been that way, very self-critical and never satisfied with anything when it comes to my performance.

Dancing with the Stars explains a lot about why I am still so passionate and excited about my career and why each day is such an adventure.

My formula is simple: Stay open to the unexpected. Learn to let go of your self-limiting thinking. Tomorrow, something unexpected is going to happen that is exciting. Let the experiences come. Don't be afraid to say *yes* a lot. Be grateful and forgiving. Stay flexible. Know that there's always another way. Keep going and never stop pushing the envelope of your potential. And stay courageous in your quest for inner peace and a life full of love.

Lastly, in case you're wondering what happened to that galloping horse, here's an update. The horse is alive and well. The horse still loves to run. It still enjoys being in the game, but with one important distinction. It doesn't have to win every race.